THE WORKS OF JOHN MILTON

THE WORKS OF
JOHN MILTON

VOLUME V

NEW YORK
Columbia University Press
1932

PRINTED IN THE UNITED STATES OF AMERICA
BY THE PRINTING HOUSE OF WILLIAM EDWIN RUDGE, INC.
MOUNT VERNON, NEW YORK

CONTENTS

	PAGE
The Tenure of Kings and Magistrates . . .	I
EDITED BY WILLIAM HALLER	
Eikonoklastes	61
EDITED BY WILLIAM HALLER	
Notes	311

ILLUSTRATIONS

PAGE

Title-page to the First Edition of The Tenure of
Kings and Magistrates, 1649   I

Title-page to the First Edition of Eikonoklastes,
1649   62

THE TENURE OF KINGS

THE TENURE OF
KINGS
AND
MAGISTRATES:
PROVING,

That it is Lawfull, and hath been
held so through all Ages, for any,
who have the Power, to call to account a
Tyrant, or wicked KING, and after
due conviction, to depose, and put
him to death; if the ordinary MA-
GISTRATE have neglected, or
deny'd to doe it.

And that they, who of late, so much blame
Deposing, are the Men that did it themselves.

The Author, J. M.

LONDON,

Printed by *Matthew Simmons*, at the Gilded
Lyon in Aldersgate Street, 1649.

THE TENURE OF
KINGS
And MAGISTRATES.

IF men within themselves would be govern'd by reason, and not generally give up thir understanding to a double tyrannie, of Custom from without, and blind affections within, they would discerne better, what it is to favour and
5 uphold the Tyrant of a Nation. But being slaves within doors, no wonder that they strive so much to have the public State conformably govern'd to the inward vitious rule, by which they govern themselves. For indeed none can love freedom heartilie, but good men; the rest love not freedom,
10 but licence; which never hath more scope or more indulgence then under Tyrants. Hence is it that Tyrants are not oft offended, nor stand much in doubt of bad men, as being all naturally servile; but in whom vertue and true worth most is eminent, them they feare in earnest, as by right thir Maisters,
15 against them lies all thir hatred and suspicion. Consequent-lie neither doe bad men hate Tyrants, but have been alwayes readiest with the falsifi'd names of *Loyalty,* and *Obedience,* to colour over thir base compliances. And although som-times for shame, and when it comes to thir owne grievances,
20 of purse especially, they would seeme good Patriots, and side with the better cause, yet when others for the deliverance of

thir Countrie, endu'd with fortitude and Heroick vertue to
feare nothing but the curse writt'n against those *That doe
the worke of the Lord negligently,** would goe on to remove,   *Jer. 48.19
not only the calamities and thraldoms of a People, but the
5 roots and causes whence they spring, streight these men, and
sure helpers at need, as if they hated only the miseries but not
the mischiefs, after they have juggl'd and palter'd with the
world, bandied and born armes against thir King, devested
him, disannointed him, nay curs'd him all over in thir Pul-
10 pits and thir Pamphlets, to the ingaging of sincere and real
men, beyond what is possible or honest to retreat from, not
only turne revolters from those principles, which only could
at first move them, but lay the staine of disloyaltie, and
worse, on those proceedings, which are the necessary conse-
15 quences of thir own former actions; nor dislik'd by themselves, were they manag'd to the intire advantages of thir
own Faction; not considering the while that he toward
whom they boasted thir new fidelitie, counted them accessory; and by those Statutes and Lawes which they so
20 impotently brandish against others, would have doom'd
them to a Traytors death, for what they have don alreadie.
'T is true, that most men are apt anough to civill Wars
and commotions as a noveltie, and for a flash hot and
active; but through sloth or inconstancie, and weakness
25 of spirit either fainting, ere thir own pretences, though
never so just, be half attain'd, or through an inbred falshood
and wickednes, betray oft times to destruction with themselves, men of noblest temper joyn'd with them for causes,

whereof they in their rash undertakings were not capable.

If God and a good cause give them Victory, the prosecution wherof for the most part, inevitably draws after it the alteration of Lawes, change of Goverment, downfal of
5 Princes with thir families; then comes the task to those Worthies which are the soule of that enterprize, to be swett and labour'd out amidst the throng and noises of Vulgar and irrational men. Some contesting for privileges, customs, forms, and that old entanglement of Iniquity, thir gibrish
10 Lawes, though the badge of thir ancient slavery. Others who have beene fiercest against thir Prince, under the notion of a Tyrant, and no mean incendiaries of the Warr against him, when God out of his providence and high disposal hath deliver'd him into the hand of thir brethren, on a suddain
15 and in a new garbe of Allegiance, which thir doings have long since cancell'd; they plead for him, pity him, extoll him, protest against those that talk of bringing him to the tryal of Justice, which is the Sword of God, superior to all mortal things, in whose hand soever by apparent signes his
20 testified will is to put it. But certainly if we consider who and what they are, on a suddain grown so pitifull, wee may conclude, thir pitty can be no true, and Christian commiseration, but either levitie and shallowness of minde, or else a carnal admiring of that worldly pomp and greatness, from
25 whence they see him fall'n; or rather lastly a dissembl'd and seditious pity, fain'd of industry to begett new discord. As for mercy, if it be to a Tyrant, under which Name they themselves have cited him so oft in the hearing of God, of

Angels, and the holy Church assembl'd, and there charg'd
him with the spilling of more innocent blood by farr, then
ever *Nero* did, undoubtedly the mercy which they pretend,
is the mercy of wicked men; and their mercies, wee read are
5 cruelties; hazarding the welfare of a whole Nation, to have
sav'd one, whom so oft they have tearm'd *Agag;* and vilifying the blood of many *Jonathans,* that have sav'd *Israel;* in-
sisting with much niceness on the unnecessariest clause of
thir Covnant wrested, wherein the feare of change, and the
10 absurd contradiction of a flattering hostilitie had hamperd
them, but not scrupling to give away for complements, to an
implacable revenge, the heads of many thousand Christians
more.

Another sort there is, who comming in the cours of these
15 affaires, to have thir share in great actions, above the form of
Law or Custom, at least to give thir voice and approbation,
begin to swerve, and almost shiver at the Majesty and gran-
deur of som noble deed, as if they were newly enter'd into a
great sin; disputing presidents, forms, and circumstances,
20 when the Commonwealth nigh perishes for want of deeds
in substance, don with just and faithfull expedition. To these
I wish better instruction, and vertue equal to thir calling;
the former of which, that is to say Instruction, I shall indeavour, as my dutie is, to bestow on them; and exhort them not
25 to startle from the just and pious resolution of adhering with
all thir strength & assistance to the present Parlament &
Army, in the glorious way wherin Justice and Victory hath
set them; the only warrants through all ages, next under

immediat Revelation, to excercise supream power, in those
proceedings which hitherto appeare equal to what hath been
don in any age or Nation heretofore, justly or magnani-
mouslie. Nor let them be discourag'd or deterr'd by any new
5 Apostate Scarcrowes, who under show of giving counsel,
send out their barking monitories and *memento's,* empty of
ought else but the spleene of a frustrated Faction. For how
can that pretended counsel bee either sound or faithfull,
when they that give it, see not for madness and vexation of
10 thir ends lost, that those Statutes and Scriptures which both
falsly and scandalously, they wrest against thir Friends and
Associates, would by sentence of the common adversarie, fall
first and heaviest upon thir own heads. Neither let milde
and tender dispositions be foolishly softn'd from thir duty
15 and perseverance, with the unmaskuline Rhetorick of any
puling Priest or Chaplain, sent as a friendly Letter of advice,
for fashion sake in privat, and forthwith publisht by the
Sender himself, that wee may know how much of friend
there was in it, to cast an odious envie upon them, to whom
20 it was pretended to be sent in charitie. Nor let any man be
deluded by either the ignorance or the notorious hypocrisie
and self-repugnance of our dancing Divines, who have the
conscience and the boldness, to come with Scripture in thir
mouthes, gloss'd and fitted for thir turnes with a double con-
25 tradictory sense, transforming the sacred verity of God, to an
Idol with two Faces, looking at once two several ways; and
with the same quotations to charge others, which in the
same case they made serve to justifie themselves. For while

the hope to bee made Classic and Provincial Lords led them
on, while pluralities greas'd them thick and deep, to the
shame and scandal of Religion, more then all the Sects and
Heresies they exclaim against, then to fight against the
5 Kings person, and no less a Party of his Lords and Commons,
or to put force upon both the Houses, was good, was lawfull,
was no resisting of Superior powers; they onely were powers
not to be resisted, who countenanc'd the good, and punish't
the evil. But now that thir censorious domineering is not
10 suffer'd to be universal, truth and conscience to be freed,
Tithes and Pluralities to be no more, though competent
allowance provided, and the warme experience of large gifts,
and they so good at taking them; yet now to exclude & seize
upon impeach't Members, to bring Delinquents without ex-
15 emption to a faire Tribunal by the common National Law
against murder, is now to be no less then *Corah, Dathan,*
and *Abiram*. He who but erewhile in the Pulpits was a
cursed Tyrant, an enemie to God and Saints, lad'n with all
the innocent blood spilt in three Kingdoms, and so to be
20 fought against, is now, though nothing penitent or alter'd
from his first principles, a lawfull Magistrate, a Sovran Lord,
the Lords anointed, not to be touch'd, though by themselves
imprison'd. As if this onely were obedience, to preserve the
meere useless bulke of his person, and that onely in prison,
25 not in the field, and to disobey his commands, deny him his
dignity and office, every where to resist his power but where
they thinke it onely surviving in thir own faction.

But who in particular is a Tyrant cannot be determin'd in

a general discours, otherwise then by supposition; his particular charge, and the sufficient proof of it must determin
that: which I leave to Magistrates, at least to the uprighter
sort of them, and of the people, though in number less by
5 many, in whom faction least hath prevaild above the Law of
nature and right reason, to judge as they find cause. But this
I dare owne as part of my faith, that if such a one there be,
by whose Commission, whole massachers have been committed on his faithfull Subjects, his Provinces offerd to pawn
10 or alienation, as the hire of those whom he had sollicited to
come in and destroy whole Citties and Countries; be he King,
or Tyrant, or Emperour, the Sword of Justice is above him;
in whose hand soever is found sufficient power to avenge the
effusion, and so great a deluge of innocent blood. For if all
15 human power to execute, not accidentally but intendedly,
the wrath of God upon evil doers without exception, be of
God; then that power, whether ordinary, or if that faile,
extraordinary so executing that intent of God, is lawfull, and
not to be resisted. But to unfold more at large this whole
20 Question, though with all expedient brevity, I shall here set
downe from first beginning, the original of Kings; how and
wherfore exalted to that dignitie above thir Brethren; and
from thence shall prove, that turning to Tyranny they may
bee as lawfully depos'd and punish'd, as they were at first
25 elected: This I shall doe by autorities and reasons, not learnt
in corners among Scisms and Heresies, as our doubling
Divines are ready to calumniat, but fetch't out of the midst
of choicest and most authentic learning, and no prohibited

Authors, nor many Heathen, but Mosaical, Christian, Orthodoxal, and which must needs be more convincing to our
Adversaries, Presbyterial.

No man who knows ought, can be so stupid to deny that
5 all men naturally were borne free, being the image and re-
semblance of God himself, and were by privilege above all
the creatures, born to command and not to obey: and that
they liv'd so. Till from the root of *Adams* transgression,
falling among themselves to doe wrong and violence, and
10 foreseeing that such courses must needs tend to the destruction of them all, they agreed by common league to bind each
other from mutual injury, and joyntly to defend themselves
against any that gave disturbance or opposition to such agreement. Hence came Citties, Townes and Common-wealths.
15 And because no faith in all was found sufficiently binding,
they saw it needfull to ordaine som authoritie, that might
restrain by force and punishment what was violated against
peace and common right. This autoritie and power of self-
defence and preservation being originally and naturally in
20 every one of them, and unitedly in them all, for ease, for
order, and least each man should be his own partial Judge,
they communicated and deriv'd either to one, whom for the
eminence of his wisdom and integritie they chose above the
rest, or to more then one whom they thought of equal de-
25 serving: the first was call'd a King; the other Magistrates.
Not to be thir Lords and Maisters (though afterward those
names in som places were giv'n voluntarily to such as had
been Authors of inestimable good to the people) but, to be

thir Deputies and Commissioners, to execute, by vertue of thir intrusted power, that justice which else every man by the bond of nature and of Cov'nant must have executed for himself, and for one another. And to him that shall consider
5 well why among free Persons, one man by civil right should beare autority and jurisdiction over another, no other end or reason can be imaginable. These for a while govern'd well, and with much equity decided all things at thir own arbitrement: till the temptation of such a power left absolute in thir
10 hands, perverted them at length to injustice and partialitie. Then did they who now by tryal had found the danger and inconveniences of committing arbitrary power to any, invent Laws either fram'd, or consented to by all, that should confine and limit the autority of whom they chose to govern
15 them: that so man, of whose failing they had proof, might no more rule over them, but law and reason abstracted as much as might be from personal errors and frailties. While as the Magistrate was set above the people, so the Law was set above the Magistrate. When this would not serve, but
20 that the Law was either not executed, or misapply'd, they were constrain'd from that time, the onely remedy left them, to put conditions and take Oaths from all Kings and Magistrates at thir first instalment to doe impartial justice by Law: who upon those termes and no other, receav'd Allegeance
25 from the people, that is to say, bond or Covnant to obey them in execution of those Lawes which they the people had themselves made, or assented to. And this ofttimes with express warning, that if the King or Magistrate prov'd unfaithfull

to his trust, the people would be disingag'd. They added also Counselors and Parlaments, nor to be onely at his beck, but with him or without him, at set times, or at all times, when any danger threatn'd to have care of the public safety.
5 Therefore saith *Claudius Sesell* a French Statesman, *The Parliament was set as a bridle to the King;* which I instance rather, not because our English Lawyers have not said the same long before, but because that French Monarchy is granted by all to be a farr more absolute then ours. That this
10 and the rest of what hath hitherto been spok'n is most true, might be copiously made appeare throughout all Stories Heathen and Christian; ev'n of those Nations where Kings and Emperours have sought meanes to abolish all ancient memory of the Peoples right by thir encroachments and
15 usurpations. But I spare long insertions, appealing to the known constitutions of both the latest Christian Empires in Europe, the Greek and German, besides the French, Italian, Arragonian, English, and not least the Scottish Histories: not forgetting this onely by the way, that *William* the
20 Norman though a Conqueror, and not unsworn at his Coronation, was compell'd the second time to take oath at S. *Albanes,* ere the people would be brought to yeild obedience.

It being thus manifest that the power of Kings and Magistrates is nothing else, but what is only derivative, transferr'd
25 and committed to them in trust from the People, to the Common good of them all, in whom the power yet remaines fundamentally, and cannot be tak'n from them, without a violation of thir natural birthright, and seeing that from hence

Aristotle and the best of Political writers have defin'd a
King, him who governs to the good and profit of his People,
and not for his own ends, it follows from necessary causes,
that the Titles of Sov'ran Lord, natural Lord, and the like,
5 are either arrogancies, or flatteries, not admitted by Emperours and Kings of best note, and dislikt by the Church both
of Jews, *Isai.* 26. 13. and ancient Christians, as appears by
Tertullian and others. Although generally the people of
Asia, and with them the Jews also, especially since the time
10 they chose a King against the advice and counsel of God, are
noted by wise Authors much inclinable to slavery.

Secondly, that to say, as is usual, the King hath as good
right to his Crown and dignitie, as any man to his inheritance, is to make the Subject no better then the Kings slave,
15 his chattell, or his possession that may be bought and sould.
And doubtless if hereditary title were sufficiently inquir'd,
the best foundation of it would be found either but in courtesie or convenience. But suppose it to be of right hereditarie,
what can be more just and legal, if a subject for certain
20 crimes be to forfet by Law from himself, and posterity, all
his inheritance to the King, then that a King for crimes pro-
portional, should forfet all his title and inheritance to the
people: unless the people must be thought created all for
him, he not for them, and they all in one body inferior to
25 him single, which were a kinde of treason against the dignitie of mankind to affirm.

Thirdly it follows, that to say Kings are accountable to
none but God, is the ouerturning of all Law and govern-

ment. For if they may refuse to give account, then all cov'-
nants made with them at Coronation; all Oathes are in
vaine, and meer mockeries, all Lawes which they sweare to
keep, made to no purpose; for if the King feare not God,
5 as how many of them doe not? we hold then our lives and
estates, by the tenure of his meer grace and mercy, as from
a God, not a mortal Magistrate, a position that none but
Court Parasites or men besotted would maintain. *Aristotle*
therefore, whom we commonly allow for one of the best
10 interpreters of nature and morality, writes in the fourth of
his politics chap. 10. that Monarchy unaccountable, is the
worst sort of Tyranny; and least of all to be endur'd by free
born men. And surely no Christian Prince, not drunk with
high mind, and prouder then those Pagan *Cæsars* that deifi'd
15 themselves, would arrogate so unreasonably above human
condition, or derogate so basely from a whole Nation of
men his Brethren, as if for him only subsisting, and to serve
his glory; valuing them in comparison of his owne brute will
and pleasure, no more then so many beasts, or vermin under
20 his Feet, not to be reasond with, but to be trod on; among
whom there might be found so many thousand Men for
wisdom, vertue, nobleness of mind, and all other respects,
but the fortune of his dignity, farr above him. Yet some
would perswade us, that this absurd opinion was King
25 *Davids;* because in the 51 *Psalm* he cries out to God, *Against
thee onely have I sinn'd;* as if *David* had imagin'd that to
murder *Uriah* and adulterate his Wife, had bin no sinn
against his Neighbour, when as that Law of *Moses* was to

the King expresly, *Deut.* 17. not to think so highly of himself above his Brethren. *David* therfore by those words
could mean no other, then either that the depth of his guiltiness was known to God onely, or to so few as had not the
5 will or power to question him, or that the sin against God
was greater beyond compare then against *Uriah.* Whatever his meaning were, any wise man will see that the pa-
thetical words of a Psalme can be no certaine decision to a
poynt that hath abundantly more certain rules to goe by.
10 How much more rationally spake the Heathen King *Demo-*
phoon in a Tragedy of *Euripides* then these Interpreters
would put upon King *David, I rule not my people by Tyr-*
anny, as if they were Barbarians, but am my self liable, if I
doe unjustly, to suffer justly. Not unlike was the speech of
15 *Trajan* the worthy Emperor, to one whom he made General
of his Prætorian Forces. Take this drawn sword, saith he,
to use for me, if I reigne well, if not, to use against me. Thus
Dion relates. And not *Trajan* onely, but *Theodosius* the
yonger, a Christian Emperor and one of the best, causd it to
20 be enacted as a rule undenyable and fit to be acknowledg'd
by all Kings and Emperors, that a Prince is bound to the
Laws; that on the autority of Law the autority of a Prince
depends, and to the Laws ought submitt. Which Edict of his
remains yet in the *Code* of *Justinian. l.* 1. *tit.* 24. as a sacred
25 constitution to all the succeeding Emperors. How then can
any King in Europe maintain and write himself accountable
to none but God, when Emperors in thir own imperial
Statutes have writt'n and decreed themselves accountable to

Law. And indeed where such account is not fear'd, he that bids a man reigne over him above Law, may bid as well a savage Beast.

It follows lastly, that since the King or Magistrate holds
5 his autoritie of the people, both originaly and naturally for their good in the first place, and not his own, then may the people as oft as they shall judge it for the best, either choose him or reject him, retaine him or depose him though no Tyrant, meerly by the liberty and right of free born Men, to
10 be govern'd as seems to them best. This, though it cannot but stand with plain reason, shall be made good also by Scripture. *Deut.* 17. 14. *When thou art come into the Land which the Lord thy God giveth thee, and shalt say I will set a King over mee, like as all the Nations about mee.* These
15 words confirme us that the right of choosing, yea of changing thir own Goverment is by the grant of God himself in the People. And therfore when they desir'd a King, though then under another form of goverment, and though thir changing displeas'd him, yet he that was himself thir King,
20 and rejected by them, would not be a hindrance to what they intended, furder then by perswasion, but that they might doe therein as they saw good, 1 *Sam.* 8. onely he reserv'd to himself the nomination of who should reigne over them. Neither did that exempt the King, as if he were to God onely
25 accountable, though by his especial command anointed. Therfore *David first made a Covnant with the Elders of Israel, and so was by them anointed King,* 2 *Sam.* 5. 3. 1 *Chron.* 11. And *Jehoiada* the Priest making *Jehoash* King,

made a Cov'nant between him and the People, 2 *Kings* 11.
17. Therfore when *Roboam* at his comming to the Crown,
rejected those conditions which the Israelites brought him,
heare what they answer him, *What portion have we in*
5 *David, or Inheritance in the son of Jesse? See to thine own
House David*. And for the like conditions not perform'd, all
Israel before that time depos'd *Samuel;* not for his own de-
fault, but for the misgoverment of his Sons. But som will
say to both these examples, it was evilly don. I answer, that
10 not the latter, because it was expressly allow'd them in the
Law to set up a King if they pleas'd; and God himself joyn'd
with them in the work; though in som sort it was at that
time displeasing to him, in respect of old *Samuel* who had
govern'd them uprightly. As *Livy* praises the Romans who
15 took occasion from *Tarquinius* a wicked Prince to gaine thir
libertie, which to have extorted, saith hee, from *Numa,* or
any of the good Kings before, had not bin seasonable. Nor
was it in the former example don unlawfully; for when
Roboam had prepar'd a huge Army to reduce the Israelites,
20 he was forbidd'n by the Prophet, 1 *Kings* 12. 24. *Thus saith
the Lord yee shall not goe up, nor fight against your brethren, for this thing is from me*. He calls them thir Brethren,
not Rebels, and forbidds to be proceeded against them, owning the thing himself, not by single providence, but by ap-
25 probation, and that not onely of the act, as in the former
example, but of the fit season also; he had not otherwise forbidd to molest them. And those grave and wise Counselors
whom *Rehoboam* first advis'd with, spake no such thing, as

our old gray headed Flatterers now are wont, stand upon
your birth-right, scorn to capitulate, you hold of God, not of
them; for they knew no such matter, unless conditionally,
but gave him politic counsel, as in a civil transaction. Ther-
5 fore Kingdom and Magistracy, whether supreme or subordinat, is without difference, call'd *a human ordinance,* 1
Pet. 2. 13. &c. which we are there taught is the will of God
wee should alike submitt to, so farr as for the punishment of
evil doers, and the encouragement of them that doe well.
10 *Submitt* saith he, *as free men.* But to any civil power unaccountable, unquestionable, and not to be resisted, no not in
wickedness, and violent actions, how can we submitt as free
men? *There is no power but of God,* saith *Paul, Rom.* 13.
as much as to say, God put it into mans heart to find out that
15 way at first for common peace and preservation, approving
the exercise therof; els it contradicts *Peter* who calls the
same autority an Ordinance of man. It must be also understood of lawfull and just power, els we read of great power
in the affaires and Kingdoms of the World permitted to the
20 Devil: for saith he to Christ, *Luke* 4. 6. *All this power will
I give thee and the glory of them, for it is deliver'd to me, &
to whomsoever I will, I give it:* neither did he ly, or Christ
gainsay what he affirm'd; for in the thirteenth of the *Revelation* wee read how the Dragon gave to the beast *his power,*
25 *his seate, and great autority:* which beast so autoriz'd most
expound to be the tyrannical powers and Kingdoms of the
earth. Therfore Saint *Paul* in the forecited Chapter tells us
that such Magistrates he meanes, as are, not a terror to the

good but to the evil; such as beare not the sword in vaine, but
to punish offenders, and to encourage the good. If such onely
be mentiond here as powers to be obeyd, and our submis-
sion to them onely requir'd, then doubtless those powers that
5 doe the contrary, are no powers ordain'd of God, and by
consequence no obligation laid upon us to obey or not to
resist them. And it may bee well observd that both these
Apostles, whenever they give this precept, express it in
termes not *concrete* but *abstract,* as Logicians are wont to
10 speake, that is, they mention the ordinance, the power, the
autoritie before the persons that execute it; and what that
power is, least we should be deceav'd, they describe exactly.
So that if the power be not such, or the person execute not
such power, neither the one nor the other is of God, but of
15 the Devil, and by consequence to bee resisted. From this exposition *Chrysostome* also on the same place dissents not;
explaining that these words were not writt'n in behalf of a
tyrant. And this is verify'd by *David,* himself a King, and
likeliest to bee Author of the *Psalm* 94. 20. which saith *Shall*
20 *the throne of iniquity have fellowship with thee?* And it
were worth the knowing, since Kings in these dayes, and
that by Scripture, boast the justness of thir title, by holding
it immediately of God, yet cannot show the time when God
ever set on the throne them or thir forefathers, but onely
25 when the people chose them, why by the same reason, since
God ascribes as oft to himself the casting down of Princes
from the throne, it should not be thought as lawful, and as
much from God, when none are seen to do it but the people,

and that for just causes. For if it needs must be a sin in them to depose, it may as likely be a sin to have elected. And contrary if the peoples act in election be pleaded by a King, as the act of God, and the most just title to enthrone him, why may not the peoples act of rejection, bee as well pleaded by the people as the act of God, and the most just reason to depose him? So that we see the title and just right of raigning or deposing, in reference to God, is found in Scripture to be all one; visible onely in the people, and depending meerly upon justice and demerit. Thus farr hath bin considerd briefly the power of Kings and Magistrates; how it was and is originally the peoples, and by them conferr'd in trust onely to bee imployed to the common peace and benefit; with liberty therfore and right remaining in them to reassume it to themselves, if by Kings or Magistrates it be abus'd; or to dispose of it by any alteration, as they shall judge most conducing to the public good.

Wee may from hence with more ease, and force of argument determin what a Tyrant is, and what the people may doe against him. A Tyrant whether by wrong or by right comming to the Crown, is he who regarding neither Law nor the common good, reigns onely for himself and his faction: Thus St. *Basil* among others defines him. And because his power is great, his will boundless and exorbitant, the fulfilling whereof is for the most part accompanied with innumerable wrongs and oppressions of the people, murders, massachers, rapes, adulteries, desolation, and subversion of Citties and whole Provinces, look how great a good and hap-

piness a just King is, so great a mischeife is a Tyrant; as
hee the public father of his Countrie, so this the common
enemie. Against whom what the people lawfully may doe,
as against a common pest, and destroyer of mankinde, I sup-
5 pose no man of cleare judgement need goe furder to be
guided then by the very principles of nature in him. But
because it is the vulgar folly of men to desert thir own reason,
and shutting thir eyes to think they see best with other mens,
I shall show by such examples as ought to have most waight
10 with us, what hath bin don in this case heretofore. The
Greeks and *Romans,* as thir prime Authors witness, held it
not onely lawfull, but a glorious and Heroic deed, rewarded
publicly with Statues and Garlands, to kill an infamous
Tyrant at any time without tryal: and but reason, that he
15 who trod down all Law, should not be voutsaf'd the benefit
of Law. Insomuch that *Seneca* the Tragedian brings in
Hercules the grand suppressor of Tyrants, thus speaking,

> ———— ———— *Victima haud ulla amplior*
> *Potest, magisque opima mactari Jovi*
> 20 *Quam Rex iniquus* ———— ———— ————
> ———— ———— *There can be slaine*
> *No sacrifice to God more acceptable*
> *Then an unjust and wicked King* ———— ————

But of these I name no more, lest it bee objected they were
25 Heathen; and come to produce another sort of men that had
the knowledge of true Religion. Among the Jews this cus-

tom of tyrant-killing was not unusual. First *Ehud,* a man whom God had raysd to deliver Israel from *Eglon* King of *Moab,* who had conquerd and rul'd over them eighteene years, being sent to him as an Ambassador with a present,

5 slew him in his own house. But hee was a forren Prince, an enemie, and *Ehud* besides had special warrant from God. To the first I answer, it imports not whether forren or native: For no Prince so native but professes to hold by Law; which when he himself overturns, breaking all the Covnants and

10 Oaths that gave him title to his dignity, and were the bond and alliance between him and his people, what differs he from an outlandish King, or from an enemie? For look how much right the King of *Spaine* hath to govern us at all, so much right hath the King of *England* to govern us tyran-

15 nically. If he, though not bound to us by any League, comming from *Spaine* in person to subdue us or to destroy us, might lawfully by the people of *England* either bee slaine in fight, or put to death in captivity, what hath a native King to plead, bound by so many Covnants, benefits and honours

20 to the welfare of his people, why he through the contempt of all Laws and Parlaments, the onely tie of our obedience to him, for his own wills sake, and a boasted prerogative unaccountable, after sev'n years warring and destroying of his best Subjects, overcom, and yeilded prisoner, should think

25 to scape unquestionable, as a thing divine, in respect of whom so many thousand Christians destroy'd, should lie unaccounted for, polluting with their slaughterd carcasses all the Land over, and crying for vengeance against the living that

should have righted them. Who knows not that there is a
mutual bond of amity and brother-hood between man and
man over all the World, neither is it the English Sea that can
sever us from that duty and relation: a straiter bond yet there
5 is between fellow-subjects, neighbours, and friends; But
when any of these doe one to another so as hostility could doe
no worse, what doth the Law decree less against them, then
op'n enemies and invaders? or if the Law be not present, or
too weake, what doth it warrant us to less then single de-
10 fence, or civil warr? and from that time forward the Law of
civil defensive warr differs nothing from the Law of forren
hostility. Nor is it distance of place that makes enmitie, but
enmity that makes distance. He therfore that keeps peace
with me, neer or remote, of whatsoever Nation, is to mee as
15 farr as all civil and human offices an Englishman and a
neighbour: but if an Englishman forgetting all Laws, human, civil and religious, offend against life and liberty, to
him offended and to the Law in his behalf, though born in
the same womb, he is no better then a Turk, a Sarasin, a
20 Heathen. This is Gospel, and this was ever Law among
equals; how much rather then in force against any King
whatever, who in respect of the people is confessd inferior and
not equal: to distinguish therfore of a Tyrant by outlandish,
or domestic is a weak evasion. To the second that he was an
25 enemie, I answer, what Tyrant is not? yet *Eglon* by the
Jewes had bin acknowledgd as thir Sovran; they had serv'd
him eighteen yeares, as long almost as we our *William* the
Conqueror, in all which time he could not be so unwise a

Statesman but to have tak'n of them Oaths of Fealty and Allegeance, by which they made themselves his proper Subjects, as thir homage and present sent by *Ehud* testify'd. To the third, that he had special warrant to kill *Eglon* in that
5 manner, it cannot bee granted, because not expressd; tis plain that he was raysd by God to be a Deliverer, and went on just principles, such as were then and ever held allowable, to deale so by a Tyrant that could no otherwise be dealt with. Neither did *Samuel* though a Profet, with his own hand
10 abstain from *Agag;* a forren enemie no doubt; but mark the reason. *As thy Sword hath made women childless;* a cause that by the sentence of Law it self nullifies all relations. And as the Law is between Brother and Brother, Father and Son, Maister and Servant, wherfore not between King or
15 rather Tyrant and People? And whereas *Jehu* had special command to slay *Jehoram* a successive and hereditarie Tyrant, it seems not the less imitable for that; for where a thing grounded so much on natural reason hath the addition of a command from God, what does it but establish the lawful-
20 ness of such an act. Nor is it likely that God who had so many wayes of punishing the house of *Ahab* would have sent a subject against his Prince, if the fact in it self, as don to a Tyrant, had bin of bad example. And if *David* refus'd to lift his hand against the Lords anointed, the matter be-
25 tween them was not tyranny, but privat enmity, and *David* as a privat person had bin his own revenger, not so much the peoples. But when any tyrant at this day can shew to be the Lords anointed, the onely mention'd reason why *David*

withheld his hand, he may then but not till then presume on the same privilege.

Wee may pass therfore hence to Christian times. And first our Saviour himself, how much he favour Tyrants, and how much intended they should be found or honourd among Christians, declares his mind not obscurely; accounting thir absolute autority no better then Gentilism, yea though they flourish'd it over with the splendid name of Benefactors; charging those that would be his Disciples to usurp no such dominion; but that they who were to bee of most autoritie among them, should esteem themselves Ministers and Servants to the public. *Matt.* 20. 25. *The Princes of the Gentiles excercise Lordship over them,* and *Mark* 10. 42. *They that seem to rule,* saith he, either slighting or accounting them no lawful rulers, *but yee shall not be so, but the greatest among you shall be your Servant.* And although hee himself were the meekest, and came on earth to be so, yet to a Tyrant we hear him not voutsafe an humble word: but *Tell that Fox, Luc.* 13. So farr we ought to be from thinking that Christ and his Gospel should be made a Sanctuary for Tyrants from justice, to whom his Law before never gave such protection. And wherfore did his Mother the Virgin *Mary* give such praise to God in her profetic song, that he had now by the comming of Christ *Cutt down Dynasta's or proud Monarchs from the throne,* if the Church, when God manifests his power in them to doe so, should rather choose all miserie and vassalage to serve them, and let them stil sit on thir potent seats to bee ador'd for doing mischief. Surely it is not for nothing that tyrants by a kind of natural instinct both hate and feare none more then the true Church and Saints of God, as the most dangerous enemies and subverters of Monarchy, though indeed of tyranny; hath not this bin 5 the perpetual cry of Courtiers, and Court Prelats? whereof no likelier cause can be alleg'd, but that they well discern'd the mind and principles of most devout and zealous men, and indeed the very discipline of Church, tending to the dissolution of all tyranny. No marvel then if since the faith of 10 Christ receav'd, in purer or impurer times, to depose a King and put him to death for Tyranny, hath bin accounted so just and requisite, that neighbour Kings have both upheld and tak'n part with subjects in the action. And *Ludovicus Pius,* himself an Emperor, and Son of *Charles* the great, being 15 made Judge, *Du Haillan* is my author, between *Milegast* King of the *Vultzes* and his Subjects who had depos'd him, gave his verdit for the Subjects, and for him whom they had chos'n in his room. Note here that the right of electing whom they please is by the impartial testimony of an Em-20 peror in the people. For, said he, *A just Prince ought to be prefer'd before an unjust, and the end of goverment before the prerogative.* And *Constantinus Leo,* another Emperor, in the *Byzantine* Laws saith, *that the end of a King is for the general good, which he not performing is but the counterfet* 25 *of a King.* And to prove that som of our own Monarchs have acknowledg'd that thir high office exempted them not from punishment, they had the Sword of St. *Edward* born before them by an officer who was call'd Earle of the Palace, eev'n

at the times of thir highest pomp and solemnities, to mind
them, saith *Matthew Paris,* the best of our Historians, that if
they errd, the Sword had power to restraine them. And what
restraint the Sword comes to at length, having both edge and
5 point, if any *Sceptic* will doubt, let him feel. It is also
affirm'd from diligent search made in our ancient books of
Law, that the Peers and Barons of England had a legal right
to judge the King: which was the cause most likely, for it
could be no slight cause, that they were call'd his Peers, or
10 equals. This however may stand immovable, so long as man
hath to deale with no better then man; that if our Law judge
all men to the lowest by thir Peers, it should in all equity
ascend also, and judge the highest. And so much I find both
in our own and forren Storie, that Dukes, Earles, and Mar-
15 queses were at first not hereditary, not empty and vain titles,
but names of trust and office, and with the office ceasing, as
induces me to be of opinion, that every worthy man in Parlament, for the word Baron imports no more, might for the
public good be thought a fit Peer and judge of the King;
20 without regard had to petty caveats, and circumstances, the
chief impediment in high affaires, and ever stood upon most
by circumstantial men. Whence doubtless our Ancestors who
were not ignorant with what rights either Nature or ancient
Constitution had endowd them, when Oaths both at Coro-
25 nation, and renewd in Parlament would not serve, thought
it no way illegal to depose and put to death thir tyrannous
Kings. Insomuch that the Parlament drew up a charge
against *Richard the second,* and the Commons requested to

have judgement decree'd against him, that the realme might
not bee endangerd. And *Peter Martyr* a Divine of formost
rank, on the third of *Judges* approves thir doings. Sir *Thomas
Smith* also a Protestant and a Statesman, in his Common-
5 welth of *England,* putting the question whether it be lawfull to rise against a Tyrant, answers that the vulgar judge
of it according to the event, and the lerned according to the
purpose of them that do it. But far before these days, *Gildas*
the most ancient of all our Historians, speaking of those
10 times wherein the Roman Empire decaying quitted and re-
linquishd what right they had by Conquest to this Iland, and
resign'd it all into the peoples hands, testifies that the people
thus re-invested with thir own original right, about the year
446, both elected them Kings, whom they thought best (the
15 first Christian Brittish Kings that ever raign'd heer since the
Romans) and by the same right, when they apprehended
cause, usually depos'd and put them to death. This is the
most fundamental and ancient tenure that any King of
England can produce or pretend to; in comparison of which,
20 all other titles and pleas are but of yesterday. If any object
that *Gildas* condemns the Britans for so doing, the answer is
as ready; that he condemns them no more for so doing, then
hee did before for choosing such, for saith he, *They anointed
them Kings, not of God, but such as were more bloody then
25 the rest.* Next hee condemns them not at all for deposing or
putting them to death, but for doing it over hastily, without
tryal or well examining the cause, and for electing others
wors in thir room. Thus we have heer both domestic and

most ancient examples that the people of Britain have depos'd and put to death thir Kings in those primitive Christian times. And to couple reason with example, if the Church
in all ages, Primitive, Romish, or Protestant, held it ever no
5 less thir duty then the power of thir Keyes, though without
express warrant of Scripture, to bring indifferently both King
and Peasant under the utmost rigor of thir Canons and Censures Ecclesiastical, eev'n to the smiting him with a final
excommunion, if he persist impenitent, what hinders but
10 that the temporal Law both may and ought, though without
a special Text or precedent, extend with like indifference the
civil Sword, to the cutting off without exemption him that
capitally offends. Seeing that justice and Religion are from
the same God, and works of justice ofttimes more acceptable.
15 Yet because that some lately, with the tongues and arguments of Malignant backsliders, have writt'n that the proceedings now in Parlament against the King, are without
precedent from any Protestant State or Kingdom, the examples which follow shall be all Protestant and chiefly
20 Presbyterian.

In the yeare 1546. The *Duke of Saxonie, Lantgrave of
Hessen,* and the whole Protestant league raysd op'n Warr
against *Charles the fifth* thir Emperor, sent him a defiance,
renounc'd all faith and allegeance towards him, and debated
25 long in Councel whither they should give him so much as
the title of *Cæsar. Sleidan. l.* 17. Let all men judge what
this wanted of deposing or of killing, but the power to doe it.

In the yeare 1559. The Scotch Protestants claiming

promise of thir Queen Regent for libertie of conscience, she answering that promises were not to be claim'd of Princes beyond what was commodious for them to grant, told her to her face in the Parlament then at *Sterling,* that if it were so, they renounc'd thir obedience; and soon after betook them to Armes. *Buchanan Hist. l.* 16. certainly when allegeance is renounc'd, that very hour the King or Queen is in effect depos'd.

In the yeare 1564. *John Knox* a most famous Divine and the reformer of *Scotland* to the Presbyterian discipline, at a general Assembly maintained op'nly in a dispute against *Lethington* the Secretary of State, that Subjects might & ought execute Gods judgements upon thir King; that the fact of *Jehu* and others against thir King having the ground of Gods ordinary command to put such and such offenders to death was not extraordinary, but to bee imitated of all that preferr'd the honour of God to the affection of flesh and wicked Princes; that Kings, if they offend, have no privilege to be exempted from the punishments of Law more then any other subject; so that if the King be a Murderer, Adulterer, or Idolater, he should suffer, not as a King, but as an offender; and this position he repeates again and again before them. Answerable was the opinion of *John Craig* another learned Divine, and that Lawes made by the tyranny of Princes, or the negligence of people, thir posterity might abrogate, and reform all things according to the original institution of Common-welths. And *Knox* being commanded by the Nobilitie to write to *Calvin* and other lerned

men for thir judgement in that question, refus'd; alleging
that both himself was fully resolv'd in conscience, and had
heard thir judgements, and had the same opinion under
handwriting of many the most godly and most lerned that
5 he knew in Europe; that if he should move the question to
them againe, what should he doe but shew his own forget-
fulness or inconstancy. All this is farr more largely in the
Ecclesiastic History of *Scotland l.* 4. with many other passages to this effect all the Book over; set out with diligence
10 by Scotchmen of best repute among them at the beginning
of these troubles, as if they labourd to inform us what wee
were to doe, and what they intended upon the like occasion.

And to let the world know that the whole Church and
Protestant State of *Scotland* in those purest times of reforma-
15 tion were of the same beleif, three years after, they met in
the feild *Mary* thir lawful and hereditary Queen, took her
prisoner yeilding before fight, kept her in prison, and the
same yeare depos'd her. *Buchan. Hist. l.* 18.

And four years after that, the Scots in justification of thir
20 deposing Queen *Mary,* sent Ambassadors to Queen *Elizabeth,* and in a writt'n Declaration alleg'd that they had us'd
toward her more lenity then shee deserv'd, that thir Ancestors had heretofore punish'd thir Kings by death or banishment; that the Scots were a free Nation, made King whom
25 they freely chose, and with the same freedom unkingd him
if they saw cause, by right of ancient laws and Ceremonies
yet remaining, and old customs yet among the High-landers
in choosing the head of thir Clanns, or Families; all which

with many other arguments bore witness that regal power was nothing else but a mutual Covnant or stipulation between King and people. *Buch. Hist. l.* 20. These were Scotchmen and Presbyterians; but what measure then have they
5 lately offerd, to think such liberty less beseeming us then themselves, presuming to put him upon us for a Maister whom thir law scarce allows to be thir own equal? If now then we heare them in another strain then heretofore in the purest times of thir Church, we may be confident it is the
10 voice of Faction speaking in them, not of truth and Reformation. Which no less in *England* then in *Scotland,* by the mouthes of those faithful witnesses commonly call'd Puritans, and Nonconformists, spake as clearly for the putting down, yea the utmost punishing of Kings, as in thir several
15 Treatises may be read; eev'n from the first raigne of *Elizabeth* to these times. Insomuch that one of them, whose name was *Gibson,* foretold K. *James,* he should be rooted out, and conclude his race, if he persisted to uphold Bishops. And that very inscription stampt upon the first Coines at his Coro-
20 nation, a naked Sword in a hand with these words, *Si mereor in me, Against me, if I deserve,* not only manifested the judgement of that State, but seem'd also to presage the sentence of Divine justice in this event upon his Son.

In the yeare 1581. the States of *Holland* in a general As-
25 sembly at the *Hague,* abjur'd all obedience and subjection to *Philip* King of *Spaine;* and in a Declaration justifie thir so doing; for that by his tyrannous goverment against faith so many times giv'n & brok'n he had lost his right to all the

Belgic Provinces; that therfore they depos'd him and declar'd it lawful to choose another in his stead. *Thuan. l. 74.*
From that time, to this, no State or Kingdom in the world
hath equally prosperd: But let them remember not to look
5 with an evil and prejudicial eye upon thir Neighbours walk-
ing by the same rule.

But what need these examples to Presbyterians, I mean
to those who now of late would seem so much to abhorr
deposing, when as they to all Christendom have giv'n the
10 latest and the liveliest example of doing it themselves. I
question not the lawfulness of raising Warr against a Tyrant
in defence of Religion, or civil libertie; for no Protestant
Church from the first *Waldenses* of *Lyons,* and *Languedoc*
to this day but have don it round, and maintain'd it lawful.
15 But this I doubt not to affirme, that the Presbyterians, who
now so much condemn deposing, were the men themselves
that deposd the King, and cannot with all thir shifting and
relapsing, wash off the guiltiness from thir own hands. For
they themselves, by these thir late doings have made it guilti-
20 ness, and turn'd thir own warrantable actions into Rebellion.

There is nothing that so actually makes a King of *England,* as rightful possession and Supremacy *in all causes both
civil and Ecclesiastical:* and nothing that so actually makes a
Subject of *England,* as those two Oaths of Allegeance and
25 Supremacy observ'd *without equivocating, or any mental
reservation.* Out of doubt then when the King shall command things already constituted in Church, or State, obedience is the true essence of a subject, either to doe, if it be

lawful, or if he hold the thing unlawful, to submitt to that
penaltie which the Law imposes, so long as he intends to
remaine a Subject. Therfore when the people or any part of
them shall rise against the King and his autority executing
5 the Law in any thing establish'd civil or Ecclesiastical, I doe
not say it is rebellion, if the thing commanded though establish'd be unlawful, and that they sought first all due means
of redress (and no man is furder bound to Law) but I say it
is an absolute renouncing both of Supremacy and Allege-
10 ance, which in one word is an actual and total deposing of
the King, and the setting up of another supreme autority over
them. And whether the Presbyterians have not don all this
and much more, they will not put mee, I suppose, to reck'n
up a seven years story fresh in the memory of all men. Have
15 they not utterly broke the Oath of Allegeance, rejecting the
Kings command and autority sent them from any part of the
Kingdom whether in things lawful or unlawful? Have they
not abjur'd the Oath of Supremacy by setting up the Parlament without the King, supreme to all thir obedience, and
20 though thir Vow and Covnant bound them in general to the
Parlament, yet somtimes adhering to the lesser part of Lords
and Commons that remaind faithful, as they terme it, and
eev'n of them, one while to the Commons without the Lords,
another while to the Lords without the Commons? Have
25 they not still declar'd thir meaning, whatever thir Oath were,
to hold them onely for supreme whom they found at any
time most yeilding to what they petition'd? Both these Oaths
which were the straitest bond of an English subject in refer-

ence to the King, being thus broke & made voide, it follows
undenyably that the King from that time was by them in
fact absolutely depos'd, and they no longer in reality to be
thought his subjects, notwithstanding thir fine clause in the
5 Covnant to preserve his person, Crown, and dignity, set there
by som dodging Casuist with more craft then sincerity to
mitigate the matter in case of ill success and not tak'n I suppose by any honest man, but as a condition subordinat to
every the least particle that might more concerne Religion,
10 liberty, or the public peace. To prove it yet more plainly that
they are the men who have depos'd the King, I thus argue.
We know that King and Subject are relatives, and relatives
have no longer being then in the relation; the relation between King and Subject can be no other then regal autority
15 and subjection. Hence I inferr past their defending, that if
the Subject who is one relative, take away the relation, of
force he takes away also the other relative; but the Presbyterians who were one relative, that is to say Subjects, have
for this sev'n years tak'n away the relation, that is to say the
20 Kings autority, and thir subjection to it, therfore the Presbyterians for these sev'n years have remov'd and extinguishd
the other relative, that is to say the King, or to speak more in
brief have depos'd him; not onely by depriving him the execution of his autoritie, but by conferring it upon others. If
25 then thir Oaths of subjection brok'n, new Supremacy obey'd,
new Oaths and Covnants tak'n, notwithstanding frivolous
evasions, have in plaine termes unking'd the King, much
more then hath thir sev'n years Warr; not depos'd him onely

but outlaw'd him, and defi'd him as an alien, a rebell to Law,
and enemie to the State. It must needs be clear to any man
not avers from reason, that hostilitie and subjection are two
direct and positive contraries; and can no more in one sub-
5 ject stand together in respect of the same King, then one
person at the same time can be in two remote places. Against
whom therfore the Subject is in act of hostility we may be
confident that to him he is in no subjection: and in whom
hostility takes place of subjection, for they can by no meanes
10 consist together, to him the King can be not onely no King,
but an enemie. So that from hence we shall not need dispute
whether they have depos'd him, or what they have defaulted
towards him as no King, but shew manifestly how much
they have don toward the killing him. Have they not levied
15 all these Warrs against him whether offensive or defensive
(for defence in Warr equally offends, and most prudently
before hand) and giv'n Commission to slay where they
knew his person could not be exempt from danger? And if
chance or flight had not sav'd him, how oft'n had they killd
20 him, directing thir Artillery without blame or prohibition to
the very place where they saw him stand? Have they not
Sequester'd him, judg'd or unjudgd, and converted his reve-
new to other uses, detaining from him as a grand Delinquent,
all meanes of livelyhood, so that for them long since he
25 might have perisht, or have starv'd? Have they not hunted
and pursu'd him round about the Kingdom with sword and
fire? Have they not formerly deny'd to Treat with him, and
thir now recanting Ministers preach'd against him, as a rep-

robate incurable, an enemy to God and his Church markt
for destruction, and therfore not to be treated with? Have
they not beseig'd him, & to thir power forbidd him Water
and Fire, save what they shot against him to the hazard of
5 his life? Yet while they thus assaulted and endangerd it with
hostile deeds, they swore in words to defend it with his
Crown and dignity; not in order, as it seems now, to a firm
and lasting peace, or to his repentance after all this blood;
but simply, without regard, without remorse, or any com-
10 parable value of all the miseries and calamities sufferd by the
poore people, or to suffer hereafter through his obstinacy or
impenitence. No understanding man can bee ignorant that
Covnants are ever made according to the present state of persons and of things; and have ever the more general laws of
15 nature and of reason included in them, though not express'd.
If I make a voluntary Covnant as with a man, to doe him
good, and he prove afterward a monster to me, I should con-
ceave a disobligement. If I covnant, not to hurt an enemie,
in favour of him & forbearance, & hope of his amendment,
20 & he, after that, shall doe me tenfould injury and mischief,
to what he had don when I so Covnanted, and stil be plotting what may tend to my destruction, I question not but that
his after actions release me; nor know I Covnant so sacred
that withholds me from demanding justice on him. How-
25 beit, had not thir distrust in a good cause, and the fast and
loos of our prevaricating Divines oversway'd, it had bin
doubtless better not to have inserted in a Covnant unneces-
sary obligations, and words not works of a supererogating

Allegeance to thir enemy; no way advantageous to themselves, had the King prevail'd, as to thir cost many would
have felt; but full of snare and distraction to our friends,
usefull onely, as we now find, to our adversaries, who under
5 such a latitude and shelter of ambiguous interpretation have
ever since been plotting and contriving new opportunities to
trouble all again. How much better had it bin, and more
becomming an undaunted vertue, to have declar'd op'nly
and boldly whom and what power the people were to hold
10 Supreme; as on the like occasion Protestants have don before,
and many conscientious men now in these times have more
then once besought the Parlament to doe, that they might
goe on upon a sure foundation, and not with a ridling Covnant in thir mouths, seeming to sweare counter almost in the
15 same breath Allegeance and no Allegeance; which doubtless
had drawn off all the minds of sincere men from siding with
them, had they not discern'd thir actions farr more deposing
him then thir words upholding him; which words made now
the subject of cavillous interpretations, stood ever in the Cov-
20 nant, by judgement of the more discerning sort, an evidence
of thir feare, not of thir fidelity. What should I return to
speak on, of those attempts for which the King himself hath
oft'n charg'd the Presbyterians of seeking his life, when as
in the due estimation of things, they might without a fallacy
25 be sayd to have don the deed outright. Who knows not that
the King is a name of dignity and office, not of person: Who
therfore kills a King, must kill him while he is a King. Then
they certainly who by deposing him have long since tak'n

from him the life of a King, his office and his dignity, they
in the truest sence may be said to have killd the King: nor
onely by thir deposing and waging Warr against him, which
besides the danger to his personal life, sett him in the fardest
5 opposite point from any vital function of a King, but by thir
holding him in prison, vanquishd and yeilded into thir absolute and *despotic* power, which brought him to the lowest
degradement and incapacity of the regal name. I say not by
whose matchless valour next under God, lest the story of thir
10 ingratitude thereupon carry me from the purpose in hand,
which is to convince them that they, which I repeat againe,
were the men who in the truest sense killd the King, not
onely as is prov'd before, but by depressing him thir King
farr below the rank of a subject to the condition of a Captive,
15 without intention to restore him, as the Chancellour of *Scotland* in a speech told him plainly at *Newcastle,* unless hee
granted fully all thir demands, which they knew he never
meant. Nor did they Treat or think of Treating with him,
till thir hatred to the Army that deliverd them, not thir love
20 or duty to the King, joyn'd them secretly with men sentenc'd
so oft for Reprobats in thir own mouthes, by whose suttle
inspiring they grew madd upon a most tardy and improper
Treaty. Whereas if the whole bent of thir actions had not
bin against the King himself, but only against his evil coun-
25 selers, as they faind, & publishd, wherfore did they not restore him all that while to the true life of a King, his office,
Crown, and Dignity, when he was in thir power, & they
themselves his neerest Counselers. The truth therfore is, both

that they would not, and that indeed they could not without
thir own certain destruction; having reduc'd him to such a
final pass, as was the very death and burial of all in him that
was regal, and from whence never King of *England* yet
5 reviv'd, but by the new re-inforcement of his own party,
which was a kind of resurrection to him. Thus having quite
extinguisht all that could be in him of a King, and from a
total privation clad him over, like another specifical thing,
with formes and habitudes destructive to the former, they
10 left in his person, dead as to Law, and all the civil right
either of King or Subject, the life onely of a Prisner, a Captive and a Malefactor. Whom the equal and impartial hand
of justice finding, was no more to spare then another ordnary
man; not onely made obnoxious to the doom of Law by a
15 charge more then once drawn up against him, and his own
confession to the first Article at *Newport,* but summond and
arraign'd in the sight of God and his people, curst & devoted
to perdition worse then any Ahab, or Antiochus, with exhortation to curse all those in the name of God that made not
20 Warr against him, as bitterly as *Meroz* was to be curs'd, that
went not out against a Canaanitish King, almost in all the
Sermons, Prayers, and Fulminations that have bin utterd this
sev'n yeares by those clov'n tongues of falshood and dissention; who now, to the stirring up of new discord, acquitt him;
25 and against thir own disciplin, which they boast to be the throne
and scepter of Christ, absolve him, unconfound him, though
unconverted, unrepentant, unsensible of all thir pretious
Saints and Martyrs whose blood they have so oft laid upon

his head: and now againe with a new sovran anointment can
wash it all off, as if it were as vile, and no more to be reckn'd
for, then the blood of so many Dogs in a time of Pestilence:
giving the most opprobrious lye to all the acted zeale that for
5 these many yeares hath filld thir bellies, and fed them fatt
upon the foolish people. Ministers of sedition, not of the
Gospel, who while they saw it manifestly tend to civil Warr
and blood shed, never ceasd exasperating the people against
him; and now that they see it likely to breed new commo-
10 tion, cease not to incite others against the people that have
sav'd them from him, as if sedition were thir onely aime,
whether against him or for him. But God, as we have cause
to trust, will put other thoughts into the people, and turn
them from giving eare or heed to these Mercenary noise-
15 makers, of whose fury, and fals prophecies we have anough
experience; and from the murmurs of new discord will incline them to heark'n rather with erected minds to the voice
of our Supreme Magistracy, calling us to liberty and the
flourishing deeds of a reformed Common-wealth; with this
20 hope that as God was heretofore angry with the Jews who
rejected him and his forme of Goverment to choose a King,
so that he will bless us, and be propitious to us who reject a
King to make him onely our leader and supreme governour
in the conformity as neer as may be of his own ancient gover-
25 ment; if we have at least but so much worth in us to entertaine the sense of our future happiness, and the courage to
receave what God voutsafes us: wherein we have the honour
to precede other Nations who are now labouring to be our

followers. For as to this question in hand what the people by thir just right may doe in change of goverment, or of gover-nour, we see it cleerd sufficiently; besides other ample au-tority eev'n from the mouths of Princes themselves. And
5 surely they that shall boast, as we doe, to be a free Nation, and not have in themselves the power to remove, or to abolish any governour supreme, or subordinat, with the goverment it self upon urgent causes, may please thir fancy with a ridic-ulous and painted freedom, fit to coz'n babies; but are indeed
10 under tyranny and servitude; as wanting that power, which is the root and sourse of all liberty, to dispose and *œconomize* in the Land which God hath giv'n them, as Maisters of Family in thir own house and free inheritance. Without which natural and essential power of a free Nation, though
15 bearing high thir heads, they can in due esteem be thought no better then slaves and vassals born, in the tenure and occupation of another inheriting Lord. Whose goverment, though not illegal, or intolerable, hangs over them as a Lordly scourge, not as a free goverment; and therfore to be
20 abrogated. How much more justly then may they fling off tyranny, or tyrants; who being once depos'd can be no more then privat men, as subject to the reach of Justice and ar-raignment as any other transgressors. And certainly if men, not to speak of Heathen, both wise and Religious have don
25 justice upon Tyrants what way they could soonest, how much more milde & human then is it, to give them faire and op'n tryal? To teach lawless Kings, and all who so much adore them, that not mortal man, or his imperious will, but

Justice is the onely true sovran and supreme Majesty upon earth. Let men cease therfore out of faction & hypocrisie to make out-cries and horrid things of things so just and honorable. Though perhaps till now no protestant State or king-
5 dom can be alleg'd to have op'nly put to death thir King, which lately some have writt'n, and imputed to thir great glory; much mistaking the matter. It is not, neither ought to be the glory of a Protestant State, never to have put thir King to death; It is the glory of a Protestant King never to have
10 deserv'd death. And if the Parlament and Military Councel doe what they doe without precedent, if it appeare thir duty, it argues the more wisdom, vertue, and magnanimity, that they know themselves able to be a precedent to others. Who perhaps in future ages, if they prove not too degenerat, will
15 look up with honour, and aspire toward these exemplary, and matchless deeds of thir Ancestors, as to the highest top of thir civil glory and emulation. Which heretofore, in the persuance of fame and forren dominion, spent it self vain-gloriously abroad; but henceforth may learn a better forti-
20 tude, to dare execute highest Justice on them that shall by force of Armes endeavour the oppressing and bereaving of Religion and thir liberty at home: that no unbridl'd Potentate or Tyrant, but to his sorrow for the future, may presume such high and irresponsible licence over mankinde, to havock
25 and turn upside-down whole Kingdoms of men, as though they were no more in respect of his perverse will then a Nation of Pismires. As for the party calld Presbyterian, of whom I believe very many to be good and faithfull Christians,

though misledd by som of turbulent spirit, I wish them
earnestly and calmly not to fall off from thir first principles;
nor to affect rigor and superiority over men not under them;
not to compell unforcible things, in Religion especially,
5 which if not voluntary, becomes a sin; nor to assist the clamor
and malicious drifts of men whom they themselves have
judg'd to be the worst of men, the obdurat enemies of God
and his Church: nor to dart against the actions of thir brethren, for want of other argument, those wrested Lawes and
10 Scriptures thrown by Prelats and Malignants against thir
own sides, which though they hurt not otherwise, yet tak'n
up by them to the condemnation of thir own doings, give
scandal to all men, and discover in themselves either ex-
treame passion, or apostacy. Let them not oppose thir best
15 friends and associats, who molest them not at all, infringe
not the least of thir liberties; unless they call it thir liberty to
bind other mens consciences, but are still seeking to live at
peace with them and brotherly accord. Let them beware an
old and perfet enemy, who though he hope by sowing dis-
20 cord to make them his instruments, yet cannot forbeare a
minute the op'n threatning of his destind revenge upon them,
when they have servd his purposes. Let them, feare therfore
if they be wise, rather what they have don already, then what
remaines to doe, and be warn'd in time they put no confi-
25 dence in Princes whom they have provok'd, lest they be
added to the examples of those that miserably have tasted the
event. Stories can informe them how *Christiern* the second,
King of *Denmark* not much above a hundred yeares past,

driv'n out by his Subjects, and receav'd againe upon new
Oaths and conditions, broke through them all to his most
bloody revenge; slaying his chief opposers when he saw his
time, both them and thir children invited to a feast for that
5   purpose. How *Maximilian* dealt with those of *Bruges,*
though by mediation of the *German* Princes reconcil'd to
them by solem and public writings drawn and seald. How
the massacre at *Paris* was the effect of that credulous peace
which the French Protestants made with *Charles* the ninth
10 thir King: and that the main visible cause which to this day
hath sav'd the *Netherlands* from utter ruin, was thir final not
beleiving the perfidious cruelty which, as a constant maxim
of State, hath bin us'd by the Spanish Kings on thir Subjects
that have tak'n Armes and after trusted them; as no later age
15 but can testifie, heretofore in *Belgia* it self, and this very
yeare in *Naples.* And to conclude with one past exception,
though farr more ancient, *David,* whose sanctify'd prudence
might be alone sufficient, not to warrant us only, but to
instruct us, when once he had tak'n Armes, never after that
20 trusted *Saul,* though with tears and much relenting he twise
promis'd not to hurt him. These instances, few of many,
might admonish them both English and Scotch not to let
thir own ends, and the driving on of a faction betray them
blindly into the snare of those enemies whose revenge looks
25 on them as the men who first begun, fomented and carri'd
on, beyond the cure of any sound or safe accommodation,
all the evil which hath since unavoidably befall'n them and
thir King.

I have somthing also to the Divines, though brief to what were needfull; not to be disturbers of the civil affairs, being in hands better able and more belonging to manage them; but to study harder, and to attend the office of good Pastors,
5 knowing that he whose flock is least among them hath a dreadfull charge, not performd by mounting twise into the chair with a formal preachment huddl'd up at the odd hours of a whole lazy week, but by incessant pains and watching *in season and out of season, from house to house* over the
10 soules of whom they have to feed. Which if they ever well considerd, how little leasure would they find to be the most pragmatical Sidesmen of every popular tumult and Sedition? And all this while are to learn what the true end and reason is of the Gospel which they teach; and what a world it differs
15 from the censorious and supercilious lording over conscience. It would be good also they liv'd so as might perswade the people they hated covetousness, which worse then heresie, is idolatry; hated pluralities and all kind of Simony; left rambling from Benefice to Benefice, like rav'nous Wolves seek-
20 ing where they may devour the biggest. Of which if som, well and warmely seated from the beginning, be not guilty, twere good they held not conversation with such as are: let them be sorry that being call'd to assemble about reforming the Church, they fell to progging and solliciting the Parla-
25 ment, though they had renounc'd the name of Priests, for a new setling of thir Tithes and Oblations; and double lin'd themselves with spiritual places of commoditie beyond the possible discharge of thir duty. Let them assemble in Con-

sistory with thir Elders and Deacons, according to ancient
Ecclesiastical rule, to the preserving of Church-discipline,
each in his several charge, and not a pack of Clergiemen by
themselves to belly-cheare in thir presumptuous Sion, or to
5 promote designes, abuse and gull the simple Laity, and stirr
up tumult, as the Prelats did, for the maintenance of thir
pride and avarice. These things if they observe, and waite
with patience, no doubt but all things will goe well without
their importunities or exclamations: and the Printed letters
10 which they send subscrib'd with the ostentation of great
Characters and little moment, would be more considerable
then now they are. But if they be the Ministers of Mammon
in stead of Christ, and scandalize his Church with the filthy
love of gaine, aspiring also to sit the closest & the heaviest of
15 all Tyrants, upon the conscience, and fall notoriously into
the same sinns, wherof so lately and so loud they accus'd
the Prelates, as God rooted out those wicked ones immediatly before, so will he root out them thir imitators: and to
vindicate his own glory and Religion, will uncover thir
20 hypocrisie to the op'n world; and visit upon thir own heads
that *curse ye Meroz,* the very *Motto* of thir Pulpits, wherwith
so frequently, not as *Meroz,* but more like Atheists they have
blasphem'd the vengeance of God, and traduc'd the zeale of
his people. And that they be not what they goe for, true
25 Ministers of the Protestant doctrine, taught by those abroad,
famous and religious men, who first reformd the Church, or
by those no less zealous, who withstood corruption and the
Bishops heer at home, branded with the name of Puritans

and Nonconformists, wee shall abound with testimonies to make appeare: that men may yet more fully know the difference between Protestant Divines, and these Pulpit-firebrands.

5   Luther.
Lib. contra Rusticos apud Sleidan. l. 5.

Is est hodie rerum status, &c. *Such is the state of things at this day, that men neither can, nor will, nor indeed ought to endure longer the domination of you Princes.*

10   Neque vero Cæsarem, &c. *Neither is Cæsar to make Warr as head of Christ'ndom, Protector of the Church, Defender of the Faith; these Titles being fals and Windie, and most Kings being the greatest Enemies to Religion. Lib: De bello contra Turcas. apud Sleid. l.* 14. What hinders then, but
15 that we may depose or punish them?

These also are recited by *Cochlæus* in his *Miscellanies* to be the words of *Luther,* or some other eminent Divine, then in *Germany,* when the Protestants there entred into solemn Covnant at *Smalcaldia.* Ut ora ijs obturem &c. *That I may*
20 *stop thir mouthes, the Pope and Emperor are not born but elected, and may also be depos'd as hath bin oft'n don.* If *Luther,* or whoever els thought so, he could not stay there; for the right of birth or succession can be no privilege in nature to let a Tyrant sit irremoveable over a Nation free
25 born, without transforming that Nation from the nature and condition of men born free, into natural, hereditary, and successive slaves. Therfore he saith furder; *To displace and throw down this Exactor, this Phalaris, this Nero, is a work*

well pleasing to God; Namely, for being such a one: which is a moral reason. Shall then so slight a consideration as his happ to be not elective simply, but by birth, which was a meer accident, overthrow that which is moral, and make un-
5 pleasing to God that which otherwise had so well pleasd him? certainly not: for if the matter be rightly argu'd, Election much rather then chance, bindes a man to content himself with what he suffers by his own bad Election. Though indeed neither the one nor other bindes any man, much less
10 any people to a necessary sufferance of those wrongs and evils, which they have abilitie and strength anough giv'n them to remove.

Zwinglius. tom. 1. *articul.* 42.

Quando vero perfidè,&c. *When Kings raigne perfidiously,*
15 *and against the rule of Christ, they may according to the word of God be depos'd.*

Mihi ergo compertum non est, &c. *I know not how it comes to pass that Kings raigne by succession, unless it be with consent of the whole people.* ibid.
20 Quum vero consensu, &c: *But when by suffrage and consent of the whole people, or the better part of them, a Tyrant is depos'd or put to death, God is the chief leader in that action.* ibid.

Nunc cum tam tepidi sumus, &c. *Now that we are so*
25 *luke warm in upholding public justice, we indure the vices of Tyrants to raigne now a dayes with impunity; justly therfore by them we are trod underfoot, and shall at length with them be punisht. Yet ways are not wanting by which Ty-*

rants may be remoov'd, but there wants public justice. ibid.

Cavete vobis ô tyranni. *Beware yee Tyrants for now the Gospell of Jesus Christ spreading farr and wide, will renew the lives of many to love innocence and justice; which if yee*
5 *also shall doe, yee shall be honourd. But if yee shall goe on to rage and doe violence, yee shall be trampl'd on by all men.* ibid.

Romanum imperium imò quodq; &c. *When the Roman Empire or any other shall begin to oppress Religion, and wee*
10 *negligently suffer it, wee are as much guilty of Religion so violated, as the Oppressors themselvs.* Idem Epist. ad Conrad. Somium.

Calvin on Daniel. c. 4. v. 25.

Hodie Monarchæ semper in suis titulis, &c. *Now adays*
15 *Monarchs pretend alwayes in thir Titles, to be Kings by the grace of God: but how many of them to this end onely pretend it, that they may raigne without controule; for to what purpose is the grace of God mentiond in the Title of Kings, but that they may acknowledge no Superiour? In the meane*
20 *while God, whose name they use, to support themselves, they willingly would tread under thir feet. It is therfore a meer cheat when they boast to raigne by the grace of God.*

Abdicant se terreni principes, &c. *Earthly Princes depose themselves while they rise against God, yea they are un-*
25 *worthy to be numberd among men: rather it behooves us to spitt upon thir heads then to obey them. On Dan: c. 6. v. 22.*

Bucer on Matth. c. 5.

Si princeps superior, &c. *If a Sovran-Prince endeavour by*

armes to defend transgressors, to subvert those things which
are taught in the word of God, they who are in autority
under him, ought first to disswade him; if they prevaile not,
and that he now beares himself not as a Prince, but as an
5 *enemie, and seekes to violate privileges and rights granted to*
inferior Magistrates or commonalities, it is the part of pious
Magistrates, imploring first the assistance of God, rather to
try all ways and means, then to betray the flock of Christ, to
such an enemie of God: for they also are to this end ordain'd,
10 *that they may defend the people of God, and maintain those*
things which are good and just. For to have supreme power
less'ns not the evil committed by that power, but makes it
the less tolerable, by how much the more generally hurtful.
Then certainly the less tolerable, the more unpardonably to
15 be punish'd.

Of *Peter Martyr* we have spoke before.

Paræus in Rom. 13.

Quorum est constituere Magistratus, &c. *They whose part*
it is to set up Magistrates, may restrain them also from out-
20 *ragious deeds, or pull them down; but all Magistrates are*
set up either by Parlament, or by Electors, or by other Mag-
istrates; They therfore who exalted them, may lawfully de-
grade and punish them.

Of the Scotch Divines I need not mention others then the
25 famousest among them, *Knox,* & and his fellow Labourers
in the reformation of *Scotland;* whose large Treatises on this
subject, defend the same Opinion. To cite them sufficiently,
were to insert thir whole Books, writt'n purposely on this

argument. *Knox Appeal;* and to the Reader; where he
promises in a Postscript that the Book which he intended to
set forth, call'd, The second blast of the Trumpet, should
maintain more at large, that the same men most justly may
5 depose, and punish him whom unadvisedly they have elected,
notwithstanding birth, succession, or any Oath of Allegeance.
Among our own Divines, *Cartwright* and *Fenner,* two of
the Lernedest, may in reason satisfy us what was held by
the rest. *Fenner* in his Book of *Theologie* maintaining, That
10 *they who have power, that is to say a Parlament, may either
by faire meanes or by force depose a Tyrant,* whom he defines to be him, that wilfully breakes all, or the principal
conditions made between him and the Common-wealth.
Fen. Sac: Theolog. c. 13. and *Cartwright* in a prefix'd
15 Epistle testifies his approbation of the whole Book.

Gilby de obedientiâ. p. 25. & 105.

*Kings have thir autoritie of the people, who may upon
occasion reassume it to themselves.*

Englands Complaint against the Canons.

20 *The people may kill wicked Princes as monsters and cruel
beasts.*

Christopher Goodman of Obedience.

When Kings or Rulers become blasphemers of God, oppressors and murderers of thir Subjects, they ought no more
25 to be accounted Kings or lawfull Magistrates, but as privat
men to be examind, accus'd, condemn'd and punisht by the
Law of God, and being convicted and punisht by that law,
it is not mans but Gods doing, *C.* 10. *p.* 139.

By the civil laws a foole or Idiot born, and so prov'd shall loose the lands and inheritance wherto he is born, because he is not able to use them aright. And especially ought in no case be sufferd to have the goverment of a whole Nation; But there is no such evil can come to the Commonwealth by fooles and idiots as doth by the rage and fury of ungodly Rulers; Such therfore being without God ought to have no autority over Gods people, who by his Word requireth the contrary. *C.* 11. *p.* 143, 144.

No person is exempt by any Law of God from this punishment, be he King, Queene, or Emperor, he must dy the death, for God hath not plac'd them above others, to transgress his laws as they list, but to be subject to them as well as others, and if they be subject to his laws, then to the punishment also, so much the more as thir example is more dangerous. *C.* 13. *p.* 184.

When Magistrates cease to doe thir Duty, the people are as it were without Magistrates, yea worse, and then God giveth the sword into the peoples hand, and he himself is become immediatly thir head. *p.* 185.

If Princes doe right and keep promise with you, then doe you owe to them all humble obedience: if not, yee are discharg'd, and your study ought to be in this case how ye may depose and punish according to the Law such Rebels against God and oppressors of thir Country. *p.* 190.

This *Goodman* was a Minister of the *English* Church at *Geneva,* as *Dudley Fenner* was at *Middleburrough,* or some other place in that Country. These were the Pastors of those

Saints and Confessors who flying from the bloudy persecution of Queen *Mary,* gather'd up at length thir scatterd members into many Congregations; wherof som in upper, some
in lower *Germany,* part of them settl'd at *Geneva;* where this
5 Author having preachd on this subject to the great liking of
certain lerned and godly men who heard him, was by them
sundry times & with much instance requir'd to write more
fully on that point. Who therupon took it in hand, and conferring with the best lerned in those parts (among whom
10 *Calvin* was then living in the same City) with their special
approbation he publisht this treatise, aiming principally, as is
testify'd by *Whittingham* in the Preface, that his Brethren of
England, the Protestants, might be perswaded in the truth
of that Doctrine concerning obedience to Magistrates. *Whit-*
15 *tingham in Prefat.*

These were the true Protestant Divines of *England,* our
fathers in the faith we hold; this was their sense, who for so
many yeares labouring under Prelacy, through all stormes
and persecutions kept Religion from extinguishing; and de-
20 liverd it pure to us, till there arose a covetous and ambitious
generation of Divines (for Divines they call themselves) who
feining on a sudden to be new converts and proselytes from
Episcopacy, under which they had long temporiz'd, op'nd
thir mouthes at length, in shew against Pluralities and Prel-
25 acy, but with intent to swallow them down both; gorging
themselves like Harpy's on those simonious places and preferments of thir outed predecessors, as the quarry for which
they hunted, not to pluralitie onely but to multiplicitie: for

possessing which they had accusd them thir Brethren, and aspiring under another title to the same authoritie and usurpation over the consciences of all men.

Of this faction diverse reverend and lerned Divines, as
5 they are stil'd in the Phylactery of thir own Title page, pleading the lawfulnes of defensive Armes against this King, in a Treatise call'd *Scripture and Reason,* seem in words to disclaime utterly the deposing of a King; but both the Scripture and the reasons which they use, draw consequences after
10 them, which without their bidding, conclude it lawfull. For if by Scripture, and by that especially to the *Romans,* which they most insist upon, Kings, doing that which is contrary to Saint *Pauls* definition of a Magistrat, may be resisted, they may altogether with as much force of consequence be de-
15 pos'd or punishd. And if by reason the unjust autority of Kings *may be forfeted in part, and his power be reassum'd in part, either by the Parlament or People, for the case in hazard and the present necessitie,* as they affirm *p.* 34, there can no Scripture be alleg'd, no imaginable reason giv'n, that
20 necessity continuing, as it may alwayes, and they in all prudence and thir duty may take upon them to foresee it, why in such a case they may not finally amerce him with the loss of his Kingdom, of whose amendment they have no hope. And if one wicked action persisted in against Religion, Laws,
25 and liberties may warrant us to thus much in part, why may not forty times as many tyrannies, by him committed, warrant us to proceed on restraining him, till the restraint become total. For the ways of justice are exactest proportion;

EIKONOKLASTES

ΕΙΚΟΝΟΚΛΑΣΤΗΣ

IN

Anſwer

To a Book Intitl'd

ΕΙΚΩΝ ΒΑΣΙΛΙΚΗ,

THE

PORTRATURE of his Sacred MAJESTY

in his *Solitudes* and *Sufferings.*

The Author I. M. *John Milton*

PROV. 28. 15, 16, 17.

15. *As a roaring Lyon, and a ranging Beare, ſo is a wicked Ruler over the poor people.*

16. *The Prince that wanteth underſtanding, is also a great oppreſſor; but he that hateth covetouſneſſe ſhall prolong his dayes.*

17. *A man that doth violence to the blood of any perſon, ſhall fly to the pit, let no man ſtay him.*

Saluſt. Conjurat. Catilin.

Regium imperium, quod initio, conſervandæ libertatis, atque augendæ reipub. causâ fuerat, in ſuperbiam, dominationemque ſe convertit.

Regibus boni, quam mali, ſuspectiores ſunt; ſemperque his aliena virtus formidoloſa eſt.

Quidlibet impunè facere, hoc ſcilicet regium eſt.

Publiſhed by Authority.

London, Printed by *Matthew Simmons*, next dore to the gilded Lyon in Alderſgate ſtreet. 1649.

The *PREFACE*

TO descant on the misfortunes of a person fall'n from so high a dignity, who hath also payd his final debt both to Nature and his Faults, is neither of it self a thing commendable, nor the intention of this discours.
5 Neither was it fond ambition, or the vanity to get a Name, present, or with Posterity, by writing against a King: I never was so thirsty after Fame, nor so destitute of other hopes and means, better and more certaine to attaine it. For Kings have gain'd glorious Titles from thir Favourers by writing
10 against privat men, as *Henry* the 8th did against *Luther;* but no man ever gain'd much honour by writing against a King, as not usually meeting with that force of Argument in such Courtly *Antagonists,* which to convince might add to his reputation. Kings most commonly, though strong in Le-
15 gions, are but weak at Arguments; as they who ever have accustom'd from the Cradle to use thir will onely as thir right hand, thir reason always as thir left. Whence unexpectedly constrain'd to that kind of combat, they prove but weak and puny Adversaries. Nevertheless for their sakes who
20 through custom, simplicitie, or want of better teaching, have not more seriously considerd Kings, then in the gaudy name of Majesty, and admire them and thir doings, as if they breath'd not the same breath with other mortal men, I shall make no scruple to take up (for it seems to be the challenge both of
25 him and all his party) to take up this Gauntlet, though a Kings, in the behalf of Libertie, and the Commonwealth.

And furder, since it appears manifestly the cunning drift
of a factious and defeated Party, to make the same advantage
of his Book, which they did before of his Regal Name and
Authority, and intend it not so much the defence of his for-
5 mer actions, as the promoting of thir own future designes,
making thereby the Book thir own rather then the Kings, as
the benefit now must be thir own more then his, now the
third time to corrupt and disorder the mindes of weaker men,
by new suggestions and narrations, either falsly or falla-
10 ciously representing the state of things, to the dishonour of
this present Goverment, and the retarding of a generall
peace, so needfull to this afflicted Nation, and so nigh obtain'd, I suppose it no injurie to the dead, but a good deed
rather to the living, if by better information giv'n them, or,
15 which is anough, by onely remembring them the truth of
what they themselves know to be heer misaffirm'd, they may
be kept from entring the third time unadvisedly into Warr
and bloodshed. For as to any moment of solidity in the Book
it self, save only that a King is said to be the Author, a name,
20 then which there needs no more among the blockish vulgar,
to make it wise, and excellent, and admir'd, nay to set it next
the Bible, though otherwise containing little els but the common grounds of tyranny and popery, drest up, the better to
deceiv, in a new Protestant guise, and trimmly garnish'd
25 over, or as to any need of answering, in respect of staid and
well-principl'd men, I take it on me as a work assign'd rather,
then by me chos'n or affected. Which was the cause both of
beginning it so late, and finishing it so leasurely, in the midst

of other imployments and diversions. And though well it
might have seem'd in vaine to write at all; considering the
envy and almost infinite prejudice likely to be stirr'd up
among the Common sort, against what ever can be writt'n
5 or gainsaid to the Kings book, so advantageous to a book it is,
only to be a Kings, and though it be an irksom labour to
write with industrie and judicious paines that which neither
waigh'd, nor well read, shall be judg'd without industry or
the paines of well judging, by faction and the easy literature
10 of custom and opinion, it shall be ventur'd yet, and the truth
not smother'd, but sent abroad, in the native confidence of
her single self, to earn, how she can, her entertainment in the
world, and to finde out her own readers; few perhaps, but
those few, such of value and substantial worth, as truth and
15 wisdom, not respecting numbers and bigg names, have bin
ever wont in all ages to be contented with.

And if the late King had thought sufficient those Answers
and Defences made for him in his life time, they who on the
other side accus'd his evil Goverment, judging that on their
20 behalf anough also hath been reply'd, the heat of this controversie was in likelyhood drawing to an end; and the furder
mention of his deeds, not so much unfortunat as faulty, had
in tenderness to his late sufferings, bin willingly forborn;
and perhaps for the present age might have slept with him
25 unrepeated; while his adversaries, calm'd and asswag'd with
the success of thir cause, had bin the less unfavorable to his
memory. But since he himself, making new appeale to Truth
and the World, hath left behind him this Book as the best

advocat and interpreter of his own actions, and that his
Friends by publishing, dispersing, commending, and almost
adoring it, seem to place therein the chiefe strength and
nerves of thir cause, it would argue doubtless in the other
5 party great deficience and distrust of themselves, not to meet
the force of his reason in any field whatsoever, the force and
equipage of whose Armes they have so oft'n met victoriously.
And he who at the Barr stood excepting against the form and
manner of his Judicature, and complain'd that he was not
10 heard, neither he nor his Friends shall have that cause now
to find fault; being mett and debated with in this op'n and
monumental Court of his own erecting; and not onely heard
uttering his whole mind at large, but answer'd. Which to doe
effectually, if it be necessary that to his Book nothing the
15 more respect be had for being his, they of his own Party can
have no just reason to exclaime. For it were too unreasonable that he, because dead, should have the liberty in his
Book to speak all evil of the Parlament; and they, because
living, should be expected to have less freedom, or any for
20 them, to speak home the plain truth of a full and pertinent
reply. As he, to acquitt himself, hath not spar'd his Adversaries, to load them with all sorts of blame and accusation,
so to him, as in his Book alive, there will be us'd no more
Courtship then he uses; but what is properly his own guilt,
25 not imputed any more to his evil Counsellors, (a Ceremony
us'd longer by the Parlament then he himself desir'd) shall
be laid heer without circumlocutions at his own dore. That
they who from the first beginning, or but now of late, by

what unhappines I know not, are so much affatuated, not
with his person onely, but with his palpable faults, and dote
upon his deformities, may have none to blame but thir own
folly, if they live and dye in such a strook'n blindness, as next
5 to that of *Sodom* hath not happ'nd to any sort of men more
gross, or more misleading. Yet neither let his enemies expect
to finde recorded heer all that hath been whisper'd in the
Court, or alleg'd op'nly of the Kings bad actions; it being the
proper scope of this work in hand, not to ripp up and relate
10 the misdoings of his whole life, but to answer only, and
refute the missayings of his book.

First then that some men (whether this were by him intended, or by his Friends) have by policy accomplish'd after
death that revenge upon thir Enemies, which in life they
15 were not able, hath been oft related. And among other examples we finde that the last will of *Cæsar* being read to the
people, and what bounteous Legacies hee had bequeath'd
them, wrought more in that Vulgar audience to the aveng-
ing of his death, then all the art he could ever use, to win thir
20 favor in his life-time. And how much their intent, who publish'd these overlate Apologies and Meditations of the dead
King, drives to the same end of stirring up the people to bring
him that honour, that affection, and by consequence, that
revenge to his dead Corps, which hee himself living could
25 never gain to his Person, it appears both by the conceited
portraiture before his Book, drawn out to the full measure of
a Masking Scene, and sett there to catch fools and silly gazers,
and by those Latin words after the end, *Vota dabunt quæ*

Bella negarunt; intimating, That what hee could not compass by Warr, he should atchieve by his Meditations. For in
words which admitt of various sense, the libertie is ours to
choose that interpretation which may best minde us of what
our restless enemies endeavor, and what wee are timely to
prevent. And heer may be well observ'd the loose and neg-
ligent curiosity of those who took upon them to adorn the
setting out of this Book: for though the Picture sett in Front
would Martyr him and Saint him to befool the people, yet
the Latin Motto in the end, which they understand not,
leaves him, as it were a politic contriver to bring about that
interest by faire and plausible words, which the force of
Armes deny'd him. But quaint Emblems and devices begg'd
from the old Pageantry of some Twelf-nights entertainment
at *Whitehall,* will doe but ill to make a Saint or Martyr; and
if the People resolve to take him Sainted at the rate of such
a Canonizing, I shall suspect thir Calendar more then the
Gregorian. In one thing I must commend his op'nness who
gave the title to this Book, Εἰκὼν Βασιλική, that is to say,
The Kings Image; and by the Shrine he dresses out for him,
certainly would have the people come and worship him. For
which reason this answer also is intitl'd *Iconoclastes,* the famous Surname of Many Greek Emperors, who in thir zeal
to the command of God, after long tradition of Idolatry in
the Church, took courage, and broke all superstitious Images to peeces. But the People, exorbitant and excessive in all
thir motions, are prone ofttimes not to a religious onely, but
to a civil kinde of Idolatry in idolizing thir Kings; though

never more mistak'n in the object of thir worship; heretofore being wont to repute for Saints, those faithful and
courageous Barons, who lost thir lives in the Field, making
glorious Warr against Tyrants for the common Liberty; as
5 *Simon de Momfort* Earl of *Leicester,* against *Henry* the
third; *Thomas Plantagenet* Earl of *Lancaster,* against *Edward* the second. But now, with a besotted and degenerate
baseness of spirit, except some few, who yet retain in them
the old English fortitude and love of Freedom, and have tes-
10 tifi'd it by thir matchless deeds, the rest, imbastardiz'd from
the ancient nobleness of thir Ancestors, are ready to fall flatt
and give adoration to the Image and Memory of this Man,
who hath offer'd at more cunning fetches to undermine our
Liberties, and putt Tyranny into an Art, then any British
15 King before him. Which low dejection and debasement of
mind in the people, I must confess I cannot willingly ascribe
to the natural disposition of an English-man, but rather to
two other causes. First, to the Prelats and thir fellow-teach-
ers, though of another Name and Sect, whose Pulpit stuff,
20 both first and last, hath bin the Doctrin and perpetual infu-
sion of servility and wretchedness to all thir hearers; whose
lives the type of worldliness and hypocrisie, without the least
true pattern of vertue, righteousness, or self-denial in thir
whole practice. I attribute it next to the factious inclination
25 of most men divided from the public by several ends and
humors of thir own. At first no man less belov'd, no man
more generally condemn'd then was the King; from the
time that it became his custom to break Parlaments at home,

and either wilfully or weakly to betray Protestants abroad, to
the beginning of these Combustions. All men inveigh'd
against him; all men, except Court-vassals, oppos'd him and
his tyrannical proceedings; the cry was universal; and this
5 full Parlament was at first unanimous in thir dislike and
Protestation against his evil Goverment. But when they
who sought themselves and not the Public, began to doubt
that all of them could not by one and the same way attain to
thir ambitious purposes, then was the King, or his Name at
10 least, as a fit property, first made use of, his doings made the
best of, and by degrees justifi'd: Which begott him such a
party, as after many wiles and struglings with his inward
fears, imbold'n'd him at length to sett up his Standard against
the Parlament. Whenas before that time, all his adherents,
15 consisting most of dissolute Sword-men and Suburb-roysters,
hardly amounted to the making up of one ragged regiment
strong anough to assault the unarmed house of Commons.
After which attempt, seconded by a tedious and bloody warr
on his subjects, wherein he hath so farr exceeded those his
20 arbitrary violences in time of Peace, they who before hated
him for his high misgoverment, nay, fought against him
with display'd banners in the field, now applaud him and
extoll him for the wisest and most religious Prince that liv'd.
By so strange a method amongst the mad multitude is a sud-
25 den reputation won, of wisdom by wilfulness and suttle
shifts, of goodness by multiplying evil, of piety by endeavouring to root out true religion.

But it is evident that the chief of his adherents never lov'd

him, never honour'd either him or his cause, but as they took
him to set a face upon thir own malignant designes; nor
bemoan his loss at all, but the loss of thir own aspiring hopes:
Like those captive women whom the Poet notes in his *Iliad*,
5 to have bewaild the death of *Patroclus* in outward show, but
indeed thir own condition.

Πάτροχλον πρόφασιν, σφῶν δ' αὐτῶν κήδε' ἑκάστη.
Hom. Iliad. τ.

And it needs must be ridiculous to any judgement unin-
10 thrall'd, that they who in other matters express so little fear
either of God or man, should in this one particular outstripp
all precisianism with thir scruples and cases, and fill mens
ears continually with the noise of thir conscientious Loyaltie
and Allegeance to the King, Rebels in the mean while to God
15 in all thir actions beside: much less that they whose profess'd Loyalty and Allegeance led them to direct Arms
against the Kings Person, and thought him nothing violated
by the Sword of Hostility drawn by them against him, should
now in earnest think him violated by the unsparing Sword
20 of Justice, which undoubtedly so much the less in vain she
bears among Men, by how much greater and in highest place
the offender. Els Justice, whether moral or political, were
not Justice, but a fals counterfet of that impartial and God-
like vertue. The onely grief is, that the head was not strook
25 off to the best advantage and commodity of them that held it
by the hair; an ingratefull and pervers generation, who hav-

ing first cry'd to God to be deliver'd from thir King, now
murmur against God that heard thir praiers, and cry as loud
for thir King against those that deliver'd them. But as to the
Author of these Soliloquies, whether it were undoubtedly the
5 late King, as is vulgarly beleev'd, or any secret *Coadjutor,*
and some stick not to name him, it can add nothing, nor shall
take from the weight, if any be, of reason which he brings.
But allegations, not reasons are the main contents of this
Book; and need no more then other contrary allegations to
10 lay the question before all men in an eev'n ballance; though
it were suppos'd that the testimony of one man in his own
cause affirming, could be of any moment to bring in doubt
the autority of a Parlament denying. But if these his fair
spok'n words shall be heer fairly confronted and laid parallel
15 to his own farr differing deeds, manifest and visible to the
whole Nation, then surely we may look on them who notwithstanding shall persist to give to bare words more credit
then to op'n deeds, as men whose judgement was not rationally evinc'd and perswaded, but fatally stupifi'd and be-
20 witch'd, into such a blinde and obstinate beleef. For whose
cure it may be doubted, not whether any charm, though
never so wisely murmur'd, but whether any prayer can be
available. This however would be remember'd and wel
noted, that while the K. instead of that repentance which
25 was in reason and in conscience to be expected from him,
without which we could not lawfully re-admitt him, persists
heer to maintain and justifie the most apparent of his evil
doings, and washes over with a Court-fucus the worst and

foulest of his actions, disables and uncreates the Parlament
it self, with all our laws and Native liberties that ask not his
leave, dishonours and attaints all Protestant Churches, not
Prelaticall, and what they piously reform'd, with the slander
5 of rebellion, sacrilege, and hypocrisie; they who seem'd of
late to stand up hottest for the Cov'nant, can now sit mute
and much pleas'd to hear all these opprobrious things utter'd
against thir faith, thir freedom, and themselves in thir own
doings made traitors to boot: The Divines also, thir wiz-
10 zards, can be so braz'n as to cry *Hosanna* to this his book,
which cries louder against them for no disciples of Christ, but
of *Iscariot;* and to seem now convinc'd with these wither'd
arguments and reasons heer, the same which in som other
writings of that party, and in his own former Declarations
15 and expresses, they have so oft'n heertofore endeavour'd to
confute and to explode; none appearing all this while to vindicate Church or State from these calumnies and reproaches,
but a small handfull of men whom they defame and spit at
with all the odious names of Schism and Sectarism. I never
20 knew that time in *England,* when men of truest Religion
were not counted Sectaries: but wisdom now, valor, justice,
constancy, prudence united and imbodied to defend Religion
and our Liberties, both by word and deed against tyranny, is
counted Schism and faction. Thus in a graceless age things
25 of highest praise and imitation under a right name, to make
them infamous and hatefull to the people, are miscall'd.
Certainly, if ignorance and perversness will needs be national
and universal, then they who adhere to wisdom and to truth,

are not therfore to be blam'd, for beeing so few as to seem a
sect or faction. But in my opinion it goes not ill with that
people where these vertues grow so numerous and well
joyn'd together, as to resist and make head against the rage
5 and torrent of that boistrous folly and superstition that pos-
sesses and hurries on the vulgar sort. This therfore we may
conclude to be a high honour don us from God, and a spe-
ciall mark of his favor, whom he hath selected as the sole
remainder, after all these changes and commotions, to stand
10 upright and stedfast in his cause; dignify'd with the defence
of truth and public libertie; while others who aspir'd to be
the topp of Zelots, and had almost brought Religion to a
kinde of trading monopoly, have not onely by thir late silence
and neutrality bely'd thir profession, but founder'd them-
15 selves and thir consciences, to comply with enemies in that
wicked cause and interest which they have too oft'n curs'd
in others, to prosper now in the same themselves.

’Εικονοκλάστης

I. *Upon the Kings calling this last Par-*
lament.

THAT which the King layes down heer as his first
foundation, and as it were the head stone of his
whole Structure, that *He call'd this last Parlament*
not more by others advice and the necessity of his affaires,
then by his own chois and inclination, is to all knowing men
so apparently not true, that a more unlucky and inauspicious
sentence, and more betok'ning the downfall of his whole
Fabric, hardly could have come into his minde. For who
knows not that the inclination of a Prince is best known
either by those next about him, and most in favor with him,
or by the current of his own actions. Those neerest to this
King and most his Favorites, were Courtiers and Prelates;
men whose chief study was to finde out which way the King
inclin'd, and to imitate him exactly. How these men stood
affected to Parlaments, cannot be forgott'n. No man but may
remember it was thir continuall exercise to dispute and
preach against them; and in thir common discours nothing
was more frequent, then that *they hoped the King should*
now have no need of Parlaments any more. And this was but
the copy which his Parasites had industriously tak'n from his
own words and actions, who never call'd a Parlament but to
supply his necessities; and having supply'd those, as suddenly and ignominiously dissolv'd it, without redressing any
one greevance of the people. Somtimes choosing rather to

miss of his Subsidies, or to raise them by illegal courses, then that the people should not still miss of thir hopes to be re-leiv'd by Parlaments.

The first he broke off at his comming to the Crown; for no other cause then to protect the Duke of *Buckingham* against them who had accus'd him, besides other hainous crimes, of no less then poysoning the deceased King his Father; concerning which matter the Declaration of *No more addresses,* hath sufficiently inform'd us. And still the latter breaking was with more affront and indignity put upon the House and her worthiest Members, then the former: In-somuch that in the fifth year of his Raign, in a Proclamation he seems offended at the very rumor of a Parlament divulg'd among the people: as if he had tak'n it for a kind of slander, that men should think him that way exorable, much less inclin'd: and forbidds it as a presumption to prescribe him any time for Parlaments, that is to say, either by perswasion or Petition, or so much as the reporting of such a rumor; for other manner of prescribing was at that time not suspected. By which feirce Edict, the people, forbidd'n to complain, as well as forc'd to suffer, began from thenceforth to despaire of Parlaments. Whereupon such illegal actions, and espe-cially to get vast summs of Money, were put in practise by the King and his new Officers, as Monopolies, compulsive Knight-hoods, Cote, Conduct and Ship money, the seizing not of one *Naboths* Vineyard, but of whole Inheritances under the pretence of Forrest, or Crown-Lands, corruption and Bribery compounded for, with impunities granted for

the future, as gave evident proof that the King never meant,
nor could it stand with the reason of his affaires, ever to recall
Parlaments; having brought by these irregular courses the
peoples interest and his own to so direct an opposition, that
5 he might foresee plainly, if nothing but a Parlament could
save the people, it must necessarily be his undoing.

Till eight or nine years after, proceeding with a high hand
in these enormities, and having the second time levied an
injurious Warr against his native Countrie *Scotland,* and
10 finding all those other shifts of raising Money, which bore
out his first expedition, now to faile him, not *of his own chois
and inclination,* as any Child may see, but urg'd by strong
necessities, and the very pangs of State, which his own violent proceedings had brought him to, hee calls a Parlament;
15 first in *Ireland,* which onely was to give him four Subsidies,
and so to expire; then in *England,* where his first demand
was but twelve Subsidies, to maintain a Scotch Warr, condemn'd and abominated by the whole Kingdom; promising
thir greevances should be consider'd afterward. Which when
20 the Parlament, who judg'd that Warr it self one of thir main
greevances, made no hast to grant, not enduring the delay
of his impatient will, or els fearing the conditions of thir
grant, he breaks off the whole Session, and dismisses them
and thir greevances with scorn and frustration.

25 Much less therfore did hee call this last Parlament by his
own chois and inclination; but having first try'd in vaine all
undue ways to procure Mony, his Army, of thir own accord,
being beat'n in the North, the Lords Petitioning, and the

general voice of the people almost hissing him and his ill-
acted regality off the Stage, compell'd at length both by his
wants, and by his feares, upon meer extremity he summon'd
this last Parlament. And how is it possible that hee should
5 willingly incline to Parlaments, who never was perceiv'd to
call them, but for the greedy hope of a whole National Bribe,
his Subsidies, and never lov'd, never fulfill'd, never promoted
the true end of Parlaments, the redress of greevances, but still
put them off, and prolong'd them, whether gratify'd or not
10 gratify'd; and was indeed the Author of all those greevances.
To say therfore that hee call'd this Parlament of his own
chois and inclination, argues how little truth wee can expect from the sequel of this Book, which ventures in the very
first period to affront more then one Nation with an untruth
15 so remarkable; and presumes a more implicit Faith in the
people of *England,* then the Pope ever commanded from the
Romish Laitie; or els a natural sottishness fitt to be abus'd
and ridd'n. While in the judgement of wise Men, by laying
the foundation of his defence on the avouchment of that
20 which is so manifestly untrue, he hath giv'n a worse foile to
his own cause, then when his whole Forces were at any time
overthrown. They therfore who think such great Service don
to the Kings affairs in publishing this Book, will find themselves in the end mistak'n: if sense and right mind, or but
25 any mediocrity of knowledge and remembrance hath not
quite forsak'n men.

But to prove his inclination to Parlaments, he affirms heer
To have always thought the right way of them, most safe for

his Crown, and best pleasing to his People. What hee thought we know not; but that hee ever took the contrary way wee saw; and from his own actions we felt long agoe what he thought of Parlaments or of pleasing his People: a surer evidence then what we hear now too late in words.

He alleges, that *the cause of forbearing to convene Parlaments, was the sparkes which some mens distempers there studied to kindle.* They were indeed not temper'd to his temper; for it neither was the Law, nor the rule by which all other tempers were to bee try'd; but they were esteem'd and chos'n for the fittest men in thir several Counties, to allay and quench those distempers which his own inordinate doings had inflam'd. And if that were his refusing to *convene,* till those men had been qualify'd to his temper, that is to say, his will, we may easily conjecture what hope ther was of Parlaments, had not fear and his insatiat poverty in the midst of his excessive wealth constrain'd him.

Hee hoped by his freedom, and their moderation to prevent misunderstandings. And wherfore not by their freedom and his moderation? But freedom he thought too high a word for them; and moderation too mean a word for himself: this was not the way to prevent misunderstandings. He still *fear'd passion and prejudice in other men;* not in himself: *and doubted not by the weight of his* own *reason, to counterpoyse any Faction;* it being so easie for him, and so frequent, to call his obstinacy, Reason, and other mens reason, Faction. Wee in the mean while must beleive, that wisdom and all reason came to him by Title, with his Crown;

Passion, Prejudice, and Faction came to others by being Subjects.

He was sorry to hear with what popular heat Elections were carry'd in many places. Sorry rather that Court Letters
5 and intimations prevail'd no more, to divert or to deterr the people from thir free Election of those men, whom they thought best affected to Religion and thir Countries Libertie, both at that time in danger to be lost. And such men they were, as by the Kingdom were sent to advise him, not sent to
10 be cavill'd at, because Elected, or to be entertaind by him with an undervalue and misprision of thir temper, judgment, or affection. In vain was a Parlament thought fittest by the known Laws of our Nation, to advise and regulate unruly Kings, if they, in stead of hearkning to advice, should be
15 permitted to turn it off, and refuse it by vilifying and traducing thir advisers, or by accusing of a popular heat those that lawfully elected them.

His own and his Childrens interest oblig'd him to seek and to preserve the love and welfare of his Subjects. Who
20 doubts it? But the same interest, common to all Kings, was never yet available to make them all seek that, which was indeed best for themselves and thir Posterity. All men by thir own and thir Childrens interest are oblig'd to honestie and justice: but how little that consideration works in privat
25 men, how much less in Kings, thir deeds declare best.

He intended to oblige both Friends and Enemies, and to exceed thir desires, did they but pretend to any modest and sober sence; mistaking the whole business of a Parlament.

Which mett not to receive from him obligations, but Justice;
nor he to expect from them thir modesty, but thir grave advice, utter'd with freedom in the public cause. His talk of
modesty in thir desires of the common welfare, argues him
not much to have understood what he had to grant, who mis-
conceav'd so much the nature of what they had to desire.
And for *sober sence* the expresion was too mean; and re-
coiles with as much dishonour upon himself, to be a King
where sober sense could possibly be so wanting in a Parlament.

*The odium and offences which some mens rigour, or re-
missness in Church and State had contracted upon his Goverment, hee resolved to have expiated with better Laws and
regulations.* And yet the worst of misdemeanors committed
by the worst of all his favourites, in the hight of thir dominion, whether acts of rigor or remissness, he hath from time to
time continu'd, own'd, and taken upon himself by public
Declarations, as oft'n as the Clergy, or any other of his Instruments felt themselves over burd'n'd with the peoples
hatred. And who knows not the superstitious rigor of his
Sundays Chappel, and the licentious remissness of his Sundays
Theater; accompanied with that reverend Statute for *Do-
minical* Jiggs and May-poles, publish'd in his own Name,
and deriv'd from the example of his Father *James.* Which
testifies all that rigor in superstition, all that remissness in
Religion to have issu'd out originally from his own House,
and from his own Autority. Much rather then may those
general miscarriages in State, his proper Sphear, be imputed

to no other person chiefly then to himself. And which of all
those oppressive Acts, or Impositions did he ever disclaim or
disavow, till the fatal aw of this Parlament hung ominously
over him. Yet heer hee smoothly seeks to wipe off all the
5 envie of his evill Goverment upon his Substitutes, and under-
Officers: and promises, though much too late, what wonders
he purpos'd to have don in the reforming of Religion; a work
wherein all his undertakings heretofore declare him to have
had little or no judgement. Neither could his Breeding, or
10 his cours of life acquaint him with a thing so Spiritual.
Which may well assure us what kind of Reformation we
could expect from him; either som politic form of an impos'd Religion, or els perpetual vexation, and persecution to
all those that comply'd not with such a form. The like amend-
15 ment hee promises in State; not a stepp furder *then his Reason and Conscience told him was fitt to be desir'd;* wishing
*hee had kept within those bounds, and not suffer'd his own
judgement to have bin over-borne in some things,* of which
things one was the Earl of *Straffords* execution. And what
20 signifies all this, but that stil his resolution was the same, to
set up an arbitrary Goverment of his own; and that all Britain was to be ty'd and chain'd to the conscience, judgement,
and reason of one Man; as if those gifts had been only his
peculiar and Prerogative, intal'd upon him with his fortune
25 to be a King. When as doubtless no man so obstinate, or so
much a Tyrant, but professes to be guided by that which he
calls his Reason, and his Judgement, though never so corrupted; and pretends also his conscience. In the mean while,

for any Parlament or the whole Nation to have either reason, judgement, or conscience, by this rule was altogether in vaine, if it thwarted the Kings will; which was easie for him to call by any other more plausible name. He himself
5 hath many times acknowledg'd to have no right over us but by Law; and by the same Law to govern us: but Law in a Free Nation hath bin ever public reason, the enacted reason of a Parlament; which he denying to enact, denies to govern us by that which ought to be our Law; interpos-
10 ing his own privat reason, which to us is no Law. And thus we find these faire and specious promises, made upon the experience of many hard sufferings, and his most mortifi'd retirements, being throughly sifted, to containe nothing in them much different from his former practices, so cross,
15 and so averse to all his Parlaments, and both the Nations of this Iland. What fruits they could in likelyhood have produc'd in his restorement, is obvious to any prudent foresight.

And this is the substance of his first section, till wee come
20 to the devout of it, model'd into the form of a privat Psalter. Which they who so much admire, either for the matter or the manner, may as well admire the Arch-Bishops late Breviary, and many other as good *Manuals,* and *Handmaids of Devotion,* the lip-work of every Prelatical Liturgist, clapt to-
25 gether, and quilted out of Scripture phrase, with as much ease, and as little need of Christian diligence, or judgement, as belongs to the compiling of any ord'nary and salable peece of English Divinity, that the Shops value. But he who from

such a kind of Psalmistry, or any other verbal Devotion, without the pledge and earnest of sutable deeds, can be perswaded of a zeale, and true righteousness in the person, hath much yet to learn; and knows not that the deepest policy of

5 a Tyrant hath bin ever to counterfet Religious. And *Aristotle* in his Politics, hath mentiond that special craft among twelve other tyrannical *Sophisms*. Neither want wee examples. *Andronicus Comnenus* the *Byzantine* Emperor, though a most cruel Tyrant, is reported by *Nicetas* to have bin a con-

10 stant reader of Saint *Pauls* Epistles; and by continual study had so incorporated the phrase & stile of that transcendent Apostle into all his familiar Letters, that the imitation seem'd to vie with the Original. Yet this availd not to deceave the people of that Empire; who notwithstanding his Saints

15 vizard, tore him to peeces for his Tyranny. From Stories of this nature both Ancient and Modern which abound, the Poets also, and som English, have bin in this point so mindfull of *Decorum,* as to put never more pious words in the mouth of any person, then of a Tyrant. I shall not instance

20 an abstruse Author, wherein the King might be less conversant, but one whom wee well know was the Closet Companion of these his solitudes, *William Shakespeare;* who introduces the Person of *Richard* the third, speaking in as high a strain of pietie, and mortification, as is utterd in any pass-

25 age of this Book; and sometimes to the same sense and purpose with some words in this place, *I intended,* saith he, *not onely to oblige my Freinds but mine enemies.* The like saith *Richard, Act 2. Scen. 1,*

I doe not know that Englishman alive,
With whom my soule is any jott at odds,
More then the Infant that is borne to night;
I thank my God for my humilitie.

5   Other stuff of this sort may be read throughout the whole
Tragedie, wherein the Poet us'd not much licence in depart-
ing from the truth of History, which delivers him a deep dis-
sembler, not of his affections onely, but of Religion.

In praying therfore, and in the outward work of Devo-
10 tion, this King wee see hath not at all exceeded the worst of
Kings before him. But herein the worst of Kings, professing
Christianism, have by farr exceeded him. They, for ought
we know, have still pray'd thir own, or at least borrow'd
from fitt Authors. But this King, not content with that
15 which, although in a thing holy, is no holy theft, to attribute
to his own making other mens whole Prayers, hath as it
were unhallow'd, and unchrist'nd the very duty of prayer
it self, by borrowing to a Christian use Prayers offer'd to a
Heathen God. Who would have imagin'd so little feare in
20 him of the true all-seeing Deitie, so little reverence of the
Holy Ghost, whose office is to dictat and present our Christian Prayers, so little care of truth in his last words, or honour
to himself, or to his Friends, or sense of his afflictions, or of
that sad howr which was upon him, as immediatly before
25 his death to popp into the hand of that grave Bishop who attended him, for a special Relique of his saintly exercises, a

Prayer stol'n word for word from the mouth of a Heathen
fiction praying to a heathen God; & that in no serious Book,
but the vain amatorious Poem of Sr *Philip Sidneys Arcadia;*
a Book in that kind full of worth and witt, but among reli-
5 gious thoughts, and duties not worthy to be nam'd; nor to be
read at any time without good caution; much less in time of
trouble and affliction to be a Christians Prayer-Book. They
who are yet incredulous of what I tell them for a truth, that
this Philippic Prayer is no part of the Kings goods, may sat-
10 isfie thir own eyes at leasure in the 3d. Book of Sir *Philips
Arcadia* p. 248. comparing Pammela's Prayer with the first
Prayer of his Majestie, deliverd to Dr. *Juxton* immediatly
before his death, and Entitl'd, *A prayer in time of Captivity*
Printed in all the best Editions of his Book. And since there
15 be a crew of lurking raylers, who in thir Libels, and thir fitts
of rayling up and down, as I hear from others, take it so cur-
rishly that I should dare to tell abroad the secrets of thir
Ægyptian Apis, to gratify thir gall in som measure yet more,
which to them will be a kinde of almes (for it is the weekly
20 vomit of thir gall which to most of them is the sole meanes
of thir feeding) that they may not starv for me, I shall gorge
them once more with this digression somwhat larger then
before: nothing troubl'd or offended at the working upward
of thir Sale-venom thereupon, though it happ'n to asperse
25 me; beeing, it seemes, thir best livelyhood and the only use
or good digestion that thir sick and perishing mindes can
make of truth charitably told them. However, to the benefit
of others much more worth the gaining, I shall proceed in

my assertion; that if only but to tast wittingly of meat or
drink offerd to an Idol, be in the doctrin of St. *Paul* judg'd
a pollution, much more must be his sin who takes a prayer,
so dedicated, into his mouth, and offers it to God. Yet hardly
5 it can be thought upon (though how sad a thing) without
som kind of laughter at the manner, and solemn transaction
of so gross a cousenage: that he who had trampl'd over us so
stately and so tragically should leave the world at last so
ridiculously in his exit, as to bequeath among his Deifying
10 friends that stood about him such a pretious peece of mockery to be publisht by them, as must needs cover both his and
their heads with shame, if they have any left. Certainly they
that will, may now see at length how much they were deceiv'd in him, and were ever like to be hereafter, who car'd
15 not, so neer the minute of his death, to deceive his best and
deerest freinds with the trumpery of such a prayer, not more
secretly then shamefully purloind; yet giv'n them as the
royall issue of his own proper Zeal. And sure it was the hand
of God to let them fal & be tak'n in such a foolish trapp, as
20 hath exposd them to all derision; if for nothing els, to throw
contempt and disgrace in the sight of all men upon this his
Idoliz'd Book, and the whole rosarie of his Prayers; thereby
testifying how little he accepted them from those who
thought no better of the living God then of a buzzard Idol,
25 fitt to be so servd and worshipt in reversion, with the polluted
orts and refuse of *Arcadia's* and *Romances,* without being
able to discern the affront rather then the worship of such an
ethnic Prayer. But leaving what might justly be offensive to

God, it was a trespass also more then usual against human
right, which commands that every Author should have the
property of his own work reservd to him after death as well
as living. Many Princes have bin rigorous in laying taxes on
5 thir Subjects by the head, but of any King heertofore that
made a levy upon thir witt, and seisd it as his own legitimat,
I have not whom beside to instance. True it is I lookt rather
to have found him gleaning out of Books writt'n purposely
to help Devotion. And if in likelyhood he have borrowd
10 much more out of Prayer-books then out of Pastorals, then
are these painted Feathers, that set him off so gay among the
people, to be thought few or none of them his own. But if
from his Divines he have borrow'd nothing, nothing out of
all the Magazin, and the rheume of thir Mellifluous prayers
15 and meditations, let them who now mourn for him as for
Tamuz, them who howle in thir Pulpits, and by thir howl-
ing declare themselvs right Wolves, remember and consider
in the midst of thir hideous faces, when they doe onely not
cutt thir flesh for him like those ruefull Preists whom *Eliah*
20 mock'd; that he who was once thir *Ahab,* now thir *Josiah,*
though faining outwardly to reverence Churchmen, yet heer
hath so extremely set at nought both them and thir praying
faculty, that being at a loss himself what to pray in Captivity,
he consulted neither with the Liturgie, nor with the Direc-
25 tory, but neglecting the huge fardell of all thir honycomb
devotions, went directly where he doubted not to find better
praying, to his mind with *Pammela* in the Countesses *Arcadia.* What greater argument of disgrace & ignominy could

have bin thrown with cunning upon the whole Clergy, then
that the King among all his Preistery, and all those number-
les volumes of thir theological distillations, not meeting with
one man or book of that coate that could befreind him with
5 a prayer in Captivity, was forc'd to robb Sr. *Philip* and his
Captive Shepherdess of thir Heathen orisons, to supply in
any fashion his miserable indigence, not of bread, but of a
single prayer to God. I say therfore not of bread, for that
want may befall a good man, and yet not make him totally
10 miserable: but he who wants a prayer to beseech God in his
necessity, tis unexpressible how poor he is; farr poorer within
himself then all his enemies can make him. And the unfit-
ness, the undecency of that pittifull supply which he sought,
expresses yet furder the deepness of his poverty.

15   Thus much be said in generall to his prayers, and in spe-
ciall to that *Arcadian* prayer us'd in his Captivity, anough to
undeceave us what esteeme wee are to set upon the rest. For
he certainly whose mind could serve him to seek a Christian
prayer out of a Pagan Legend, and assume it for his own,
20 might gather up the rest God knows from whence; one perhaps out of the French *Astræa,* another out of the Spanish
Diana; Amadis and *Palmerin* could hardly scape him. Such
a person we may be sure had it not in him to make a prayer
of his own, or at least would excuse himself the paines and
25 cost of his invention, so long as such sweet *rapsodies* of
Heathenism and Knighterrantry could yeild him prayers.
How dishonourable then, and how unworthy of a Christian
King were these ignoble shifts to seem holy and to get a Saint-

ship among the ignorant and wretched people; to draw them
by this deception, worse then all his former injuries, to go a
whoring after him. And how unhappy, how forsook of
grace, and unbelovd of God that people who resolv to know
5 no more of piety or of goodnes, then to account him thir
cheif Saint and Martyr, whose bankrupt devotion came not
honestly by his very prayers; but having sharkd them from
the mouth of a Heathen worshipper, detestable to teach him
prayers, sould them to those that stood and honourd him
10 next to the Messiah, as his own heav'nly compositions in adversity, for hopes no less vain and presumptuous (and death
at that time so imminent upon him) then by these goodly
reliques to be held a Saint and Martyr in opinion with the
People.

15   And thus farr in the whole Chapter we have seen and consider'd, and it cannot but be cleer to all men, how, and for
what ends, what concernments, and necessities the late King
was no way induc'd, but every way constrain'd to call this
last Parlament: yet heer in his first prayer he trembles not to
20 avouch as in the eares of God, *That he did it with an upright
intention, to his glory, and his peoples good:* Of which
dreadfull attestation how sincerely meant, God, to whom it
was avow'd, can onely judge; and he hath judg'd already;
and hath writt'n his impartial Sentence in Characters legible
25 to all Christ'ndom; and besides hath taught us, that there be
som, whom he hath giv'n over to delusion; whose very mind
and conscience is defil'd; of whom Saint *Paul* to *Titus* makes
mention.

II. *Upon the Earle of Straffords Death.*

THIS next Chapter is a penitent confession of the King, and the strangest, if it be well weigh'd, that ever was Auricular. For hee repents heer of giving
5 his consent, though most unwillingly, to the most seasonable and solemn peece of Justice, that had bin don of many yeares in the Land: But his sole conscience thought the contrary. And thus was the welfare, the safety, and within a little, the unanimous demand of three populous Nations to have at-
10 tended stil on the singularity of one mans opinionated con-science; if men had bin always so tame and spiritless; and had not unexpectedly found the grace to understand, that if his conscience were so narrow and peculiar to it selfe, it was not fitt his Authority should be so ample and Universall over
15 others. For certainly a privat conscience sorts not with a pub-lic Calling; but declares that Person rather meant by nature for a private fortune. And this also we may take for truth, that hee whose conscience thinks it sin to put to death a capital Offendor, will as oft think it meritorious to kill a righteous
20 Person. But let us heare what the sin was that lay so sore upon him, and, as one of his Prayers giv'n to Dr. *Juxton* testifies, to the very day of his death; it was his signing the Bill of *Straffords* execution: a man whom all men look'd upon as one of the boldest and most impetuous instruments
25 that the King had to advance any violent or illegal designe. He had rul'd *Ireland,* and som parts of *England* in an Ar-bitrary manner, had indeavour'd to subvert Fundamental

Lawes, to subvert Parlaments, and to incense the King against them; he had also endeavor'd to make Hostility between *England* and *Scotland:* He had counceld the King to call over that Irish Army of Papists, which he had cunningly
5 rais'd, to reduce *England,* as appear'd by good Testimony then present at the Consultation. For which, and many other crimes alledg'd and prov'd against him in 28. Articles, he was condemnd of high Treason by the Parlament. The Commons by farr the greater number cast him; the Lords, after they
10 had bin satisfi'd in a full discours by the Kings Sollicitor, and the opinions of many Judges deliver'd in thir House, agreed likewise to the Sentence of Treason. The People universally cri'd out for Justice. None were his Friends but Courtiers, and Clergimen, the worst at that time, and most corrupted
15 sort of men; and Court Ladies, not the best of Women; who when they grow to that insolence as to appeare active in State affaires, are the certain sign of a dissolute, degenerat, and pusillanimous Common-wealth. Last of all the King, or rather first, for these were but his Apes, was not satisfi'd in
20 conscience to condemn him of High Treason; and declar'd to both Houses, *That no fears or respects whatsoever should make him alter that resolution founded upon his conscience.* Either then his resolution was indeed not founded upon his conscience, or his conscience receav'd better information, or
25 else both his conscience and this his strong resolution strook saile, notwithstanding these glorious words, to his stronger fear. For within a few dayes after, when the Judges at a privie Counsel, and four of his elected Bishops had pick'd

the thorn out of his conscience, he was at length perswaded
to signe the Bill for *Straffords* Execution. And yet perhaps
that it wrung his conscience to condemn the *Earle* of high
Treason is not unlikely: not because he thought him guilt-
5 less of highest Treason, had half those crimes bin committed
against his own privat Interest or Person, as appear'd plainly
by his charge against the six Members, but because he knew
himself a Principal in what the *Earl* was but his accessory,
and thought nothing Treason against the Common-wealth,
10 but against himself only.

Had he really scrupl'd to sentence that for Treason which
he thought not Treasonable, why did he seeme resolv'd by
the Judges and the Bishops? And if by them resolv'd, how
comes the scruple heer again? It was not then, as he now
15 pretends, *The importunities of some and the feare of many*
which made him signe, but the satisfaction giv'n him by
those Judges & Ghostly Fathers of his own choosing. Which
of him shall we believe? For hee seemes not one, but double;
either heer we must not beleeve him professing that his satis-
20 faction was but seemingly receav'd & out of feare, or els wee
may as well beleeve that the scruple was no real scruple, as
we can beleeve him heer against himself before, that the satisfaction then receiv'd was no real satisfaction: of such a
variable and fleeting conscience what hold can be tak'n? But
25 that indeed it was a facil conscience? and could dissemble
satisfaction when it pleas'd, his own ensuing actions declar'd:
being soon after found to have the chief hand in a most detested conspiracy against the Parlament and Kingdom, as by

Letters and examinations of *Percy, Goring,* and other Conspirators came to light; that his intention was to rescue the
Earle of *Strafford,* by seizing on the Towre of *London;* to
bring up the English Army out of the North, joyn'd with
eight thousand Irish Papists rais'd by *Strafford,* and a French
Army to be landed at *Portsmouth* against the Parlament and
thir Friends. For which purpose the King, though requested
by both Houses to disband those Irish Papists, refus'd to do
it, and kept them still in Armes to his own purposes. No
marvel then, if being as deeply criminous as the Earle himself, it stung his conscience to adjudge to death those misdeeds whereof himself had bin the chiefe Author: no marvel
though in stead of blaming and detesting his ambition, his
evil Counsel, his violence and oppression of the people, he
fall to praise his great *Abilities;* and with Scolastic flourishes beneath the decencie of a King, compares him to *the
Sun,* which in all figurative use, and significance beares allusion to a King, not to a Subject: No marvel though he knit
contradictions as close as words can lye together, *not approving in his judgement,* and yet approving in his subsequent
reason all that *Strafford* did, as *driv'n by the necessity of
times and the temper of that people;* for this excuses all his
misdemeanors: Lastly, no marvel that he goes on building
many faire and pious conclusions upon false and wicked
premises, which deceive the common Reader not well discerning the antipathy of such connexions: but this is the
marvel, & may be the astonishment of all that have a conscience, how he durst in the sight of God (and with the same

words of contrition wherwith *David* repents the murdering
of *Uriah*) repent his lawfull compliance to that just act of
not saving him, whom he ought to have deliver'd up to
speedy punishment; though himself the guiltier of the two.
5 If the deed were so sinfull to have put to death so great a
malefactor, it would have tak'n much doubtless from the
heaviness of his sin, to have told God in his confession, how
he labour'd, what dark plots he had contriv'd, into what a
league enterd, and with what Conspirators against his Parla-
10 ment and Kingdoms, to have rescu'd from the claime of
Justice so notable and so deare an Instrument of Tyranny:
Which would have bin a story, no doubt as pleasing in the
eares of Heav'n, as all these equivocal repentances. For it was
feare, and nothing els, which made him faine before both
15 the scruple and the satisfaction of his conscience, that is to
say, of his mind: his first feare pretended conscience that he
might be born with to refuse signing; his latter feare being
more urgent made him finde a conscience both to signe and
to be satisfy'd. As for repentance it came not on him till a
20 long time after; when he saw *he could have sufferd nothing
more, though he had deny'd that Bill*. For how could he
understandingly repent of letting that be Treason which
the Parlament and whole Nation so judg'd? This was that
which repented him, to have giv'n up to just punishment
25 so stout a Champion of his designes, who might have bin
so usefull to him in his following civil Broiles. It was a
worldly repentance not a conscientious; or els it was a
strange Tyranny which his conscience had got over him, to

vex him like an evil spirit for doing one act of Justice, and by
that means to *fortifie his resolution* from ever doing so any
more. That mind must needs be irrecoverably deprav'd,
which either by chance or importunity tasting but once of
5 one just deed, spatters at it, and abhorrs the relish ever after.
To the Scribes and Pharises, woe was denounc'd by our Saviour, for straining at a Gnatt and swallowing a Camel;
though a Gnatt were to be straind at: But to a conscience
with whom one good deed is so hard to pass down, as to en-
10 danger almost a choaking, and bad deeds without number
though as bigg and bulkie as the ruin of three Kingdoms,
goe down currently without straining, certainly a farr greater
woe appertaines. If his conscience were come to that unnat-
ural *dyscrasie,* as to digest poyson and to keck at wholsom
15 food, it was not for the Parlament, or any of his Kingdoms
to feed with him any longer. Which to concele he would perswade us that the Parlament also in their conscience escap'd
not *some touches of remorse* for putting *Strafford* to death,
in forbidding it by an *after act* to be a precedent for the fu-
20 ture. But in a fairer construction, that act imply'd rather a
desire in them to pacifie the Kings mind, whom they perceav'd by this meanes quite alienated: in the mean while not
imagining that this after act should be retorted on them to tie
up Justice for the time to come upon like occasion, whether
25 this were made a precedent or not, no more then the want of
such a precedent, if it had bin wanting, had bin available to
hinder this.

But how likely is it that this after act argu'd in the Par-

lament thir least repenting for the death of *Strafford,* when
it argu'd so little in the King himself: who notwithstanding
this after act which had his own hand and concurrence, if
not his own instigation, within the same yeare accus'd of
5 high Treason no less then six Members at once for the same
pretended crimes which his conscience would not yeeld to
think treasonable in the Earle. So that this his suttle Argument to fast'n a repenting, and by that means a guiltiness of
Straffords death upon the Parlament, concludes upon his
10 own head; and shews us plainly that either nothing in his
judgment was Treason against the Common-wealth, but
onely against the Kings Person, a tyrannical Principle, or
that his conscience was a perverse and prevaricating conscience, to scruple that the Common-wealth should punish
15 for treasonous in one eminent offender, that which he himself sought so vehemently to have punisht in six guiltless persons. If this were *that touch of conscience which he bore
with greater regrett,* then for any sin committed in his life,
whether it were that proditory Aid sent to *Rochel* and Re-
20 ligion abroad, or that prodigality of shedding blood at home,
to a million of his Subjects lives not valu'd in comparison of
one *Strafford,* we may consider yet at last, what true sense
and feeling could be in that conscience, and what fitness to
be the maister conscience of three Kingdoms.
25　　But the reason why he labours that wee should take notice
of so much *tenderness and regrett in his soule* for *having any
hand in Straffords death,* is worth the marking ere we conclude. *He hop'd it would be som evidence before God and*

Man to all posteritie that he was farr from bearing that vast load and guilt of blood layd upon him by others. Which hath the likeness of a suttle dissimulation; bewailing the blood of one man, his commodious Instrument, put to death most
5 justly, though by him unwillingly, that we might think him too tender to shed willingly the blood of those thousands, whom he counted Rebels. And thus by dipping voluntarily his fingers end, yet with shew of great remorse in the blood of *Strafford,* wherof all men cleer him, he thinks to scape
10 that Sea of innocent blood wherein his own guilt inevitably hath plung'd him all over. And we may well perceave to what easie satisfactions and purgations he had inur'd his secret conscience, who thaught, by such weak policies and ostentations as these, to gaine beleif and absolution from un-
15 derstanding Men.

III.   *Upon his going to the House of Commons.*

CONCERNING his unexcusable, and hostile march from the Court to the House of Commons, there
20 needs not much be said. For he confesses it to be an act which most men, whom he calls *his enemies* cry'd shame upon; *indifferent men* grew *jealous of and fearfull, and many of his Friends resented as a motion rising rather from passion then reason:* He himself, in one of his Answers to
25 both Houses, made profession to be convinc'd that it was a plaine breach of thir Privilege: Yet heer like a rott'n build-

ing newly trimm'd over he represents it speciously and
fraudulently to impose upon the simple Reader; and seeks
by smooth and supple words not heer only, but through his
whole Book, to make som beneficial use or other ev'n of his
5 worst miscarriages.

These Men, saith he, meaning his Friends, *knew not the
just motives and pregnant grounds with which I thought my
selfe furnish'd;* to wit, against the five Members, whom hee
came to dragg out of the House. His best Friends indeed
10 knew not, nor could ever know his motives to such a riotous
act: and had he himself known any just grounds, he was not
ignorant how much it might have tended to his justifying,
had he nam'd them in this place, and not conceal'd them.
But suppose them real, suppose them known, what was this
15 to that violation and dishonor put upon the whole House,
whose very dore forcibly kept op'n, and all the passages neer
it he besett with Swords and Pistols cockt and menac'd in the
hands of about three hunderd Swaggerers and Ruffians, who
but expected, nay audibly call'd for the word of onset to be-
20 ginn a slaughter.

*He had discover'd as he thought unlawfull correspondencies
which they had us'd, and ingagements to imbroile his Kingdomes,* and remembers not his own unlawfull correspondencies, and conspiracies with the Irish Army of Papists, with the
25 French to land at *Portsmouth,* and his tampering both with
the English and the Scotch Army, to come up against the
Parlament: the least of which attempts by whomsoever, was
no less then manifest Treason against the Common-wealth.

If to demand Justice on the five Members were his Plea, for that which they with more reason might have demanded Justice upon him (I use his own Argument) *there needed not so rough assistance.* If hee had *resolv'd to bear that re-*
5 *pulse with patience,* which his Queen by her words to him at his return little thought he would have done, wherfore did he provide against it, with such an armed and unusual force? But his heart serv'd him not to undergoe the hazzard that such a desperate scuffle would have brought him to. But
10 wherfore did he goe at all, it behooving him to know there were two Statutes that declar'd he ought first to have ac-quainted the Parlament, who were the Accusers, which he re-fus'd to doe, though still professing to govern by Law, and still justifying his attempts against Law. And when he saw
15 it was not permitted him to attaint them but by a faire tryal, as was offerd him from time to time, for want of just matter which yet never came to light, he let the business fall of his own accord; and all those *pregnancies,* and *just motives* came to just nothing.
20 *He had no temptation of displeasure or revenge against those men:* None, but what he thirsted to execute upon them, for the constant opposition which they made against his tyrannous proceedings, and the love and reputation which they therfore had among the People, but most immediatly,
25 for that they were suppos'd the cheif by whose activity those 12. protesting Bishops were but a week before committed to the Tower.

He mist but little to have produc'd Writings under some

mens own hands. But yet he mist, though thir Chambers, Trunks, and Studies were seal'd up and search'd; yet not found guilty. *Providence would not have it so.* Good Providence, that curbs the raging of proud Monarchs, as well as
5 of madd multitudes. *Yet he wanted not such probabilities* (for his pregnant is come now to probable) *as were sufficient to raise jealousies in any Kings heart.* And thus his pregnant *motives* are at last prov'd nothing but a Tympany, or a Queen *Maries* Cushion: For in any Kings heart, as Kings
10 goe now, what shadowie conceit, or groundless toy will not create a jealousie.

    That he had design'd to assault the House of Commons, taking God to witness, he utterly denies; yet, in his Answer to the City, maintaines that *any course of violence had bin*
15 *very justifiable.* And we may then guess how farr it was from his designe. However it discover'd in him an excessive eagerness to be aveng'd on them that cross'd him; and that to have his will, he stood not to doe things never so much below him. What a becomming sight it was to see the King
20 of *England* one while in the House of Commons, by and by in the *Guild-Hall* among the Liveries and Manufactures, prosecuting so greedily the track of five or six fled Subjects; himself not the Sollicitor onely, but the Pursivant and the Apparitor of his own partial cause. And although, in his An-
25 swers to the Parlament, hee hath confess'd, first that his manner of prosecution was illegal, next, *that as hee once conceiv'd hee had ground anough to accuse them; so at length that hee found as good cause to desert any prosecution of*

them, yet heer he seems to reverse all, and against promise takes up his old deserted accusation, that he might have something to excuse himself, instead of giving due reparation; which he always refus'd to give them, whom he had so
5 dishonor'd.

That I went, saith he of his going to the House of Commons, *attended with some Gentlemen;* Gentlemen indeed; the ragged Infantrie of Stewes and Brothels; the spawn and shiprack of Taverns and Dicing Houses: and then he pleads
10 *it was no unwonted thing for the Majesty and safety of a King to be so attended, especially in discontented times.* An illustrious Majestie no doubt, so attended: a becomming safety for the King of *England,* plac'd in the fidelity of such Guards and Champions: Happy times; when Braves and
15 Hacksters, the onely contented Members of his Goverment, were thought the fittest and the faithfullest to defend his Person against the discontents of a Parlament and all good Men. Were those the chos'n ones to *preserve reverence to him,* while he enterd *unassur'd,* and full of suspicions into his
20 great and faithfull Councel? Let God then and the World judge whether the cause were not in his own guilty and unwarrantable doings: The House of Commons upon several examinations of this business declar'd it sufficiently prov'd, that the comming of those soldiers, Papists and others with
25 the King, was to take away some of thir Members, and in case of opposition or denyal, to have fal'n upon the House in a hostile manner. This the King heer denies; adding a fearful imprecation against his own life, *If he purposed any vio-*

lence or oppression against the Innocent, then, saith he, *let the Enemie persecute my soule, and tred my life to the ground and lay my honor in the dust.* What need then more disputing? He appeal'd to Gods Tribunal, and behold God
5 hath judg'd, and don to him in the sight of all men according to the verdict of his own mouth. To be a warning to all Kings hereafter how they use presumptuously the words and protestations of *David,* without the spirit and conscience of *David.* And the Kings admirers may heer see thir madness
10 to mistake this Book for a monument of his worth and wisdom, when as indeed it is his *Doomsday Booke;* not like that of *William* the *Norman* his Predecessor, but the record and memorial of his condemnation: and discovers whatever hath befal'n him, to have bin hast'nd on from Divine Justice by
15 the rash and inconsiderat appeal of his own lipps. But what evasions, what pretences, though never so unjust and emptie, will he refuse in matters more unknown, and more involv'd in the mists and intricacies of State, who, rather then not justifie himself in a thing so generally odious, can flatter his integ-
20 ritie with such frivolous excuses against the manifest dissent of all men, whether Enemies, Neuters, or Friends. But God and his judgements have not bin mock'd; and good men may well perceive what a distance there was ever like to be between him and his Parlament, and perhaps between him
25 and all amendment, who for one good deed, though but consented to, askes God forgiveness; and from his worst deeds don, takes occasion to insist upon his righteousness.

IV. *Upon the Insolency of the Tumults.*

WEE have heer, I must confess, a neat and well-couch'd invective against Tumults; expressing a true feare of them in the Author, but yet
5 so handsomly compos'd, and withall so feelingly, that, to make a Royal comparison, I beleeve *Rehoboam* the Son of *Solomon* could not have compos'd it better. Yet *Rehoboam* had more cause to inveigh against them; for they had ston'd his Tribute-gatherer, and perhaps had as little spar'd his own
10 Person, had hee not with all speed betak'n him to his Charret. But this King hath stood the worst of them in his own House without danger, when his Coach and Horses, in a Panic fear, have bin to seek, which argues that the Tumults at *Whitehall* were nothing so dangerous as those at *Sechem.*
15 But the matter heer considerable, is not whether the King, or his Houshold *Rhetorician* have made a pithy declamation against Tumults, but first whether these were Tumults or not, next if they were, whether the King himself did not cause them. Let us examin therfore how things at that time
20 stood. The King, as before hath bin prov'd, having both call'd this Parlament unwillingly, and as unwillingly from time to time condescended to thir several acts, carrying on a disjoynt and privat interest of his own, and not enduring to be so cross'd and overswaid, especially in the executing of his chief
25 & boldest Instrument, the Deputy of *Ireland,* first tempts the English Army, with no less reward then the spoil of *London,* to come up, and destroy the Parlament. That being discover'd

by some of the Officers, who, though bad anough, yet abhorr'd
so foul a deed, the K. hard'nd in his purpose, tempts them the
2d time at *Burrow* Bridge, promises to pawn his Jewels for
them, & that they should be mett & assisted (would they but
5 march on) with a gross body of hors under the E. of *Newcastle.*
He tempts them yet the third time, though after discovery, &
his own abjuration to have ever tempted them, as is affirmd
in the Declaration of *no more addresses.* Neither this succeeding, he turnes him next to the Scotch Army; & by his own
10 credential Letters giv'n to *Oneal* and Sr *John Hinderson,*
baites his temptation with a richer reward; not only to have
the sacking of *London,* but four Northern Counties to be
made Scottish; with Jewels of great value to be giv'n in pawn
the while. But neither would the Scots, for any promise of
15 reward, be bought to such an execrable and odious treachery; but with much honesty gave notice of the Kings designe,
both to the Parlament and City of *London.* The Parlament
moreover had intelligence, and the people could not but discern, that there was a bitter & malignant party grown up now
20 to such a boldness, as to give out insolent and threatning
speeches against the Parlament it self. Besides this, the Rebellion in *Ireland* was now broke out; and a conspiracy in
Scotland had bin made, while the King was there, against
some chief Members of that Parlament; great numbers heer
25 of unknown, and suspicious persons resorted to the City; the
King being return'd from *Scotland* presently dismisses that
Guard which the Parlament thought necessary in the midst
of so many dangers to have about them; and puts another

Guard in thir place, contrary to the Privilege of that high
Court, and by such a one commanded, as made them no less
doubtfull of the Guard it self. Which they therfore, upon
som ill effects thereof first found, discharge; deeming it more
5 safe to sitt free, though without a Guard in op'n danger,
then inclos'd with a suspected safety. The people therfore,
lest thir worthiest and most faithfull Patriots, who had expos'd themselves for the public, and whom they saw now left
naked, should want aide, or be deserted in the midst of these
10 dangers, came in multitudes, though unarm'd, to witness
thir fidelitie and readiness in case of any violence offer'd to
the Parlament. The King both envying to see the Peoples
love thus devolv'd on another object, and doubting lest it
might utterly disable him to doe with Parlaments as he was
15 wont, sent a message into the City forbidding such resorts.
The Parlament also both by what was discover'd to them,
and what they saw in a Malignant Party (some of which had
already drawn blood in a Fray or two at the Court Gate, and
eev'n at thir own Gate, in *Westminster Hall*) conceaving
20 themselves to be still in danger where they sat, sent a most
reasonable and just Petition to the King, that a Guard might
be allow'd them out of the City, wherof the Kings own
Chamberlaine, the Earl of *Essex* might have command; it
being the right of inferiour Courts to make chois of thir own
25 Guard. This the King refus'd to doe, and why he refus'd,
the very next day made manifest. For on that day it was, that
he sallied out from *White Hall,* with those trusty *Myrmi-
dons,* to block up, or give assault to the House of Commons.

He had, besides all this, begun to fortifie his Court, and entertaind armed Men not a few; who standing at his Palace
Gate, revil'd, and with drawn Swords wounded many of the
People, as they went by unarm'd, and in a peaceable manner,
5 whereof some dy'd. The passing by of a multitude, though
neither to Saint *Georges* Feast, nor to a Tilting, certainly of
it self was no Tumult; the expression of thir Loyalty and
stedfastness to the Parlament, whose lives and safeties by
more then slight rumours they doubted to be in danger, was
10 no Tumult. If it grew to be so, the cause was in the King
himself and his injurious retinue, who both by Hostile preparations in the Court, and by actual assailing of the People, gave
them just cause to defend themselves.

Surely those unarmed and Petitioning People needed not
15 have bin so formidable to any, but to such whose consciences
misgave them how ill they had deserv'd of the People; and
first began to injure them, because they justly fear'd it from
them; and then ascribe that to popular Tumult which was
occasion'd by thir own provoking.

20 And that the King was so emphatical and elaborat on this
Theam against Tumults, and express'd with such a vehemence his hatred of them, will redound less perhaps, then he
was aware, to the commendation of his Goverment. For besides that in good Goverments they happ'n seldomest, and
25 rise not without cause, if they prove extreme and pernicious,
they were never counted so to Monarchy, but to Monarchical
Tyranny; and extremes one with another are at most Antipathy. If then the King so extremely stood in fear of Tumults,

the inference will endanger him to be the other extreme.
Thus farr the occasion of this discours against Tumults; now
to the discours it self, voluble anough, and full of sentence,
but that, for the most part, either specious rather then solid,
5 or to his cause nothing pertinent.

*He never thought any thing more to presage the mischiefes
that ensu'd, then those Tumults.* Then was his foresight but
short, and much mistak'n. Those Tumults were but the
milde effects of an evil and injurious raigne; not signes of
10 mischeifs to come, but seeking releef for mischeifs past; those
signes were to be read more apparent in his rage and purpos'd revenge of those free expostulations, and clamours of
the People against his lawless Goverment. *Not any thing,*
saith he, *portends more Gods displeasure against a Nation
15 then when he suffers the clamours of the Vulgar to pass all
bounds of Law & reverence to Authority.* It portends rather
his displeasure against a Tyrannous King, whose proud
Throne he intends to overturn by that contemptible Vulgar;
the sad cries and oppressions of whom his Royaltie regarded
20 not. As for that supplicating People they did no hurt either
to Law or Autority, but stood for it rather in the Parlament
against whom they fear'd would violate it.

That *they invaded the Honour and Freedome of the two
Houses,* is his own officious accusation, not seconded by the
25 Parlament, who had they seen cause, were themselves best
able to complain. And if they *shook & menac'd* any, they
were such as had more relation to the Court, then to the Common-wealth; enemies, not patrons of the People. But if thir

petitioning unarm'd were an invasion of both Houses, what
was his entrance into the House of Commons, besetting it
with armed men, in what condition then was the honour,
and freedom of that House?

5   *They forbore not rude deportments, contemptuous words
and actions to himself and his Court.*

It was more wonder, having heard what treacherous hostility he had design'd against the City, and his whole Kingdome, that they forbore to handle him as people in thir rage
10 have handl'd Tyrants heertofore for less offences.

They were not a short ague, but a fierce quotidian feaver:
He indeed may best say it, who most felt it; for the shaking
was within him; and it shook him by his own description
worse then a storme, worse then an earthquake, Belshazzars
15 Palsie. Had not worse feares, terrors, and envies made within
him that commotion, how could a multitude of his Subjects,
arm'd with no other weapon then Petitions, have shak'n all
his joynts with such a terrible ague. Yet that the Parlament
should entertaine the least feare of bad intentions from him
20 or his Party, he endures not; but would perswade us that *men
scare themselves and others without cause;* for he thought
feare would be to them a kind of armor, and his designe was,
if it were possible, to disarme all, especially of a wise feare
and suspicion; for that he knew would find weapons.

25   He goes on therfore with vehemence to repeat the mischeifs don by these Tumults. *They first Petition'd, then protected, dictate next, and lastly overaw the Parlament. They
remov'd obstructions, they purg'd the Houses, cast out rott'n*

members. If there were a man of iron, such as *Talus,* by our Poet *Spencer,* is fain'd to be the page of Justice, who with his iron flaile could doe all this, and expeditiously, without those deceitfull formes and circumstances of Law, worse then
5 ceremonies in Religion; I say God send it don, whether by one *Talus,* or by a thousand.

But they subdu'd the men of conscience in Parlament, back'd and abetted all seditious and schismatical Proposals against government ecclesiastical and civil.

10   Now wee may perceave the root of his hatred whence it springs. It was not the Kings grace or princely goodness, but this iron flaile the People, that drove the Bishops out of thir Baronies, out of thir Cathedrals, out of the Lords House, out of thir Copes and Surplices, and all those Papistical innova-
15 tions, threw down the High Commission and Star-chamber, gave us a Triennial Parlament, and what we most desir'd; in revenge whereof he now so bitterly enveighs against them; these are those seditious and scismatical Proposals, then by him condescended to, as acts of grace, now of another name;
20 which declares him, touching matters of Church and State, to have bin no other man in the deepest of his solitude, then he was before at the highest of his Sovrantie.

But this was not the worst of these Tumults, they plaid the hasty *midwives,* and *would not stay the ripening, but*
25 *went streight to ripping up, and forcibly cut out abortive Votes.*

They would not stay perhaps the Spanish demurring, and putting off such wholsome acts and counsels, as the Politic

Cabin at *White Hall* had no mind to. But all this is complain'd heer as don to the Parlament, and yet we heard not
the Parlament at that time complaine of any violence from
the people, but from him. Wherfore intrudes he to plead the
5 cause of Parlament against the People, while the Parlament
was pleading thir own cause against him; and against him
were forc'd to seek refuge of the people? 'Tis plaine then that
those confluxes and resorts interrupted not the Parlament,
nor by them were thought Tumultuous, but by him onely
10 and his Court Faction.

   *But what good Man had not rather want any thing he
most desir'd for the public good, then attain it by such unlawfull and irreligious meanes;* as much as to say, Had not
rather sit still and let his Country be Tyranniz'd, then that
15 the people, finding no other remedie, should stand up like
Men and demand thir Rights and Liberties. This is the arti-
ficialest peece of fineness to perswade men into slavery that
the wit of Court could have invented. But heare how much
better the Moral of this Lesson would befitt the Teacher.
20 What good man had not rather want a boundless and arbitrary power, and those fine Flowers of the Crown, call'd Prerogatives, then for them to use force and perpetual vexation
to his faithfull Subjects, nay to wade for them through blood
and civil warr? So that this and the whole bundle of those
25 following sentences may be apply'd better to the convince-
ment of his own violent courses, then of those pretended
Tumults.
   Who were the chiefe Demagogues to send for those Tu-

mults, some alive are not ignorant. Setting aside the affright-
ment of this Goblin word; for the King by his leave cannot
coine English as he could Money, to be current (and tis beleev'd this wording was above his known stile and Orthog-
5 raphie, and accuses the whole composure to be conscious of
som other Author) yet if the people *were sent for, emboldn'd and directed* by those *Demagogues,* who, saving his
Greek, were good Patriots, and by his own confession *Men
of some repute for parts and pietie,* it helps well to assure us
10 there was both urgent cause, and the less danger of thir comming.

Complaints were made, yet no redress could be obtain'd.
The Parlament also complain'd of what danger they sate in
from another party, and demanded of him a Guard, but it
15 was not granted. What marvel then if it chear'd them to see
some store of thir Friends, and in the Roman not the petti-
fogging sense, thir Clients so neer about them; a defence due
by nature both from whom it was offer'd, and to whom; as
due as to thir Parents; though the Court storm'd, and fretted
20 to see such honour giv'n to them, who were then best Fathers of the Common-wealth. And both the Parlament and
people complain'd, and demanded Justice for those assaults,
if not murders don at his own dores, by that crew of Rufflers,
but he, in stead of doing Justice on them, justifi'd and abet-
25 ted them in what they did, as in his public Answer to a Petition from the City may be read. Neither is it slightly to be
pass'd over, that in the very place where blood was first
drawn in this cause, as the beginning of all that follow'd,

there was his own blood shed by the Executioner. According to that sentence of Divine justice, *In the place where Dogs lick'd the blood of* Naboth, *shall Dogs lick thy blood, eev'n thine.*

5   From hence he takes occasion to excuse that improvident and fatal error of his absenting from the Parlament. *When he found that no Declaration of the Bishops could take place against those Tumults.* Was that worth his considering, that foolish and self-undoing Declaration of twelve Cypher Bish-
10 ops, who were immediatly appeacht of Treason for that audacious Declaring? The Bishops peradventure were now and then pulld by the Rochets, and deserv'd another kind of pulling; but what amounted this to *the feare of his own person in the streets?* Did he not the very next day after his
15 irruption into the House of Commons, then which nothing had more exasperated the people, goe in his Coach unguarded into the City? did hee receave the least affront, much less violence in any of the Streets, but rather humble demeanours, and supplications? Hence may be gather'd,
20 that however in his own guiltiness hee might have justly fear'd, yet that hee knew the people so full of aw and reverence to his Person, as to dare commit himself single among the thickest of them, at a time when he had most provok'd them. Besides in *Scotland* they had handl'd the Bishops in a
25 more robustious manner; *Edinburrow* had bin full of Tumults, two Armies from thence had enterd *England* against him; yet after all this, he was not fearfull, but very forward to take so long a journey to *Edinburrow;* which argues first,

as did also his rendition afterward to the Scotch Army, that to *England* he continu'd still, as he was indeed, a stranger, and full of diffidence; to the Scots onely a native King, in his confidence, though not in his dealing towards them. It shews us
5 next beyond doubting, that all this his feare of Tumults was but a meer colour and occasion tak'n of his resolved absence from the Parlament, for some other end not difficult to be guess'd. And those instances wherein valour is not to be question'd for not *scuffling with the Sea, or an undisciplind*
10 *Rabble,* are but subservient to carry on the solemn jest of his fearing Tumults: if they discover not withall, the true reason why he departed; onely to turne his slashing at the Court Gate, to slaughtering *in the Field;* his disorderly bickering, to an orderly invading: which was nothing els but a more
15 orderly disorder.

Some suspected and affirm'd, that he meditated a Warr when he went first from White Hall. And they were not the worst heads that did so, nor did *any of his former acts weak'n him* to that, as he alleges for himself, or if they had, they
20 cleere him onely for the time of passing them, not for what ever thoughts might come after into his mind. Former actions of improvidence or fear, not with him unusual, cannot absolve him of all after meditations.

He goes on protesting his *no intention to have left White*
25 *Hall,* had these horrid Tumults giv'n him but *Faire Quarter,* as if he himself, his Wife and Children had bin in peril. But to this anough hath bin answer'd.

Had this Parlament as it was in its first Election, Namely,

with the Lord and Baron Bishops, *sate full and free,* he doubts
not but all had gon well. What warrant this of his to us?
Whose not doubting was all good mens greatest doubt.

    He was resolv'd to heare reason, and to consent so farr as
5 *he could comprehend.* A hopefull resolution; what if his
reason were found by oft experience to comprehend nothing
beyond his own advantages, was this a reason fit to be intrusted with the common good of three Nations?

    But, saith he, *as Swine are to gardens, so are Tumults to*
10 *Parlaments.* This the Parlament, had they found it so, could
best have told us. In the meane while, who knows not that
one great Hogg may doe as much mischief in a Garden, as
many little Swine.

    He was sometimes prone to think that had he call'd this
15 *last Parlament to any other place in England, the sad conse-*
quences might have bin prevented. But change of ayr changes
not the mind. Was not his first Parlament at *Oxford* dissolv'd
after two Subsidies giv'n him, and no Justice receav'd? Was
not his last in the same place, where they sat with as much
20 freedom, as much quiet from Tumults, as they could desire,
a Parlament both in his account, and thir own, consisting of
all his Friends, that fled after him, and suffer'd for him, and
yet by him nicknam'd, and casheer'd for a *Mungrill Parla-*
ment that vext his Queen with thir base and mutinous mo-
25 *tions,* as his Cabinet letter tells us? Wherby the World may
see plainly, that no shifting of place, no sifting of members
to his own mind, no number, no paucity, no freedom from
tumults, could ever bring his arbitrary wilfulness, and tyran-

nical Designes to brook the lest shape or similitude, the lest counterfet of a Parlament.

Finally instead of praying for his people as a good King should doe, hee prayes to be deliver'd from them, as *from* *wild Beasts, Inundations, and raging Seas, that had overborn* *all Loyalty, Modesty, Laws, Justice, and Religion.* God save the people from such Intercessors.

V. *Upon the Bill for Trienniall Parla-ments, And for setling this* &c.

THE Bill for a Triennial Parlament was but the third part of one good step toward that which in times past was our annual right. The other Bill for setling this Parlament was new indeed, but at that time very necessary; and in the Kings own Words no more then what the World *was fully confirm'd hee might in Justice, Reason,* *Honour, and Conscience grant them;* for to that end he affirms to have don it.

But wheras he attributes the passing of them to his own act of grace and willingness, as his manner is to make vertues of his necessities, and giving to himself all the praise, heaps ingratitude upon the Parlament, a little memory will sett the cleane contrary before us; that for those Beneficial acts we ow what wee ow to the Parlament; but to his granting them neither praise nor thanks. The first Bill granted much less then two former Statutes yet in force by *Edward* the third; that a Parlament should be call'd every yeare, or ofter if need

were; nay from a farr ancienter Law Book call'd the *Mirror,*
it is affirm'd in a late Treatise call'd *Rights of the Kingdom,*
that Parlaments by our old Laws ought twice a year to be at
London. From twice in one year to once in three year, it may
5 be soon cast up how great a loss we fell into of our ancient
liberty by that act, which in the ignorant and Slavish mindes
we then were, was thought a great purchase. Wisest men perhaps were contented, for the present at least by this act to
have recoverd Parlaments, which were then upon the brink of
10 danger to be forever lost. And this is that which the King
preaches heer for a special tok'n of his Princely favour, to
have abridg'd & over reach'd the people five parts in six of
what thir due was, both by ancient Statute, and originally.
And thus the taking from us all but a Triennial remnant of
15 that English Freedom which our Fathers left us double, in a
fair annuity enrowl'd, is set out, and sould to us heer for the
gracious, and over liberal giving of a new enfranchisment.
How little, may we think, did he ever give us, who in the
Bill of his pretended givings writes down *Imprimis* that
20 benefit or privilege once in three year giv'n us, which by
so giving, he more then twice every year illegally took from
us. Such givers as give single to take away sixfold, be to our
Enemies. For certainly this Common-wealth, if the Statutes
of our Ancestors be worth ought, would have found it hard
25 and hazardous to thrive under the dammage of such a guile-
full liberaltie. The other act was so necessary that nothing in
the power of Man, more seem'd to be the stay & support of
all things from that steep ruin, to which he had nigh brought

them, then that Act obtain'd. He had by his ill Stewardship,
and, to say no worse, the needless raising of two Armies,
intended for a civil War, begger'd both himself and the Public: and besides had left us upon the score of his needy Ene-
5 mies, for what it cost them in thir own defence against him.
To disingage him and the Kingdom, great sums were to be
borrow'd, which would never have bin lent, nor could ever
be repaid, had the King chanc'd to dissolve this Parlament as
heertofore. The errors also of his Goverment had brought the
10 Kingdom to such extremes, as were incapable of all recovery
without the absolute continuance of a Parlament. It had bin
els in vaine to goe about the setling of so great distempers, if
hee who first caus'd the malady, might when he pleas'd reject the remedy. Notwithstanding all which, that he granted
15 both these Acts unwillingly, and as a meer passive Instrument, was then visible eev'n to most of those Men who now
will see nothing.

At passing of the former Act he himself conceal'd not his
unwillingness; and testifying a general dislike of thir actions,
20 which they then proceeded in with great approbation of the
whole Kingdom, he told them with a maisterly Brow, that
*by this Act he had oblig'd them above what they had de-
serv'd,* and gave a peece of Justice to the Common-wealth six
times short of his Predecessors, as if he had bin giving som
25 boon or begg'd Office to a sort of his desertless Grooms.

That he pass'd the latter Act against his will, no man in
reason can hold it questionable. For if the *February* before
he made so dainty, and were so loath to bestow a Parlament

once in three yeare upon the Nation, because this had so oppos'd his courses, was it likely that the *May* following he
should bestow willingly on this Parlament an indissoluble
sitting, when they had offended him much more, by cutting
5 short and impeaching of high Treason his chief Favorites?
It was his feare then, not his favor which drew from him that
Act, lest the Parlament, incens'd by his Conspiracies against
them about the same time discover'd, should with the people
have resented too hainously those his doings, if to the suspi-
10 cion of thir danger from him, he had also added the denyal
of this onely meanes to secure themselves.

From these Acts therfore in which he glories, and wherwith so oft he upbraids the Parlament, he cannot justly expect to reape aught but dishonour and dispraise; as being both
15 unwillingly granted, and the one granting much less then
was before allow'd by Statute, the other being a testimony of
his violent and lawless Custom, not onely to break Privileges,
but whole Parlaments; from which enormity they were constrain'd to bind him first of all his Predecessors; never any
20 before him having giv'n like causes of distrust and jealousie
to his People. As for this Parlament, how farr he was from
being advis'd by them, as he ought, let his own words express.

He taxes them with *undoing what they found well done:*
and yet knows they undid nothing in the Church but Lord
25 Bishops, Liturgies, Ceremonies, High Commission, judg'd
worthy by all true Protestants to bee thrown out of the
Church. They undid nothing in the State but irregular and
grinding Courts, the maine grievances to be remov'd; & if

these were the things which in his opinion they found well don, we may againe from hence be inform'd with what unwillingness he remov'd them; and that those gracious Acts wherof so frequently he makes mention, may be english'd
5 more properly Acts of feare and dissimulation against his mind and conscience.

The bill preventing dissolution of this Parlament he calls *An unparalell'd Act out of the extreme confidence that his Subjects would not make ill use of it.* But was it not a greater
10 confidence of the people to put into one mans hand so great a power, till he abus'd it, as to summon and dissolve Parlaments? Hee would be thankt for trusting them, and ought to thank them rather for trusting him: the trust issuing first from them, not from him.

15 And that it was a meer trust, and not his Prerogative, to call and dissolve Parlaments at his pleasure, And that Parlaments were not to be dissolv'd, till all Petitions were heard, all greevances redrest, is not onely the assertion of this Parlament, but of our ancient Law Books, which averr it to be
20 an unwritt'n Law of common Right, so ingrav'n in the hearts of our Ancestors, and by them so constantly enjoy'd and claim'd, as that it needed not enrouling. And if the Scots in thir Declaration could charge the King with breach of their Lawes, for breaking up that Parlament without their con-
25 sent, while matters of greatest moment were depending, it were unreasonable to imagin that the wisdom of *England* should be so wanting to it self through all Ages, as not to provide by som known Law writt'n or unwritt'n, against the

not calling, or the arbitrary dissolving of Parlaments; or that
they who ordain'd thir summoning twice a yeare, or as oft as
need requir'd, did not tacitly enact also, that as necessity of
affaires call'd them, so the same necessity should keep them
5 undissolv'd, till that were fully satisfi'd. Were it not for that,
Parlaments, and all the fruit and benefit we receave by having them, would turne soon to meer abusion. It appeares then
that if this Bill of not dissolving were an unparallel'd Act, it
was a known and common Right which our Ancestors un-
10 der other Kings enjoyd as firmly as if it had bin grav'n in
Marble; and that the infringement of this King first brought
it into a writt'n Act: Who now boasts that, as a great favour
don us, which his own less fidelity then was in former Kings
constrain'd us onely of an old undoubted Right to make a
15 new writt'n Act. But what needed writt'n Acts, when as
anciently it was esteem'd part of his Crown Oath not to dissolve Parlaments, till all greevances were consider'd; wherupon, the old *Modi of Parlament* calls it flat perjury, if he
dissolve them before; as I find cited in a Booke mention'd at
20 the beginning of this Chapter, to which and other Law-
tractats I referr the more Lawyerlie mooting of this point:
which is neither my element, nor my proper work heer; since
the Book which I have to Answer pretends reason, not Au-
toritys and quotations: and I hold reason to be the best Arbi-
25 trator, and the Law of Law it self.

Tis true that *good Subjects think it not just that the Kings
condition should be worse by bettering theirs.* But then the
King must not be at such a distance from the people, in judg-

ing what is better and what worse; which might have bin
agreed, *had he known* (for his own words condemn him)
*as well with moderation to use, as with earnestness to desire
his own advantages.*

5   *A continual Parlament he thought would keep the Common-wealth in tune.* Judge Common wealth, what proofs he
gave, that this boasted profession was ever in his thought.

Some, saith he, *gave out that I repented me of that setling
Act.* His own actions gave it out beyond all supposition. For
10 doubtless it repented him to have establish'd that by Law,
which he went about so soon after to abrogat by the Sword.

He calls those Acts which he confesses, *tended to thir good,
not more Princely then friendly contributions.* As if to doe
his dutie were of curtesie, and the discharge of his trust a
15 parcell of his liberality; so nigh lost in his esteem was the
birthright of our Liberties, that to give them back againe
upon demand stood at the mercy of his *Contribution.*

*He doubts not but the affections of his People will com-
pensate his sufferings for those acts of confidence.* And im-
20 putes his sufferings to a contrary cause. Not his confidence,
but *his distrust* was that which brought him to those sufferings, from the time that he forsook his Parlament; and trusted
them ne're the sooner for what he tells *of thir pietie and religious strictness,* but rather hated them as Puritans, whom
25 he always sought to extirpat.

He would have it beleev'd, that *to bind his hands by these
Acts argu'd very short foresight of things, and extreme fa-
tuity of mind in him,* if he had meant a Warr. If we should

conclude so, that were not the onely Argument: Neither did it argue that he meant peace, knowing that what he granted for the present out of feare, he might as soon repeale by force, watching his time; and deprive them the fruit of those Acts, 5 if his own designes, wherin he put his trust, took effect.

Yet he complaines, *That the tumults threatn'd to abuse all acts of grace and turne them into wantonness.* I would they had turn'd his wantonness into the grace of not abusing Scripture. Was this becomming such a Saint as they would 10 make him, to adulterat those Sacred words from the grace of God to the acts of his own grace? *Herod* was eat'n up of Wormes for suffering others to compare his voice to the voice of God; but the Borrower of this phrase gives much more cause of jealousie that he lik'n'd his own acts of grace to the 15 acts of Gods grace.

From profaneness he scars comes off with perfet sense, *I was not then in a capacity to make Warr,* therfore *I intended not: I was not in a capacity,* therfore *I could not have giv'n my Enemies greater advantage then by so unprincely incon-* 20 *stancy to have scatter'd them by Armes, whom but lately I had settl'd by Parlament.* What place could there be for his inconstancy in that thing wherto he was in no capacity? Otherwise his inconstancy was not so unwonted or so nice, but that it would have easily found pretences to scatter those 25 in revenge, whom he settl'd in feare.

It had bin a course full of sin as well as of hazzard and dishonour. True, but if those considerations withheld him not from other actions of like nature, how can we beleeve they were of strength sufficient to withhold him from this? And that they withheld him not, the event soon taught us.

His letting some men goe up to the Pinnacle of the Temple was a temptation to them to cast him down headlong. In this
5 *Simily* we have himself compar'd to *Christ,* the Parlament to the *Devill,* and his giving them that Act of settling, to his letting them goe up to the *Pinnacle of the Temple.* A tottring and giddy Act rather then a settling. This was goodly use made of Scripture in his Solitudes. But it was no Pinnacle of
10 the Temple, it was a Pinnacle of *Nebuchadnezzars* Palace, from whence hee and Monarchy fell headlong together.

He would have others see that *All the Kingdomes of the World are not worth gaining by the wayes of sin which hazzard the Soule;* and hath himself left nothing unhazzarded
15 to keep three. He concludes with sentences that rightly scannd make not so much for him as against him, and confesses that *The Act of settling was no sin of his will,* and wee easily beleeve him, for it hath bin clearly prov'd a sin of his unwillingness.

20 With his Orisons I meddle not, for he appeals to a high Audit. This yet may be noted, that at his Prayers he had before him the sad presage of his ill success, *As of a dark and dangerous Storme which never admitted his returne to the Port from whence he set out.* Yet his Prayer-Book no sooner
25 shut, but other hopes flatter'd him; and thir flattering was his destruction.

VI. *Upon his Retirement from* West-minster.

THE Simily wherwith he begins I was about to have found fault with, as in a garb somwhat more Poetical then for a Statist: but meeting with many straines of like dress in other of his Essaies, and hearing him reported a more diligent reader of Poets, then of Politicians, I begun to think that the whole Book might perhaps be intended a peece of Poetrie. The words are good, the fiction smooth and cleanly; there wanted onely Rime, and that, they say, is bestow'd upon it lately. But to the Argument.

I stai'd at White Hall till I was driven away by shame more then feare. I retract not what I thought of the fiction, yet heer, I must confess, it lies too op'n. In his Messages, and Declarations, nay in the whole Chapter next but one before this, he affirmes that *The danger, wherin his Wife, his Children, and his own Person* were by those Tumults, was the maine cause that drove him from *White Hall,* and appeales to God as witness: he affirmes heer that it was *shame more then feare.* And *Digby,* who knew his mind as well as any, tells his new-listed Guard, *That the principal cause of his Majesties going thence, was to save them from being trodd in the dirt.* From whence we may discerne what false and frivolous excuses are avow'd for truth, either in those Declarations, or in this Penitential Book. Our forefathers were of that courage and severity of zeale to Justice, and thir native Liberty, against the proud contempt and misrule of thir Kings, that when *Richard* the Second departed but from a Committie of Lords, who sat preparing matter for the Parlament not yet assembl'd, to the removal of his evil Counselors, they first vanquish'd and put to flight *Robert de Vere*

5 his chief Favorite; and then comming up to *London* with a huge Army, requir'd the King then withdrawn for feare, but no furder off then the Tower, to come to *Westminster.* Which he refusing, they told him flatly, that unless he came, they would choose another. So high a crime it was accounted

10 then, for Kings to absent themselves, not from a Parlament, which none ever durst, but from any meeting of his Peeres and Counselors, which did but tend towards a Parlament. Much less would they have suffer'd that a King, for such trivial and various pretences, one while for feare of tumults,

15 another while *for shame to see them,* should leav his Regal Station, and the whole Kingdom bleeding to death of those wounds which his own unskilful and pervers Goverment had inflicted.

Shame then it was that drove him from the Parlament, but

20 the shame of what? Was it not the shame of his manifold errours and misdeeds, and to see how weakly he had plaid the King? No; *But to see the barbarous rudeness of those Tumults to demand any thing.* We have started heer another, and, I beleeve, the truest cause of his deserting the Parla-

25 ment. The worst and strangest of that *Any thing* which the people then demanded, was but the unlording of Bishops, and expelling them the House, and the reducing of Church Discipline to a conformity with other Protestant Churches:

this was the *Barbarism* of those Tumults; and that he might avoid the granting of those honest and pious demands, as well demanded by the Parlament as the People, for this very cause, more then for feare, by his own confession heer, he left
5 the City; and in a most tempestuous season forsook the Helme, and steerage of the Common-wealth. This was that terrible *Any thing* from which his *Conscience* and *his Reason* chose to run rather then not deny. To be importun'd the removing of evil Counselors, and other greevances in Church
10 and State, was to him *an intollerable oppression*. If the peoples demanding were so burd'nsome to him, what was his denial and delay of Justice to them?

But as the demands of his people were to him a burd'n and oppression, so was the advice of his Parlament esteem'd
15 a bondage; *Whose agreeing Votes,* as he affirmes, *Were not by any Law or reason conclusive to his judgement.* For the Law, it ordaines a Parlament to advise him in his great affaires; but if it ordaine also that the single judgement of a King shall outballance all the wisdom of his Parlament, it
20 ordaines that which frustrats the end of its own ordaining. For where the Kings judgement may dissent, to the destruction, as it may happ'n, both of himself and the Kingdom, there advice, and no furder, is a most insufficient, and frustraneous meanes to be provided by Law, in case of so high
25 concernment. And where the main & principal Law of common preservation against tyranny is left so fruitless and infirm, there it must needs follow that all lesser Laws are to thir severall ends and purposes much more weak, and un-

effectual. For that Nation would deserv to be renownd and
Chronicl'd for folly & stupidity, that should by Law provide
force against privat and petty wrongs, advice only against
tyranny and public ruin. It being therfore most unlike a
5 Law, to ordain a remedy so slender and unlawlike, to be the
utmost meanes of all our safety, or prevention, as advice is,
which may at any time be rejected by the sole judgement of
one man, the King, and so unlike the Law of *England,*
which Lawyers say is the quintessence of reason and mature
10 wisdom, wee may conclude that the Kings negative voice
was never any Law, but an absurd and reasonless Custom,
begott'n and grown up either from the flattery of basest
times, or the usurpation of immoderat Princes. Thus much
to the Law of it, by a better evidence then Rowles and Rec-
15 ords, Reason.

But it is possible he should pretend also to reason, that the
judgement of one man, not as a wise or good man, but as a
King, and oft times a wilfull, proud, and wicked King, should
outweigh the prudence, and all the vertue of an elected Par-
20 lament? What an abusive thing were it then to summon
Parlaments, that by the Major part of voices greatest matters
may be there debated and resolv'd, when as one single voice
after that, shall dash all thir Resolutions?

He attempts to give a reason why it should, *Because the*
25 *whole Parlament represents not him in any kind.* But mark
how little he advances; for if the Parlament represent the
whole Kingdom, as is sure anough they doe, then doth
the King represent onely himself; and if a King without his

Kingdom be in a civil sense nothing, then without or against
the Representative of his whole Kingdom he himself represents nothing, and by consequence his judgement and his
negative is as good as nothing; and though we should allow
5 him to be something, yet not equivalent, or comparable to
the whole Kingdom, and so neither to them who represent
it: much less that one syllable of his breath putt into the scales
should be more ponderous then the joynt voice and efficacy
of a whole Parlament, assembl'd by election, and indu'd with
10 the plenipotence of a free Nation, to make Laws, not to be
deny'd Laws, and with no more but No, a sleevless reason, in
the most pressing times of danger and disturbance, to be sent
home frustrat, and remediless.

Yet heer he maintains *To be no furder bound to agree*
15 *with the Votes of both Houses, then he sees them to agree*
with the will of God, with his just Rights as a King, and the
generall good of his People. As to the freedom of his agreeing or not agreeing, limited with due bounds, no man rep-
rehends it; this is the Question heer, or the Miracle rather,
20 why his onely not agreeing should lay a negative barr and
inhibition upon that which is agreed to by a whole Parlament, though never so conducing to the Public good or
safety? To know the will of God better then his whole Kingdom, whence should he have it? Certainly Court-breeding
25 and his perpetual conversation with Flatterers, was but a bad
Schoole. To judge of his own Rights could not belong to him,
who had no right by Law in any Court to judge of so much
as Fellony or Treason, being held a party in both these Cases,

much more in this; and his Rights however should give place
to the general good, for which end all his Rights were giv'n
him. Lastly to suppose a clearer insight and discerning of the
general good, allotted to his own singular judgement, then
5 to the Parlament and all the People, and from that self-opinion of discerning, to deny them that good which they being
all Freemen seek earnestly, and call for, is an arrogance and
iniquity beyond imagination rude and unreasonable: they
undoubtedly having most autoritie to judge of the public
10 good, who for that purpose are chos'n out, and sent by the
People to advise him. And if it may be in him to see oft *the
major part of them not in the right,* had it not bin more his
modestie to have doubted their seeing him more oft'n in the
wrong?

15   Hee passes to another reason of his denials, *Because of
some mens hydropic unsatiableness, and thirst of asking, the
more they drank, whom no fountaine of regall bountie was
able to overcome.* A comparison more properly bestow'd on
those that came to guzzle in his Wine-cellar, then on a free-
20 born People that came to claime in Parlament thir Rights and
Liberties, which a King ought therfore to grant, because of
right demanded; not to deny them for feare his bounty
should be exhaust, which in these demands (to continue the
same Metaphor) was not so much as Broach'd; it being his
25 duty, not his bounty to grant these things. He who thus re-
fuses to give us Law, in that refusal gives us another Law,
which is his will, another name also, and another condition;
of Freemen to become his vassals.

Putting off the Courtier he now puts on the Philosopher,
and sententiously disputes to this effect, *that reason ought to
be us'd to men, force and terror to Beasts; that he deserves to
be a slave who captivates the rationall soverantie of his soule,*
5 *and liberty of his will to compulsion; that he would not for-
feit that freedome which cannot be deni'd him, as a King, because it belongs to him as a Man and a Christian, though to
preserve his Kingdom, but rather dye injoying the Empire of
his soule, then live in such a vassalage as not to use his reason*
10 *and conscience to like or dislike as a King.* Which words, of
themselves, as farr as they are sense, good and Philosophical,
yet in the mouth of him who to engross this common libertie
to himself, would tred down all other men into the condition
of Slaves and beasts, they quite loose thir commendation. He
15 confesses a rational sovrantie of soule, and freedom of will in
every man, and yet with an implicit repugnancy would have
his reason the sovran of that sovranty, and would captivate
and make useless that natural freedom of will in all other men
but himself. But them that yeeld him this obedience he so
20 well rewards, as to pronounce them worthy to be Slaves.
They who have lost all to be his Subjects, may stoop and take
up the reward. What that freedom is, which *cannot be deni'd
him as a King, because it belongs to him as a Man, and a
Christian,* I understand not. If it be his negative voice, it con-
25 cludes all men who have not such a negative as his against a
whole Parlament, to be neither Men, nor Christians: and
what was he himself then, all this while that we deni'd it him
as a King? Will hee say that hee enjoy'd within himself the

less freedom for that? Might not he, both as a Man, and as a
Christian have raignd within himself, in full sovranty of
soule, no man repining, but that his outward and imperious
will must invade the civil Liberties of a Nation? Did wee
5 therfore not permit him to use his reason or his conscience,
not permitting him to bereave us the use of ours? And might
not he have enjoy'd both, as a King, governing us as Free
men by what Laws we our selves would be govern'd? It was
not the inward use of his reason and of his conscience that
10 would content him, but to use them both as a Law over all
his Subjects, *in whatever he declar'd as a King to like or dislike*. Which use of reason, most reasonless and unconscion-
able, is the utmost that any Tyrant ever pretended over his
Vassals.

15   In all wise Nations the Legislative power, and the judicial
execution of that power have bin most commonly distinct,
and in several hands: but yet the former supreme, the other
subordinat. If then the King be only set up to execute the
Law, which is indeed the highest of his office; he ought no
20 more to make or forbidd the making of any law agreed upon
in Parlament, then other inferior Judges, who are his Deputies. Neither can he more reject a Law offerd him by the
Commons, then he can new make a Law which they reject.
And yet the more to credit and uphold his cause, he would
25 seeme to have Philosophie on his side; straining her wise dictates to unphilosophical purposes. But when Kings come so
low, as to fawn upon Philosophie, which before they neither
valu'd nor understood, tis a signe that failes not, they are then

put to thir last Trump. And Philosophie as well requites
them, by not suffering her gold'n sayings either to become
their lipps, or to be us'd as masks and colours of injurious and
violent deeds. So that what they presume to borrow from
5 her sage and vertuous rules, like the Riddle of *Sphinx* not
understood, breaks the neck of thir own cause.

But now againe to Politics, *He cannot think the Majestie*
of the Crowne of England to be bound by any Coronation
Oath in a blind and brutish formalitie, to consent to what-
10 *ever its Subjects in Parlament shall require.* What Tyrant
could presume to say more, when he meant to kick down all
Law, Goverment, and bond of Oath? But why he so desires
to absolve himself the Oath of his Coronation would be worth
the knowing. It cannot but be yeelded, that the Oath which
15 bindes him to performance of his trust, ought in reason to
contain the summ of what his chief trust and Office is. But
if it neither doe enjoyn, nor mention to him, as a part of his
duty, the making or the marring of any Law or scrap of Law,
but requires only his assent to those Laws which the people
20 have already chos'n, or shall choose (for so both the Latin
of that Oath, and the old English, and all Reason admits, that
the People should not lose under a new King what freedom
they had before) then that negative voice so contended for,
to deny the passing of any Law which the Commons choose,
25 is both against the Oath of his Coronation, and his Kingly
Office. And if the King may deny to pass what the Parlament hath chos'n to be a Law, then doth the King make himself Superiour to his whole Kingdom; which not onely the

general Maxims of Policy gainsay, but eev'n our own standing Laws, as hath bin cited to him in Remonstrances heertofore, that *The King hath two Superiours, the Law and his
Court of Parlament.* But this he counts to be a blind and
5 brutish formality, whether it be Law, or Oath, or his duty,
and thinks to turn it off with wholsom words and phrases,
which he then first learnt of the honest People, when they
were so oft'n compell'd to use them against those more truely
blind and brutish formalities thrust upon us by his own com-
10 mand, not in civil matters onely but in Spiritual. And if his
Oath to perform what the People require, when they Crown
him, be in his esteem a brutish formality, then doubtless those
other Oaths of Allegiance and Supremacy, tak'n absolute
on our part, may most justly appear to us in all respects as
15 brutish and as formal; and so by his own sentence no more
binding to us then his Oath to him.

As for his instance in case *He and the House of Peers attempted to enjoyne the House of Commons,* it beares no
equalitie; for hee and the Peers represent but themselves, the
20 Commons are the whole Kingdom.

Thus he concludes *his Oath to be fully discharg'd in Governing by Laws already made,* as being not bound to pass any
new, *if his Reason bids him deny.* And so may infinite mischeifs grow, and he with a pernicious negative may deny us
25 all things good, or just, or safe, wherof our ancestors in times
much differing from ours, had either no foresight, or no
occasion to foresee; while our general good and safety shall
depend upon the privat and overweening Reason of one ob-

stinat Man; who against all the Kingdom, if he list, will interpret both the Law and his Oath of Coronation by the tenor of his own will. Which he himself confesses to be an arbitrary power, yet doubts not in his Argument to imply, as if he
5 thought it more fit the Parlament should be subject to his will, then he to their advice, a man neither by nature nor by nurture wise. How is it possible that he in whom such Principles as these were so deep rooted, could ever, though restor'd again, have raign'd otherwise then Tyrannically.

10 He objects *That force was but a slavish method to dispell his error*. But how oft'n shall it be answer'd him that no force was us'd to dispell the error out of his head, but to drive it from off our necks: for his error was imperious, and would command all other men to renounce thir own reason and un-
15 derstanding, till they perish'd under the injunction of his all-ruling error.

He alleges the uprightness of his intentions to excuse his possible failings; a position fals both in Law and Divinity: Yea contrary to his own better principles, who affirmes in the
20 twelfth Chapter, that *The goodness of a mans intention, will not excuse the scandall, and contagion of his example*. His not knowing, through the corruption of flattery and Court Principles, what he ought to have known, will not excuse his not doing what he ought to have don: no more then the small
25 skill of him who undertakes to be a *Pilot,* will excuse him to be misledd by any wandring Starr mistak'n for the Pole. But let his intentions be never so upright, what is that to us? What answer for the reason and the National Rights which

God hath giv'n us, if having Parlaments, and Laws and the power of making more to avoid mischeif, wee suffer one mans blind intentions to lead us all with our eyes op'n to manifest destruction.

5   And if Arguments prevaile not with such a one, force is well us'd; not *to carry on the weakness of our Counsels, or to convince his error,* as he surmises, but to acquitt and rescue our own reason, our own consciences from the force and prohibition laid by his usurping error upon our Liberties & un-
10 derstandings.

Never thing pleas'd him more then when his judgement concurr'd with theirs. That was to the applause of his own judgement, and would as well have pleas'd any selfconceited man.

15   *Yea in many things he chose rather to deny himself then them.* That is to say in trifles. For *of his own Interests* and Personal Rights he conceavs himself *Maister.* To part with, if he please, not to contest for, against the Kingdom which is greater then he, whose Rights are all subordinat to the King-
20 doms good: And *in what concernes truth, Justice, the right of Church or his Crown, no man shall gaine his consent against his mind.* What can be left then for a Parlament, but to sit like Images, while he still thus either with incomparable arrogance assumes to himself the best abilitie of judging
25 for other men what is Truth, Justice, Goodness, what his own, or the Churches Right, or with unsufferable Tyranny restraines all men from the enjoyment of any good, which his judgement, though erroneous, thinks not fit to grant

them; notwithstanding that the Law and his Coronal Oath requires his undeniable assent to what Laws the Parlament agree upon.

He had rather wear a Crown of Thorns with our Saviour.
5 Many would be all one with our Saviour, whom our Saviour will not know. They who govern ill those Kingdoms which they had a right to, have to our Saviours Crown of Thornes no right at all. Thornes they may find anow, of thir own gathering, and thir own twisting: for Thornes and Snares,
10 saith *Solomon,* are in the way of the froward; but to weare them as our Saviour wore them is not giv'n to them that suffer by thir own demerits. Nor is a Crown of Gold his due who cannot first wear *a Crown of Lead;* not onely for the weight of that great Office, but for the compliance which it ought to
15 have with them who are to counsel him, which heer he termes in scorne *An imbased flexibleness to the various and oft contrary dictates of any Factions,* meaning his Parlament; for the question hath bin all this while between them two. And to his Parlament, though a numerous and chois Assem-
20 bly of whom the Land thought wisest, he imputes rather then to himself, *want of reason, neglect of the Public, interest of parties, and particularitie of private will and passion;* but with what modesty or likelihood of truth it will be wearisom to repeat so oft'n.
25 He concludes with a sentence faire in seeming, but fallacious. For if the conscience be ill edifi'd, the resolution may more befitt a foolish then a Christian King, to preferr a selfwill'd conscience before a Kingdoms good; especially in the

deniall of that which Law and his Regal Office by Oath bids
him grant to his Parlament, and whole Kingdom rightfully
demanding. For we may observe him throughout the discours to assert his Negative power against the whole King-
5 dom; now under the specious Plea of his conscience and his
reason, but heertofore in a lowder note, *Without us, or
against our consent, the Votes of either or of both Houses
together, must not, cannot, shall not: Declar. May 4. 1642.*

With these and the like deceavable Doctrines he levens
10 also his Prayer.

VII. *Upon the Queens departure.*

TO this Argument we shall soon have said; for what
concerns it us to hear a Husband divulge his Houshold privacies, extolling to others the vertues of his
15 Wife; an infirmity not seldom incident to those who have
least cause. But how good shee was a Wife, was to himself,
and be it left to his own fancy; how bad a Subject, is not
much disputed. And being such, it need be made no wonder, though shee left a Protestant Kingdom with as little
20 honour as her Mother left a Popish.

That this *Is the first example of any Protestant Subjects
that have tak'n up Armes against thir King a Protestant,* can
be to Protestants no dishonour; when it shal be heard that he
first levied Warr on them, and to the interest of Papists more
25 then of Protestants. He might have giv'n yet the precedence
of making warr upon him to the subjects of his own Nation;

who had twice oppos'd him in the op'n Feild, long ere the
English found it necessary to doe the like. And how groundless, how dissembl'd is that feare, least shee, who for so many
yeares had bin averse from the Religion of her Husband, and
5 every yeare more and more, before these disturbances broke
out, should for them be now the more alienated from that
to which we never heard shee was inclin'd. But if the feare
of her Delinquency and that Justice which the Protestants
demanded on her, was any cause of her alienating the more,
10 to have gain'd her by indirect means had bin no advantage
to Religion; much less then was the detriment to loose her
furder off. It had bin happy if his own actions had not giv'n
cause of more scandal to the Protestants, then what they did
against her could justly scandalize any Papist.

15 Them who accus'd her, well anough known to be the
Parlament, he censures for *Men yet to seeke thir Religion,
whether Doctrine, Discipline, or good manners;* the rest he
soothes with the name of true English Protestants, a meer
scismatical name, yet he so great an enemy of Scism.

20 He ascribes *Rudeness and barbarity worse then Indian* to
the English Parlament, and *all vertue* to his Wife, in straines
that come almost to Sonnetting: How fitt to govern men,
undervaluing and aspersing the great Counsel of his Kingdom, in comparison of one Woman. Examples are not farr
25 to seek, how great mischeif and dishonour hath befall'n to
Nations under the Goverment of effeminate and Uxorious
Magistrates. Who being themselves govern'd and overswaid
at home under a Feminine usurpation, cannot but be farr

short of spirit and autority without dores, to govern a whole Nation.

Her tarrying heer he could not think safe among them who were shaking hands with Allegiance to lay faster hold 5 *on Religion;* and taxes them of a duty rather then a crime, it being just to obey God rather then Man, and impossible to serve two Maisters. I would they had quite shak'n off what they stood shaking hands with; the fault was in thir courage, not in thir cause.

10 In his Prayer he prayes that *The disloyaltie of his Protestant Subjects may not be a hindrance to her love of the true Religion;* and never prays that the dissoluteness of his Court, the scandals of his Clergy, the unsoundness of his own judgement, the lukewarmness of his life, his Letter of compliance 15 to the Pope, his permitting Agents at *Rome,* the Popes *Nuntio,* and her Jesuited Mother here, may not be found in the sight of God farr greater hindrances to her conversion.

But this had bin a suttle Prayer indeed, and well pray'd, though as duely as a *Pater-noster,* if it could have charm'd us 20 to sit still, and have Religion and our Liberties one by one snatch'd from us, for fear least rising to defend our selves, wee should fright the Queen a stiff Papist from turning Protestant. As if the way to make his Queen a Protestant had bin to make his Subjects more then half way Papists.

25 He prays next *That his constancy may be an antidote against the poyson of other mens example.* His constancy in what? Not in Religion, for it is op'nly known that her Religion wrought more upon him, then his Religion upon her,

and his op'n favouring of Papists, and his hatred of them call'd Puritants, the ministers also that prayd in Churches for her Conversion, being checkt from Court, made most men suspect she had quite perverted him. But what is it that the
5 blindness of hypocrisy dares not doe? It dares pray, and thinks to hide that from the eyes of God, which it cannot hide from the op'n view of man.

VIII. *Upon His repulse at* Hull, *and the fate of the* Hothams.

10 HULL, a town of great strength and opportunitie both to sea and land affaires, was at that time the Magazin of all those armes which the King had bought with mony most illegally extorted from his subjects of *England,* to use in a causless and most unjust civil warr
15 against his Subjects of *Scotland.* The King in high discontent and anger had left the Parlament and was gon toward the *North;* the Queen into Holland, where she pawn'd and set to sale the Crown-Jewels (a crime heretofore counted treasonable in Kings) and to what intent these summs were rais'd,
20 the Parlament was not ignorant. His going northward in so high a chafe they doubted was to possess himself of that strength, which the storehouse and situation of *Hull* might add suddenly to his malignant party. Having first therfore in many Petitions earnestly pray'd him to dispose and settle,
25 with consent of both Houses, the military power in trusty hands, and he as oft refusing, they were necessitated by the

turbulence and danger of those times to put the Kingdom by
thir own autority into a posture of defence; and very timely
sent sir *John Hotham* a member of the House, and Knight
of that county, to take *Hull* into his custody, and some of
5 the Train'd bands to his assistance. For besides the General
danger they had, before the Kings going to *York,* notice
giv'n them of his privat Commissions to the Earl of *Newcastle,* and to Colonel *Legg,* one of those imploid to bring the
Army up against the Parlament; who had already made som
10 attempts, & the latter of them under a disguise, to surprise
that place for the Kings party. And letters of the Lord *Digby*
were intercepted, wherin was wisht that the K. would declare himself, and retire to som safe place; other information came from abroad, that *Hull* was the place design'd for
15 some new enterprise. And accordingly *Digby* himself not
long after, with many other Commanders, and much forrain
Ammunition landed in those parts. But these attempts not
succeeding, and that Town being now in custody of the Parlament, he sends a message to them, that he had firmely re-
20 solv'd to go in person into *Ireland;* to chastise those wicked
Rebels (for these and wors words he then gave them) and
that toward this work he intended forthwith to raise by his
commissions, in the Counties neere *Westchester,* a guard for
his own person, consisting of 2000. foot, and 200. horse,
25 that should be arm'd from his Magazin at Hull. On the other
side, the Parlament forseeing the Kings drift, about the same
time send him a Petition, that they might have leave for necessary causes to remoove the magazin of *Hull* to the Towre

of *London;* to which the King returnes his denial; and soon after going to *Hull,* attended with about 400. Horse, requires the Governour to deliver him up the Town; wherof the Governour besought humbly to be excus'd, till he could
5 send notice to the Parlament who had intrusted him; wherat the King much incens'd proclaims him Traitor before the Town Walls; and gives immediat order to stop all passages between him and the Parlament. Yet he himself dispatches post after post to demand justice, as upon a Traitor: using a
10 strange iniquitie to require justice upon him whom he then way layd and debarr'd from his appearance. The Parlament no sooner understood what had pass'd, but they declare that Sir *John Hotham* had don no more then was his duty, and was therfore no Traitor.

15 This relation, being most true, proves that which is affirm'd heer to be most fals; seeing the Parlament, whom he accounts his *greatest Enemies,* had *more confidence to abett and own* what Sir *John Hotham* had don, then the King had confidence to let him answer in his own behalf.

20 To speake of his patience, and in that solemn manner, he might better have forborne; *God knows* saith he, *it affected me more with sorrow for others then with anger for my self; nor did the affront trouble me so much as their sin.* This is read, I doubt not, and beleev'd: and as there is some use of
25 every thing, so is there of this Book, were it but to shew us, what a miserable, credulous, deluded thing that creature is, which is call'd the Vulgar; who notwithstanding what they might know, will beleeve such vain-glories as these. Did not

that choleric, and vengefull act of proclaiming him Traitor before due process of Law, having bin convinc'd so late before of his illegallity with the five Members, declare his anger to be incens'd? doth not his own relation confess as much?
5 and his second Message left him fuming three dayes after, and in plaine words testifies *his impatience of delay* till *Hotham* be severely punish'd, for that which he there termes an insupportable affront.

Surely if his sorrow for Sir *John Hothams* sin were greater
10 then his anger for the affront, it was an exceeding great sorrow indeed, and wondrous charitable. But if it stirr'd him so vehemently to have Sir *John Hotham* punisht, and not at all, that we heare, to have him repent, it had a strange operation to be call'd a sorrow for his sin. Hee who would perswade
15 us of his sorrow for the sins of other men, as they are sins, not as they are sin'd against himself, must give us first some testimony of a sorrow for his own sins, and next for such sins of other men as cannot be suppos'd a direct injury to himself. But such compunction in the King no man hath yet observ'd;
20 and till then, his sorrow for Sir *John Hothams* sin will be call'd no other then the resentment of his repulse; and his labour to have the sinner onely punish'd, will be call'd by a right name, his revenge.

And *the hand of that cloud which cast all soon after into*
25 *darkness and disorder,* was his own hand. For assembling the Inhabitants of *York-shire,* and other Counties, Horse and Foot, first under colour of a new Guard to his Person, soon after, being suppli'd with ammunition from *Holland,* bought

with the Crown Jewels, he begins an op'n Warr by laying
Seige to *Hull*. Which Town was not his own, but the Kingdoms; and the Armes there, public Armes, bought with the
public Mony, or not his own. Yet had they bin his own by as
5 good right as the privat House and Armes of any man are his
own, to use either of them in a way not privat, but suspicious
to the Common-wealth, no Law permitts. But the King had
no proprietie at all either in *Hull* or in the Magazin. So that
the following *Maxims* which he cites *of bold and disloyall*
10 *undertakers* may belong more justly to whom he least meant
them. After this he againe relapses into the praise of his patience at *Hull,* and by his overtalking of it, seems to doubt
either his own conscience, or the hardness of other mens beleif. To me, the more he praises it in himself, the more he
15 seems to suspect that in very deed it was not in him; and that
the lookers on so likewise thought.

Thus much of what he suffer'd by *Hotham,* and with
what patience; now of what *Hotham* suffer'd, as he judges,
for opposing him. *He could not but observe how God not*
20 *long after pleaded and aveng'd his cause.* Most men are too
apt, and commonly the worst of men, so to interpret and expound the judgements of God, and all other events of providence or chance, as makes most to the justifying of thir own
cause, though never so evill; and attribute all to the particu-
25 lar favour of God towards them. Thus when *Saul* heard that
David was in *Keilah, God,* saith he, *hath deliver'd him into*
my hands, for he is shut in. But how farr that King was deceav'd in his thought that God was favouring to his cause,

that story unfolds; and how little reason this King had to
impute the death of *Hotham* to Gods avengement of his
repuls at *Hull,* may easily be seen. For while *Hotham* continu'd faithfull to his trust, no man more safe, more success-
5　full, more in reputation then hee. But from the time he first
sought to make his peace with the King, and to betray into
his hands that Town, into which before he had deny'd him
entrance, nothing prosper'd with him. Certainly had God
purpos'd him such an end for his opposition to the King, he
10　would not have deferr'd to punish him till then when of an
Enemy he was chang'd to be the Kings Friend, nor have
made his repentance and amendment the occasion of his
ruin. How much more likely is it, since he fell into the act of
disloyalty to his charge, that the judgement of God concurr'd
15　with the punishment of man, and justly cut him off for revolting to the King. To give the World an example, that
glorious deeds don to ambitious ends, find reward answerable, not to thir outward seeming, but to thir inward ambition. In the mean while what thanks he had from the King
20　for revolting to his cause, and what good opinion for dying
in his service, they who have ventur'd like him, or intend,
may heer take notice.

　　Hee proceeds to declare, not onely in general wherfore
Gods judgement was upon *Hotham,* but undertakes by fan-
25　sies, and allusions to give a criticism upon every particular.
That his head was divided from his body, because his heart
was divided from the King: two heads cut off in one family
for affronting the head of the Common-wealth; the eldest

son being infected with the sin of his Father, against the Father of his Countrie. These petty glosses and conceits on the high and secret judgements of God, besides the boldness of unwarrantable commenting, are so weake and shallow, 5 and so like the quibbl's of a Court Sermon, that we may safely reck'n them either fetcht from such a pattern, or that the hand of some houshold preist foisted them in; least the World should forget how much he was a Disciple of those Cymbal Doctors. But that argument by which the Author 10 would commend them to us, discredits them the more. For if they be so *obvious to every fancy,* the more likely to be erroneous, and to misconceive the mind of those high secrecies, wherof they presume to determin. For God judges not by human fansy.

15   But however God judg'd *Hotham,* yet he had the Kings pitty; but marke the reason how preposterous; so farr he had his pitty, *as he thought he at first acted more against the light of his conscience then many other men in the same cause.* Questionless they who act against conscience, whether at the 20 barr of human, or Divine Justice, are pittied least of all. These are the common grounds and verdicts of Nature, wherof when he who hath the judging of a Whole Nation, is found destitute, under such a Governour, that Nation must needs be miserable.

25   By the way he jerkes at *some mens reforming to models of Religion, and that they think all is gold of pietie that doth but glister with a shew of Zeale.* We know his meaning; and apprehend how little hope there could be of him from such

language as this: But are sure that the pietie of his prelatic modell, glister'd more upon the posts and pillars which thir Zeale and fervencie guilded over, then in the true workes of spiritual edification.

He is sorry that Hotham felt the Justice of others, and fell not rather into the hands of his mercy. But to cleare that, he should have shewn us what mercy he had ever us'd to such as fell into his hands before, rather then what mercy he intended to such as never could come to aske it. Whatever mercy one man might have expected, tis too well known, the whole Nation found none; though they besought it oft'n, and so humbly; but had bin swallow'd up in blood and ruin, to set his privat will above the Parlament, had not his strength faild him. *Yet clemency he counts a debt, which he ought to pay to those that crave it; since we pay not any thing to God for his mercy, but prayers and praises.* By this reason we ought as freely to pay all things to all men; for of all that we receive from God, what doe we pay for, more then prayers and praises? we look'd for the discharge of his Office, the payment of his dutie to the Kingdom, and are payd Court payment with empty sentences, that have the sound of gravity, but the significance of nothing pertinent.

Yet again after his mercy past and granted, he returnes back to give sentence upon *Hotham;* and whom he tells us he would so fain have sav'd alive, him he never leaves killing with a repeated condemnation, though dead long since. It was ill that sombody stood not neer to whisper him, that a reiterating Judge is worse then a tormentor. *He pitties him, he*

rejoyces not, he pitties him again, but still is sure to brand him
at the taile of his pitty, with som ignominious mark either
of ambition or disloyaltie. And with a kind of censorious
pitty, aggravats rather then less'ns or conceals the fault: To
5 pitty thus is to triumph.

He assumes to foreknow that *after times will dispute
whether Hotham were more infamous at Hull or at Towerhill.* What knew he of after times, who while he sits judging
and censuring with out end the fate of that unhappy Father
10 and his son at Towerhill, knew not that the like fate attended
him, before his own Palace Gate; and as little knew whether
after times reserve not a greater infamy to the story of his
own life and raigne.

He saies but over again in his prayer, what his Sermon hath
15 Preacht; How acceptably to those in heav'n we leave to be
decided by that precept which forbidds *Vaine Repetitions.*
Sure anough it lies as heavie as he can lay it, upon the head of
poore *Hotham.*

Needs he will fast'n upon God a peece of revenge as done
20 for his sake; and takes it for a favor, before he know it was
intended him: which in his closet had bin excusable, but in a
Writt'n and publish'd prayer, too presumptuous. *Ecclesiastes*
hath a right name for such kind of Sacrifices.

Going on he prayes thus, *Let not thy Justice prevent the
25 objects and opportunities of my mercy.* To folly, or to blas-
phemy, or to both shall we impute this? Shall the Justice of
God give place, and serv to glorifie the mercies of a man? All
other men, who know what they ask, desire of God that thir

doings may tend to his glory; but in this prayer God is requir'd that his justice would forbeare to prevent, and as good
have said to intrench upon the glory of a mans mercy. If God
forbeare his Justice it must be, sure, to the magnifying of his
5 own mercy: How then can any mortal man, without presumption little less then impious, take the boldness to aske
that glory out of his hand. It may be doubted now by them
who understand Religion, whether the King were more unfortunat in this his prayer, or *Hotham* in those his sufferings.

IX. *Upon the listing and raising Armies,* &c.

IT were an endless work to walk side by side with the
Verbosity of this Chapter; onely to what already hath
not bin spok'n, convenient answer shall be giv'n. Hee
15 begins againe with Tumults; all demonstration of the Peoples Love and Loyaltie to the Parlament was Tumult; thir
Petitioning, Tumult; thir defensive Armies were but *listed*
Tumults, and will take no notice that those about him, those
in a time of peace listed into his own House, were the begin-
20 ners of all these Tumults; abusing and assaulting not onely
such as came peaceably to the Parlament at *London,* but those
that came Petitioning to the King himself at *York.* Neither
did they abstain from doing violence and outrage to the Messengers sent from Parlament; he himself either count'nanc-
25 ing, or conniving at them.

He supposes that *His recess gave us confidence that he*

might be conquer'd. Other men suppose both that, and all
things els, who knew him neither by nature Warlike, nor ex-
perienc'd, nor fortunate; so farr was any man that discern'd
aught, from esteeming him unconquerable; yet such are
5 readiest to imbroile others.

But he had a soule invincible. What praise is that? The
stomach of a Child is ofttimes invincible to all correction.
The unteachable man hath a soule to all reason and good advice invincible; and he who is intractable, he whom nothing
10 can perswade, may boast himself invincible; whenas in some
things to be overcome is more honest and laudable then to
conquer.

He labours to have it thought that *his fearing God more
then Man* was the ground of his sufferings; but he should
15 have known that a good principle not rightly understood,
may prove as hurtfull as a bad; and his feare of God may be
as faulty as a blind zeale. He pretended to feare God more
then the Parlament; who never urg'd him to doe otherwise;
he should also have fear'd God more then he did his Cour-
20 tiers and the Bishops, who drew him, as they pleas'd, to
things inconsistent with the feare of God. Thus boasted *Saul*
to have *perform'd the Commandment of God,* and stood in
it against *Samuel;* but it was found at length that he had
fear'd the people more then God, in saving those fatt Oxen
25 for the worship of God, which were appointed for destruction. Not much unlike, if not much wors, was that fact of
his, who for feare to displease his Court, and mungrel Clergy,
with the dissolutest of the people, upheld in the Church of

God, while his power lasted, those Beasts of *Amalec,* the
Prelats against the advice of his Parlament and the example
of all Reformation; in this more unexcusable then *Saul,* that
Saul was at length convinc'd, he to the howr of death fix'd
5 in his fals perswasion; and sooths himself in the flattering
peace of an erroneous and obdurat conscience, singing to his
soul vain Psalms of exultation, as if the Parlament had assail'd
his reason with the force of Arms, and not he on the contrary
their reason with his Armes; which hath bin prov'd already,
10 and shall be more heerafter.

He twitts them with *his Acts of grace;* proud, and unself-
knowing words in the mouth of any King, who affects not to
be a God, and such as ought to be as odious in the ears of a
free Nation. For if they were unjust acts, why did he grant
15 them as of grace? If just, it was not of his grace, but of his
duty and his Oath to grant them.

A glorious King he would be, though *by his sufferings:*
But that can never be to him whose sufferings are his own
doings. He faines *a hard chois* put upon him *either to kill his*
20 *own Subjects or be kill'd.* Yet never was King less in danger
of any violence from his Subjects, till he unsheath'd his Sword
against them; nay long after that time, when he had spilt the
blood of thousands, they had still his person in a foolish ven-
eration.

25 Hee complaines, *That civil Warr must be the fruits of his*
seventeen yeares raigning with such a measure of Justice,
Peace, and Plenty, and Religion, as all Nations either admir'd
or envi'd. For the Justice we had, let the Counsel-Table,

Starr-Chamber, High Commission speak the praise of it; not forgetting the unprincely usage, and, as farr as might be, the abolishing of Parlaments, the displacing of honest Judges, the sale of Offices, Bribery and Exaction not found out to be
5 punish'd, but to be shar'd in, with impunity for the time to come. Who can number the extortions, the oppressions, the public robberies, and rapines, committed on the Subject both by Sea and Land, under various pretences? Thir possessions also tak'n from them, one while as Forrest Land, another
10 while as Crown-Land; nor were thir Goods exempted, no not the Bullion in the Mint; Piracy was become a project own'd and authoriz'd against the Subject.

For the peace we had, what peace was that which drew out the English to a needless and dishonourable voyage against
15 the *Spaniard* at *Cales?* Or that which lent our shipping to a treacherous and Antichristian Warr against the poore Protestants of Rochell our suppliants? What peace was that which fell to rob the *French* by Sea, to the imbarring of all our Merchants in that Kingdom? which brought forth that
20 unblest expedition to the Ile of *Rhee,* doubtfull whether more calamitous in the success or in the designe, betraying all the flowre of our military youth, and best Commanders to a shamefull surprisal and execution. This was the peace we had, and the peace we gave, whether to freinds or to foes
25 abroad. And if at home any peace were intended us, what meant those *Irish* billeted Souldiers in all parts of the Kingdom, and the designe of German Horse, to subdue us in our peacefull Houses?

For our Religion where was there a more ignorant, profane, and vitious Clergy, learned in nothing but the antiquitie of thir pride, thir covetousnes and superstition; whose unsincere and levenous Doctrine corrupting the people, first
5 taught them loosness, then bondage; loosning them from all sound knowledge and strictness of life, the more to fit them for the bondage of Tyranny and superstition. So that what was left us for other Nations not to pitty rather then admire or envy, all those seaventeen yeares, no wise man could see.
10 For wealth and plenty in a land where Justice raignes not, is no argument of a flourishing State, but of a neerness rather to ruin or commotion.

These were not *some miscariages* onely of Goverment, *which might escape,* but a universal distemper, and reduce-
15 ment of law to arbitrary power; not through the evil counsels of *some men,* but through the constant cours & practise of al that were in highest favour: whose worst actions frequently avowing he took upon himself; and what faults did not yet seem in public to be originally his, such care he took by pro-
20 fessing, and proclaiming op'nly, as made them all at length his own adopted sins. The persons also when he could no longer protect, he esteem'd and favour'd to the end; but never, otherwise then by constraint, yeilded any of them to due punishment; thereby manifesting that what they did was
25 by his own Autority and approbation.

Yet heer he asks *Whose innocent blood he hath shed, What widdows or Orphans teares can witness against him?* After the suspected Poysoning of his Father, not inquir'd

into, but smother'd up, and him protected and advanc'd to
the very half of his Kingdom, who was accus'd in Parlament
to be Author of the fact; (with much more evidence, then
Duke *Dudley* that fals Protector is accus'd upon record, to
5 have poison'd *Edward* the sixt) after all his rage and persecution, after so many Yeares of cruel Warr on his People in
three Kingdoms. Whence the Author of *Truths manifest,* a
Scotchman not unacquainted with affaires, positively affirmes *That there hath bin more Christian blood shed by the*
10 *Commission, approbation, and connivance of King Charles,*
and his Father James in the latter end of thir raigne, then in
the Ten Roman Persecutions. Not to speake of those many
whippings, Pillories, and other corporal inflictions wherwith
his raign also before this Warr was not unbloodie; some have
15 dy'd in Prison under cruel restraint, others in Banishment,
whose lives were shortn'd through the rigour of that persecution wherwith so many yeares he infested the true Church.
And those six Members all men judg'd to have escap'd no
less then capital danger; whom he so greedily pursuing into
20 the House of Commons, had not there the forbearance to
conceal how much it troubl'd him, *That the Birds were*
flowne. If som Vultur in the Mountains could have op'nd
his beak intelligibly and spoke, what fitter words could he
have utter'd at the loss of his prey? The Tyrant *Nero,* though
25 not yet deserving that name, sett his hand so unwillingly to
the execution of a condemned Person, as to wish *He had not*
known letters. Certainly for a King himself to charge his
Subjects with high treason, and so vehemently to prosecute

them in his own cause, as to doe the Office of a Searcher,
argu'd in him no great aversation from shedding blood, were
it but *to satisfie his anger,* and that revenge was no unpleas-
ing morsel to him, wherof he himself thought not much to
5 be so diligently his own Caterer. But we insist rather upon
what was actual then what was probable.

He now falls to examin the causes of this Warr, as a difficulty which he had long *studied* to find out. *It was not* saith
he, *my withdrawing from White Hall; for no account in*
10 *reason could be giv'n of those Tumults, where an orderly*
Guard was granted. But if it be a most certain truth that the
Parlament could never yet obtain of him any Guard fit to be
confided in, then by his own confession some account of those
pretended Tumults *may in reason be giv'n:* and both con-
15 cerning them and the Guards anough hath bin said alreadie.

Whom did he protect against the Justice of Parlament?
Whom did he not to his utmost power? Endeavouring to
have rescu'd *Strafford* from thir Justice, though with the destruction of them and the City; to that end expressly com-
20 manding the admittance of new Soldiers into the Tower,
rais'd by *Suckling* and other Conspirators, under pretence for
the *Portugall;* though that Embassador, beeing sent to, utterly deny'd to know of any such Commission from his Maister. And yet that listing continu'd. Not to repeat his other
25 Plot of bringing up the two Armies. But what can be disputed with such a King in whose mouth and opinion the
Parlament it self was never but a *Faction,* and thir Justice no
Justice, but *The dictates and oversqaying insolence of Tu-*

mults and Rabbles; and under that excuse avouches himself
op'nly the generall Patron of most notorious Delinquents, and
approves their flight out of the Land, whose crimes were
such, as that the justest and the fairest tryal would have soon-
5 est condemn'd them to death. But did not *Catiline* plead in
like manner against the *Roman* Senat and the injustice of thir
trial, and the justice of his flight from *Rome? Cæsar* also,
then hatching Tyranny, injected the same scrupulous de-
murrs to stop the sentence of death in full and free Senat de-
10 creed on *Lentulus* and *Cethegus* two of *Catilines* accomplices,
which were renew'd and urg'd for *Strafford.* He voutsafes
to the Reformation by both Kingdoms intended, no better
name then *Innovation and ruine both in Church and State.*
And what we would have learnt so gladly of him in other
15 passages before, to know wherin, he tells us now of his own
accord. The expelling of Bishops out of the House of Peers,
this was *ruin to the State,* the *removing* them *root and branch,*
this was *ruin to the Church.* How happy could this Nation be
in such a Governour who counted that thir ruin, which they
20 thought thir deliverance, the ruin both of Church and State,
which was the recovery and the saving of them both.

To the passing of those Bills against Bishops, how is it
likely that the House of Peers gave so hardly thir consent,
which they gave so easily before to the attaching them of
25 High Treason, 12. at once, onely for protesting that the Parlament could not act without them. Surely if thir rights and
privileges were thought so undoubted in that House, as is
heer maintain'd; then was that Protestation being meant and

intended in the name of thir whole spiritual Order, no Treason: and so that House it self will becom liable to a just
construction either of Injustice to appeach them for so con-
senting, or of usurpation, representing none but themselves,
5 to expect that their voting or not voting should obstruct the
Commons. Who not for *five repulses of the Lords,* no not for
fifty, were to desist from what in name of the whole Kingdom they demanded, so long as those Lords were none of our
Lords. And for the Bil against root and branch, though it
10 pass'd not in both Houses till many of the Lords and some
few of the Commons, either intic'd away by the King, or
overaw'd by the sense of thir own Malignancy not prevailing, deserted the Parlament, and made a fair riddance of
themselves, that was no warrant for them who remain'd
15 faithfull, beeing farr the greater number, to lay aside that
Bill of root and branch, till the returne of thir fugitives; a
Bill so necessary and so much desir'd by themselves as well as
by the People.

This was the *partiality,* this degrading of the Bishops, a
20 thing so wholsom in the State, and so Orthodoxal in the
Church both ancient and reformed; which the King rather
then assent to, *will either hazard both his own and the Kingdomes ruin,* by our just defence against his force of armes, or
prostrat our consciences in a blind obedience to himself, and
25 *those men whose superstition Zealous* or unzealous would in-
force upon us an Antichristian tyranny in the Church, neither
Primitive, Apostolicall, nor more *anciently universal,* then
som other manifest corruptions.

But *he was bound besides his judgement by a most strict and undispensable Oath to preserve that Order and the rights of the Church*. If he mean the Oath of his Coronation, and that the letter of that Oath admitt not to be interpreted either
5 by equity, reformation, or better knowledge, then was the King bound by that Oath to grant the clergie all those customs, franchises, and Canonical privileges granted to them by *Edward* the Confessor; and so might one day, under pretence of that Oath, and his conscience, have brought us all again to
10 popery. But had he so well rememberd, as he ought, the words to which he swore, he might have found himself no otherwise oblig'd there, then *according to the Lawes of God and true profession of the Gospel*. For if those following words, *Establish'd in this Kingdome,* be set there to limit and
15 lay prescription on the Laws of God and truth of the Gospel by mans establishment, nothing can be more absurrd or more injurious to Religion. So that however the German Emperors, or other Kings have levied all those Warrs on thir Protestant Subjects under the colour of a blind and literal observ-
20 ance to an Oath, yet this King had least pretence of all; both sworn to the Laws of God, and Evangelic truth, and disclaiming, as we heard him before, *to be bound by any Coronation Oath, in a blind and brutish formality*. Nor is it to be imagin'd, if what shall be establish'd come in question, but that
25 the Parlament should oversway the King, and not he the Parlament. And by all Law and Reason that which the Parlament will not, is no more establish'd in this Kingdom, neither is the King bound by Oath to uphold it as a thing

establish'd. And that the King who of Princely grace, as he professes, hath so oft abolisht things that stood firm by Law, as the Star-chamber, & High Commission, ever thought himself bound by Oath to keep them up, because establisht, he
5 who will beleiv, must at the same time condemn him of as many perjuries as he is well known to have abolisht both Laws and Jurisdictions, that wanted no establishment.

Had he gratifi'd, he thinks, *their Antiepiscopal Faction with his consent, and sacrific'd the Church-goverment and*
10 *Revennues to the fury of their covetousness, &c.* an Army had not bin rais'd. Wheras it was the fury of his own hatred to the professors of true Religion, which first incited him to persecute them with the Sword of Warr, when Whipps, Pillories, Exiles, and impris'nments were not thought sufficient.
15 To colour which, he cannot finde wherwithall, but that stale pretence of *Charles* the fifth, and other Popish Kings, that the Protestants had onely an intent to lay hands upon Church-revennues, a thing never in the thoughts of this Parlament, till exhausted by his endless Warr upon them, thir necessity
20 seis'd on that for the Common-wealth, which the luxury of Prelats had abus'd before to a common mischeif.

His consent to the unlording of Bishops (for to that he himself consented, and at *Canterbury* the cheif seat of thir pride, so God would have it) *was from his firm perswasion*
25 *of thir contentedness to suffer a present diminution of thir rights.* Can any man, reading this, not discern the pure mockery of a Royal consent, to delude us onely for *the present,* meaning, it seems, when time should serve, to revoke all: By

this reckning his consents and his denials come all to one
pass: and we may hence perceav the small wisdom and integrity of those Votes which Voted his Concessions at the Ile
of *Wight,* for grounds of a lasting Peace. This he alleges, this
5 controversie about Bishops, *to be the true state* of that difference between him and the Parlament. For he held Episcopacy *both very Sacred and Divine.* With this judgement and
for this cause he withdrew from the Parlament, and confesses
that some men knew *he was like to bring againe the same*
10 *judgement which he carried with him.* A fair and unex-
pected justification from his own mouth afforded to the Parlament; who notwithstanding what they knew of his obstinat
mind, omitted not to use all those means and that patience to
have gain'd him.

15   As for Delinquents, *he allowes them to be but the neces-*
sary consequences of his & their withdrawing and defend-
ing. A pretty shift to mince the name of a delinquent into a
necessary consequent: what is a Traitor but the necessary consequence of his Treason, what a Rebell, but of his Rebellion?
20 From this conceit he would inferr a *pretext* onely in the Parlament *to fetch in Delinquents,* as if there had indeed bin no
such cause, but all the Delinquency in London Tumults.
Which is the overworn theme, and stuffing of all his discourses.

25   This he thrice repeats to be the true State and reason of
all that Warr and devastation in the Land, and that *of all the*
Treaties and Propositions offer'd him, he was resolv'd *never*
to grant the abolishing of Episcopal, or the establishment of

Presbyterian Goverment. I would demand now of the *Scots* and Covnanteers (For so I call them as misobservers of the Covnant) how they will reconcile *the preservation of Religion and their liberties and the bringing of delinquents to* 5 *condign punishment,* with the *freedom, honour and safety* of this vow'd resolution here, that esteems all the Zeale of thir prostituted Covnant no better then *a noise and shew of pietie, a heat for Reformation, filling them with prejudice and obstructing all equality and clearness of judgment in* 10 *them.* With these principles who knows but that at length he might have come to take the Covnant, as others, whom they brotherly admitt, have don before him; and then all, no doubt, had gon well, and ended in a happy peace.

His prayer is most of it borrow'd out of *David;* but what 15 if it be answerd him as the *Jewes,* who trusted in *Moses,* were answerd by our *Saviour.* There is one that accuseth you, eev'n *David* whom you misapply.

He tells God *that his Enemies are many,* but tells the people, when it serves his turn, they are but *a faction of some* 20 *few, prevailing over the Major part of both Houses.*

God knows he had no passion, designe or preparation to imbroyle his Kingdom in a civill Warr. True; for he thought his Kingdom to be *Issachar* a *strong Ass that* would have *couch'd downe betweene two burd'ns,* the one of prelatical 25 superstition, the other of civil tyrannie: but what passion and designe, what close and op'n preparation he had made, to subdue us to both these by terror and preventive force, all the Nation knows.

The *confidence of som men had almost perswaded him to suspect his own innocence.* As the words of Saint *Paul* had almost perswaded *Agrippa* to be a Christian. But almost in the work of repentance is as good as not at all.

5 *God,* saith he, *will find out bloody and deceitfull men, many of whom have not liv'd out half thir days.* It behoov'd him to have bin more cautious how he tempted Gods finding out of blood and deceit, till his own yeares had bin furder spent, or that he had enjoy'd longer *the fruits of his* own *vio-*
10 *lent Counsels.*

But in stead of wariness, he adds another temptation, charging God, *To know that the chief designe of this Warr was either to destroy his Person or to force his judgement.* And thus his prayer from the evil practice of unjust accusing
15 men to God, arises to the hideous rashness of accusing God before Men to know that for truth, which all Men know to be most fals.

He praies *That God would forgive the people, for they know not what they doe.* It is an easie matter to say over what
20 our Saviour said; but how he lov'd the People, other Arguments then affected sayings must demonstrat. He who so oft hath presum'd rashly to appeale the knowledge and testimony of God, in things so evidently untrue, may be doubted what beleif or esteem he had of his forgiveness, either to him-
25 self, or those for whom he would so fain that men should heare he pray'd.

X. *Upon their seizing the Magazins, Forts,*
&c.

TO put the matter soonest out of controversy who was
the first beginner of this civil Warr, since the begin-
ing of all Warr may be discern'd not onely by the
first Act of hostilitie, but by the Counsels and preparations
foregoing, it shall evidently appeare, that the King was still
formost in all these. No King had ever at his first comming
to the Crown, more love and acclamation from a people;
10 never any people found wors requital of thir Loyaltie and
good affection: First by his extraordinary feare and mistrust
that thir Liberties and Rights, were the impairing and dimin-
ishing of his regal power, the true Original of Tyranny:
Next by his hatred to all those who were esteem'd Religious;
15 doubting that thir principles too much asserted libertie. This
was quickly seen by the vehemence, and the causes alleg'd
of his persecuting, the other by his frequent and opprobrious
dissolution of Parlaments; after he had demanded more
Mony of them, and they to obtain thir rights had granted
20 him, then would have bought the *Turk* out of *Morea,* and set
free all the Greeks. But when he sought to extort from us, by
way of Tribute, that which had bin offerd him conditionally
in Parlament, as by a free People, and that those extortions
were now consum'd and wasted by the luxurie of his Court,
25 he began then (for still the more he did wrong, the more he
fear'd) before any Tumult or insurrection of the People, to
take counsel how he might totally subdue them to his own

will. Then was the designe of German Horse, while the Duke
raignd, and which was worst of all, som thousands of the
Irish Papists were in several parts billeted upon us, while a
Parlament was then sitting. The Pulpits resounded with no
5 other Doctrine then that which gave all property to the King,
and passive obedience to the Subject. After which, innumerable formes and shapes of new exactions and Exacters over-
spread the Land. Nor was it anough to be impoverish'd,
unless wee were disarm'd. Our Train'd Bands, which are the
10 trustiest and most proper strength of a free Nation not at
warr within it self, had thir Arms in divers Counties tak'n
from them; other Ammunition by designe was ingross'd, and
kept in the Tower, not to be bought without a Licence, and
at a high rate.

15   Thus farr, and many other waies were his Counsels and
preparations before hand with us, either to a civil Warr, if it
should happ'n, or to subdue us without a Warr, which is all
one, untill the raising of his two Armies against the Scots,
and the latter of them rais'd to the most perfidious breaking
20 of a solemn Pacification: The articles wherof, though subscrib'd with his own hand, he commanded soon after to be
burnt op'nly by the Hangman. What enemy durst have don
him that dishonour and affront which he did therin to
himself.

25   After the beginning of this Parlament, whom he saw so
resolute and unanimous to releeve the Common-wealth, and
that the Earl of *Strafford* was condemn'd to die, other of his
evil Counselers impeach'd and imprison'd, to shew there

wanted not evil counsel within himself sufficient to begin a
warr upon his Subjects, though no way by them provok'd,
he sends an Agent with Letters to the King of *Denmark*, requiring aid against the parlament; and that aid was com-
5 ming, when Divine providence to divert them, sent a sudden
torrent of *Swedes* into the bowels of *Denmark*. He then endeavours to bring up both Armies, first the English, with
whom 8000 Irish Papists rais'd by *Strafford,* and a *French*
Army were to joyne; then the *Scots* at *Newcastle,* whom he
10 thought to have encourag'd by telling them what Mony and
Horse he was to have from *Denmark*. I mention not the
Irish conspiracie till due place. These and many other were
his Counsels toward a civil Warr. His preparations, after
those two Armies were dismiss'd, could not suddenly be too
15 op'n: Nevertheless there were 8000 *Irish* Papists which he
refus'd to disband, though intreated by both Houses, first for
reasons best known to himself, next under pretence of lend-
ing them to the *Spaniard;* and so kept them undisbanded till
very neere the Mounth wherin that Rebellion broke forth.
20 He was also raising Forces in London, pretendedly to serve
the *Portugall,* but with intent to seise the Tower. Into which
divers Canoneers were by him sent with many fire works,
and Granado's; and many great battering peeces were
mounted against the City. The Court was fortifi'd with Am-
25 munition, and Souldiers new listed, who follow'd the King
from *London,* and appear'd at *Kingston* som hunders of
Horse, in a warlike manner, with Waggons of Ammunition
after them; the Queen in *Holland* was buying more, of which

the Parlament had certain knowledge, and had not yet so much as once demanded the *Militia* to be settl'd, till they knew both of her going over sea, and to what intent. For she had pack'd up the Crown Jewels to have bin going long be-
5 fore, had not the Parlament suspecting by the discoveries at *Burrow Bridge* what was intended with the Jewells, us'd meanes to stay her journey till the winter. *Hull* and the Magazin there had bin secretly attempted under the Kings hand; from whom though in his declarations renouncing all thought
10 of Warr, notes were sent over sea for supply of Armes: which were no sooner come, but the inhabitants of *Yorkshire* and other Counties were call'd to Arms, and actual forces rais'd, while the Parlament were yet Petitioning in peace, and had not one man listed.

15 As to the Act of Hostilitie, though not much material in whom first it began, or by whose Commissions dated first, after such Counsels and preparations discover'd, and so farr advanc'd by the King, yet in that act also he will be found to have had precedency, if not at *London* by the assault of his
20 armed Court upon the naked People, and his attempt upon the House of Commons, yet certainly at *Hull,* first by his close practices on that Town, next by his seige. Thus whether Counsels, preparations, or Acts of hostilitie be considerd, it appeares with evidence anough, though much more might
25 be said, that the King is truly charg'd to bee the first beginner of these civil Warrs. To which may be added as a close, that in the Ile of *Wight* he charg'd it upon himself, at the public Treaty, and acquitted the Parlament.

But as for the securing of *Hull* and the public stores therin,
and in other places, it was no *Surprisall of his strength;* the
custody wherof by Autority of Parlament was committed
into hands most fitt, and most responsible for such a trust. It
5 were a folly beyond ridiculous to count our selves a free Nation, if the King not in Parlament, but in his own Person and
against them, might appropriate to himself the strength of a
whole Nation as his proper goods. What the Lawes of the
Land are, a Parlament should know best, having both the life
10 and death of Lawes in thir Lawgiving power: And the Law
of England is at best but the reason of Parlament. The Parlament therfore taking into thir hands that wherof most
properly they ought to have the keeping, committed no surprisal. If they prevented him, that argu'd not at all either *his*
15 *innocency or unpreparedness,* but their timely foresight to
use prevention.

But what needed that? *They knew his chiefest Armes left*
him were those onely which the ancient Christians were wont
to use against thir Persecuters, Prayers and Teares. O sacred
20 Reverence of God, Respect and Shame of Men, whither were
yee fled, when these hypocrisies were utterd? Was the Kingdom then at all that cost of blood to remove from him none
but Praiers and Teares? What were those thousands of blas-
pheming Cavaliers about him, whose mouthes let fly Oaths
25 and Curses by the voley; were those the Praiers? and those
Carouses drunk to the confusion of all things good or holy,
did those minister the Teares? Were they Praiers and Teares
that were listed at *York,* muster'd on *Heworth* Moore, and

laid Seige to *Hull* for the guard of his Person? Were Praiers
and Teares at so high a rate in *Holland* that nothing could
purchase them but the Crown Jewels? Yet they in *Holland*
(such word was sent us) sold them for Gunns, Carabins,
5 Morter-peeces, Canons, and other deadly Instruments of
Warr, which when they came to *York,* were all no doubt but
by the merit of some great Saint, suddenly transform'd into
Praiers and Teares; and being divided into Regiments and
Brigads were the onely Armes that mischiev'd us in all those
10 Battels and Incounters.

These were his chief Armes, whatever we must call them,
and yet such Armes, as they who fought for the Common-
wealth have by the help of better Praiers vanquish'd and
brought to nothing.

15 He bewailes his want of the Militia *Not so much in refer-*
ence to his own protection as the Peoples, whose many and
sore oppressions greeve him. Never considering how ill for
seventeen yeares together hee had protected them, and that
these miseries of the people are still his own handy work,
20 having smitt'n them like a forked Arrow so sore into the
Kingdoms sides, as not to be drawn out and cur'd without
the incision of more flesh.

He tells us that *what he wants in the hand of power* he has
in *the wings of Faith and Prayer.* But they who made no
25 reckning of those Wings while they had that power in thir
hands, may easily mistake the Wings of Faith for the Wings
of presumption, and so fall headlong.

We meet next with a comparison, how apt let them judge

who have travell'd to *Mecca, That the Parlament have hung the majestie of Kingship in an airy imagination of regality between the Privileges of both Houses, like the Tombe of Mahomet.* Hee knew not that he was prophecying the death and
5 burial of a Turkish Tyranny, that spurn'd down those Laws, which gave it life and being so long as it endur'd to be a regulated Monarchy.

He counts it an injury *Not to have the sole power in himself to help or hurt any;* and that the *Militia which he holds*
10 *to be his undoubted Right should be dispos'd as the Parlament thinks fitt.* And yet confesses that if he had it in his actual disposing, he would defend those whom he calls *His good Subjects from those mens violence and fraud, who would perswade the World that none but Wolves are fitt to*
15 *be trusted with the custody of the Shepheard and his Flock.* Surely if we may guess whom he meanes heer, by knowing whom he hath ever most oppos'd in this controversie, we may then assure our selves that by violence and fraud he meanes that which the Parlament hath don in settling the Militia,
20 and those the Wolves, into whose hands it was by them intrusted: which drawes a cleer confession from his own mouth, that if the Parlament had left him sole power of the *Militia,* he would have us'd it to the destruction of them and thir Freinds.

25 As for sole power of the *Militia,* which he claimes as a Right no less undoubted then the Crown, it hath bin oft anough told him, that he hath no more authority over the Sword then over the Law; over the Law he hath none, either

to establish or to abrogate, to interpret, or to execute, but onely by his Courts and in his Courts, wherof the Parlament is highest, no more therfore hath he power of the *Militia* which is the Sword, either to use or to dispose; but with con-
5 sent of Parlament; give him but that, and as good give him in a lump all our Laws and Liberties. For if the power of the Sword were any where separate and undepending from the power of Law, which is originally seated in the highest Court, then would that power of the Sword be soon maister of the
10 law, & being at one mans disposal, might, when he pleas'd, controule the Law, and in derision of our *Magna Charta,* which were but weak resistance against an armed Tyrant, might absolutely enslave us. And not to have in our selves, though vanting to be free-born, the power of our own free-
15 dom, and the public safety, is a degree lower then not to have the property of our own goods. For liberty of persons and the right of selfpreservation, is much neerer, much more natural, and more worth to all men, then the propriety of thir goods, and wealth. Yet such power as all this did the King in op'n
20 termes challenge to have over us; and brought thousands to help him win it; so much more good at fighting then at understanding, as to perswade themselves that they fought then for the Subjects Libertie.

He is contented, because he knows no other remedy, to
25 resigne this power, *for his owne time, but not for his successors.* So diligent and carefull he is, that we should be slaves, if not to him, yet to his Posterity, and faine would leave us the legacy of another warr about it. But the Parlament have

don well to remove that question: whom as his manner is to dignify with some good name or other, he calls now *a many headed hydra of Goverment, full of factious distractions and not more eyes then mouthes.* Yet surely not more Mouthes, 5 or not so wide, as the dissolute rabble of all his Courtiers had, both hees and shees, if there were any Males among them.

He would prove that to govern by Parlament hath *a monstrositie rather then perfection;* and grounds his argument upon two or three eminent absurdities: First by placing 10 Counsel in the senses, next by turning the senses out of the head, and in lieu therof placing power, *supreme* above sense & reason; which be now the greater Monstrosities? Furder to dispute what kind of Goverment is best, would be a long debate, it sufficeth that his reasons heer for Monarchy are 15 found weake and inconsiderable.

He bodes *much horror and bad influence after his ecclips.* He speaks his wishes: But they who by weighing prudently things past, foresee things to come, the best Divination, may hope rather all good success and happiness by removing that 20 darkness which the mistie cloud of his prerogative made between us and a peacefull Reformation, which is our true Sun light, and not he, though he would be tak'n for our sun it self. And wherfore should we not hope to be Govern'd more happily without a King, when as all our miserie, and trouble 25 hath bin either by a King, or by our necessary vindication and defence against him.

He would be thought *inforc'd to perjurie* by having granted the Militia, by which his Oath bound him to protect the

People. If he can be perjur'd in granting that, why doth he
refuse for no other cause the abolishing of Episcopacy? But
never was any Oath so blind as to sweare him to protect Delinquents against Justice, but to protect all the people in that
5 order, and by those hands which the Parlament should advise
him to, and the protected confide in; not under the shew of
protection to hold a violent and incommunicable Sword over
us, as readie to be let fall upon our own necks, as upon our
Enemies; nor to make our own hands and weapons fight
10 against our own Liberties.

By his parting with the *Militia* he takes to himself much
praise of his *assurance in Gods protection;* & to the Parlament
imputes the fear *of not daring to adventure the injustice of
their actions upon any other way of safety.* But wherfore came
15 not this assurance of Gods protection to him, till the *Militia*
was wrung out of his hands? It should seem by his holding
it so fast, that his own actions and intentions had no less of
injustice in them, then what he charges upon others; whom
he terms *Chaldeans, Sabeans, and the Devill himself.* But *Job*
20 us'd no such *Militia* against those enemies, nor such a Magazin as was at *Hull,* which this King so contended for, and
made Warr upon us, that he might have wherewithall to
make warr against us.

He concludes, that *Although they take all from him, yet
25 can they not obstruct his way to Heaven.* It was no hand-
som occasion, by faining obstructions where they are not, to
tell us whither he was going: he should have shut the dore,
and pray'd in secret, not heer in the High Street. Privat

praiers in publick, ask something of whom they ask not, and that shall be thir reward.

XI. *Upon the Nineteen Propositions,* &c.

O F the Nineteen Propositions he names none in particular, neither shall the Answer. But he insists
upon the old Plea of *his Conscience, honour, and
Reason;* using the plausibility of large and indefinite words,
to defend himself at such a distance as may hinder the eye of
common judgement from all distinct view & examination of
his reasoning. *He would buy the peace of his People at any
rate, save onely the parting with his Conscience and Honour.*
Yet shews not how it can happ'n that the peace of a People,
if otherwise to be bought at any rate, should be inconsistent
or at variance with the Conscience and Honour of a King.
Till then, we may receave it for a better sentence, that nothing should be more agreeable to the Conscience and Honour
of a King, then to preserve his Subjects in peace; especially
from civil Warr.

And which of the Propositions were *obtruded on him with
the point of the Sword,* till he first with the point of the
Sword thrust from him both the Propositions and the Pro-
pounders? He never reck'ns those violent and merciless ob-
trusions which for almost twenty years he had bin forcing
upon tender consciences by all sorts of Persecution; till
through the multitude of them that were to suffer, it could
no more be call'd a Persecution, but a plain Warr. From

which when first the Scots, then the English were constrain'd
to defend themselves, this thir just defence is that which he
cals heer, *Thir making Warr upon his soul.*

He grudges that *So many things are requir'd of him, and*
5 *nothing offerd him in requital of those favours which he had*
granted. What could satiate the desires of this man, who being king of *England,* and Maister of almost two millions
yearly what by hook or crook, was still in want; and those
acts of Justice which he was to doe in duty, counts don as fa-
10 vours; and such favors as were not don without the avari-
tious hope of other rewards besides supreme honour, and the
constant Revennue of his place.

This honour, he saith, *they did him to put him on the*
giving part. And spake truer then he intended, it beeing
15 meerly for honours sake that they did so; not that it belong'd
to him of right. For what can he give to a Parlament, who
receaves all he hath from the People, and for the Peoples
good. Yet now he brings his own conditional rights to contest and be preferr'd before the Peoples good; and yet unless
20 it be in order to their good, he hath no rights at all; raigning
by the Laws of the Land, not by his own; which Laws are in
the hands of Parlament to change or abrogate, as they shall
see best for the Common-wealth; eev'n to the taking away of
King-ship it self, when it grows too Maisterfull and Burd'n-
25 some. For every Common-wealth is in general defin'd, a
societie sufficient of it self, in all things conducible to well
being and commodious life. Any of which requisit things if
it cannot have without the gift and favour of a single person,

or without leave of his privat reason, or his conscience, it cannot be thought sufficient of it self, and by consequence no Common-wealth, nor free; but a multitude of Vassalls in the Possession and domaine of one absolute Lord; and wholly
5 obnoxious to his will. If the King have power to give or deny any thing to his Parlament, he must doe it either as a Person several from them or as one greater; neither of which will be allow'd him; not to be consider'd severally from them, for as the King of England can doe no wrong, so neither can he doe
10 right but in his Courts and by his Courts; and what is legally don in them, shall be deem'd the Kings assent, though he as a several Person shall judge or endeavour the contrary. So that indeed without his Courts or against them, he is no King. If therfore he obtrude upon us any public mischeif, or with-
15 hold from us any general good, which is wrong in the highest degree, he must doe it as a Tyrant, not as a King of England, by the known Maxims of our Law. Neither can he as one greater give aught to the Parlament which is not in thir own power, but he must be greater also then the Kingdom which
20 they represent. So that to honour him with the giving part was a meer civility, and may be well term'd the courtesie of *England,* not the Kings due.

But the *incommunicable Jewell of his conscience* he will not give, *but reserve to himself.* It seemes that his conscience
25 was none of the Crown Jewels; for those we know were, in *Holland,* not incommunicable to buy Armes against his Subjects. Being therfore but a privat Jewel, he could not have don a greater pleasure to the Kingdom then by reserving it to

himself. But he, contrary to what is heer profess'd, would
have his conscience not an incommunicable, but a universal
conscience, the whole Kingdoms conscience. Thus what he
seemes to feare least we should ravish from him, is our cheif
5 complaint that he obtruded upon us; we never forc'd him to
part with his conscience, but it was he that would have forc'd
us to part with ours.

Som things he taxes them to have offer'd him, *which while
he had the maistery of his Reason he would never consent to.*
10 Very likely; but had his reason maisterd him, as it ought,
and not bin maisterd long agoe by his sense and humour (as
the breeding of most Kings hath bin ever sensual and most
humour'd) perhaps he would have made no difficulty. Mean
while at what a fine pass is the Kingdom, that must depend
15 in greatest exigencies upon the fantasie of a Kings reason, be
he wise or foole, who arrogantly shall answer all the wisdom
of the Land, that what they offer seemes to him unreasonable.

He preferrs his *love of Truth* before his love of the People.
His love of Truth would have ledd him to the search of
20 Truth, and have taught him not to lean so much upon his
own understanding. He met at first with Doctrines of unaccountable Prerogative; in them he rested, because they pleas'd
him; they therfore pleas'd him, because they gave him all;
and this he calls his love of Truth, and preferrs it before the
25 love of his peoples peace.

Som things they propos'd *which would have wounded the
inward peace of his conscience.* The more our evil happ, that
three Kingdoms should be thus pesterd with one Conscience;

who chiefly scrupl'd to grant us that, which the parlament
advis'd him to, as the chief meanes of our public welfare and
Reformation. These scruples to many perhaps will seem pretended, to others, upon as good grounds, may seem real, and
5 that it was the just judgement of God, that he who was so
cruel and so remorseless to other mens consciences, should
have a conscience within him as cruel to himself; constrain-
ing him, as he constrain'd others, and insnaring him in such
waies and counsels, as were certain to be his destruction.

10   *Other things though he could approve, yet in honour and
policy, he thought fit to deny, lest he should seem to dare
deny nothing.* By this meanes he will be sure, what with
reason, conscience, honour, policy, or puntilios, to be found
never unfurnisht of a denyal: Whether it were his envy, not
15 to be overbounteous, or that the submissness of our asking
stirr'd up in him a certain pleasure of denying. Good Princes
have thought it thir chief happiness to be alwayes granting;
if good things, for the things sake, if things indifferent, for
the peoples sake: while this man sits calculating varietie of
20 excuses how he may grant least; as if his whole strength and
royaltie were plac'd in a meer negative.

   Of one Proposition especially he laments him much, that
they would bind him *to a generall and implicit consent for
what ever they desir'd.* Which though I find not among the
25 nineteene, yet undoubtedly the Oath of his coronation binds
him to no less; neither is he at all by his Office to interpose
against a Parlament in the making or not making of any
Law; but to take that for just and good legally, which is

there decreed, and to see it executed accordingly. Nor was
he set over us to vie wisdom with his Parlament, but to be
guided by them: *any of whome possibly* may as farr excell
him in the gift of wisdom, as he them in place and dignitie.
5 But much neerer is it to impossibilitie that any King alone
should be wiser then all his councel; sure anough it was not
he, though no King ever before him so much contended to
have it thought so. And if the Parlament so thought not, but
desir'd him to follow their advice and deliberation in things
10 of public concernment, he accounts it the same proposition,
as if *Sampson* had bin mov'd *to the putting out his eyes, that
the Philistims might abuse him.* And thus out of an unwise,
or pretended feare least others should make a scorn of him
for yeilding to his Parlament, he regards not to give cause of
15 worse suspicion, that he made a scorn of his regal Oath.

But *to exclude him from all power of deniall seemes an
arrogance;* in the Parlament he means; what in him then to
deny against the Parlament? None at all, by what he argues:
For *by Petitioning they confess thir inferioritie and that
20 obliges them to rest, if not satisfi'd, yet quieted with such an
Answer as the will and reason of their Superior thinks fit to
give.* First Petitioning, in better English, is no more then re-
questing or requiring, and men require not favours onely,
but thir due; and that not onely from Superiors, but from
25 Equals, and Inferiors also. The noblest Romans, when they
stood for that which was a kind of Regal honour, the Con-
sulship, were wont in a submissive manner to goe about
and begg that highest Dignity of the meanest *Plebeians,*

naming them man by man; which in their tongue was call'd *Petitio consulatus*. And the Parlament of *England* Petition'd the King, not because all of them were inferior to him, but because he was superior to any one of them, which they did of civil custom, and for fashions sake, more then of duty; for by plaine Law cited before, the Parlament is his Superiour.

But what law in any trial or dispute enjoynes a free man to rest quieted, though not satisfi'd, with the will and reason of his Superior? It were a mad law that would subject reason to superioritie of place. And if our highest consultations and purpos'd lawes must be terminated by the Kings will, then is the will of one man our Law, and no suttletie of dispute can redeem the Parlament, and Nation from being Slaves, neither can any Tyrant require more then that his will or reason, though not satisfying, should yet be rested in, and determin all things. We may conclude therfore that when the Parlament petition'd the King, it was but meerly forme, let it be as *foolish and absurd* as he pleases. It cannot certainly be so absurd as what he requires, that the Parlament should confine thir own and all the Kingdoms reason to the will of one man, because it was his hap to succeed his Father. For neither God nor the Lawes have subjected us to his will, nor sett his reason to be our sovran above Law (which must needs be, if he can strangle it in the birth) but sett his person over us in the sovran execution of such Laws as the Parlament establish. The Parlament therfore without any usurpation hath had it alwaies in thir power to limit and confine the

exorbitancie of Kings, whether they call it thir will, thir reason, or thir conscience.

But this above all was never expected, nor is to be endur'd,
that a King, who is bound by law and Oath to follow the
5 advice of his Parlament, should be permitted to except against
them as *young Statesmen,* and proudly to suspend his following thir advice, *untill his seven yeares experience had shewn
him how well they could govern themselves.* Doubtless the
Law never suppos'd so great an arrogance could be in one
10 man; that he whose seventeen yeares unexperience had almost ruin'd all, should sit another seven yeares Schoolmaster,
to tutor those who were sent by the whole Realme to be his
Counselers and teachers. And with what modesty can he pretend to be a Statesman himself, who with his Fathers King-
15 craft and his own, did never that of his own accord which
was not directly opposit to his professed Interest both at home
and abroad; discontenting and alienating his Subjects at
home, weakning and deserting his Confederats abroad, and
with them the Common cause of Religion. So that the whole
20 course of his raign by an example of his own furnishing hath
resembl'd *Phaeton* more then *Phœbus;* and forc'd the Parlament to drive like *Jehu;* which *Omen* tak'n from his own
mouth, God hath not diverted.

And he on the other side might have rememberd that the
25 Parlament sit in that body, not *as his Subjects* but as his Superiors, call'd, not by him but by the Law; not onely twice
every yeare, but as oft as great affaires require, *to be his Counselers and Dictators* though he stomac it, nor to be dissolv'd

at his pleasure, but when all greevances be first remov'd, all
Petitions heard, and answer'd. This is not onely Reason, but
the known Law of the Land.

When he heard that Propositions would be sent him, he
5 satt conjecturing what they would propound; and because
they propounded what he expected not, he takes that to be a
warrant for his denying them. But what did he expect? he
expected that the Parlament would reinforce *some old Laws.*
But if those Laws were not a sufficient remedy to all greev-
10 ances, nay were found to be greevances themselves, when did
we loose that other part of our freedom to establish new? He
thought *some injuries done by himself and others to the*
Common-wealth were to be repair'd. But how could that be,
while he the chief offender took upon him to be sole Judge
15 both of the injury and the reparation. *He staid till the advan-*
tages of his Crown consider'd might induce him to condi-
scend to the Peoples good. Whenas the Crown it self with all
those advantages were therfore giv'n him, that the peoples
good should be first consider'd; not bargain'd for, and bought
20 by inches with the bribe of more *offertures* and advantages to
his Crown. He look'd *for moderate desires of due Reforma-*
tion; as if any such desires could be immoderate: He lookd
for such a Reformation, *both in Church and State as might*
preserve the roots of every greevance and abuse in both still
25 growing (which he calls *The foundation and essentials*) and
would have onely the excrescencies of evil prun'd away for
the present, as was plotted before, that they might grow fast
anough between Triennial Parlaments, to hinder them by

worke anough besides, from ever striking at the root. He
alleges *They should have had regard to the Laws in force, to
the wisdom and pietie of former Parlaments to the ancient
and universall practise of Christian Churches.* As if they who
5 come with full autority to redress public greevances, which
ofttimes are Laws themselves, were to have thir hands bound
by Laws in force, or the supposition of more pietie and wisdom in thir Ancestors, or the practise of Churches heertofore, whose Fathers, notwithstanding all these pretences,
10 made as vast alterations to free themselves from ancient Popery. For all antiquity that adds or varies from the Scripture,
is no more warranted to our safe imitation, then what was
don the Age before at *Trent.* Nor was there need to have
despair'd of what could be establish'd in lieu of what was to
15 be annull'd, having before his eyes the Goverment of so many
Churches beyond the Seas; whose pregnant and solid reasons
wrought so with the Parlament, as to desire a uniformity
rather with all other Protestants, then to be a scism divided
from them under a conclave of thirty Bishops, and a crew of
20 irreligious Priests, that gap'd for the same preferment.

   And wheras he blames those propositions for not containing what they ought, what did they mention but to vindicate
and *restore the Rights of Parlament invaded* by Cabin councels, the Courts of *Justice obstructed, and the Government* of
25 Church innovated and corrupted? All these things he might
easily have observ'd in them, which he affirmes he could **not**
find: But found *those demanding* in Parlament who were
lookt upon before, as factious in the State, and scismaticall in

the Church; and demanding not onely Tolerations for them-
selves in thir vanity, noveltie and confusion, but also an ex-
tirpation of that Goverment whose Rights they had a mind
to invade. Was this man ever likely to be advis'd, who with
5 such a prejudice and disesteem sets himself against his chos'n
and appointed Counselers; likely ever to admitt of Reformation, who censures all the Goverment of other Protestant
Churches, as bad as any Papist could have censur'd them?
And what King had ever his whole Kingdom in such con-
10 tempt, so to wrong and dishonour the free elections of his
people, as to judge them whom the Nation thought worthiest
to sitt with him in Parlament, few els but such as were *pun-*
ishable by Lawes: yet knowing that time was, when to be a
Protestant, to be a Christian was by Law as punishable as to
15 be a Traitor, and that our Saviour himself comming to reform his Church, was accus'd of an intent to invade *Cæsars*
right, as good a right as the prelat Bishops ever had; the one
being got by force, the other by spiritual usurpation: and
both by force upheld.

20 He admires and falls into an extasie that the Parlament
should send him such a *horrid Proposition,* as the removal of
Episcopacy. But expect from him in an extasie no other
reasons of his admiration then the dream and tautology of
what he hath so oft repeated, Law, Antiquitie, Ancestors,
25 prosperity and the like, which will be therfore not worth a
second answer, but may pass with his own comparison *Into*
the common sewer of other Popish arguments.

Had the two Houses su'd out thir Liverie from the ward-

ship of Tumults, he could sooner have beleiv'd them. It concernd them first to sue out thir Livery from the unjust wardship of his encroaching Prerogative. And had he also redeem'd his overdated minority from a Pupillage under Bish-
5 ops, he would much less have mistrusted his Parlament; and never would have set so base a Character upon them as to count them no better then the Vassals of certain nameless men whom he charges to be such as *hunt after Faction with their Hounds the Tumults.* And yet the Bishops could have
10 told them, that *Nimrod,* the first that hunted after Faction is reputed, by ancient Tradition, the first that founded Monarchy; whence it appeares that to hunt after Faction is more properly the Kings Game; and those Hounds, which he calls the Vulgar, have bin oft'n hollow'd to from Court; of whom
15 the mungrel sort have bin entic'd; the rest have not lost thir sent; but understood aright, that the Parlament had *that part to act* which he had fail'd in: that *trust to discharge,* which he had brok'n; that *estate and honour to preserve,* which was farr beyond his, the estate and honour of the Common-
20 wealth, which he had imbezl'd.

Yet so farr doth self-opinion or fals principles delude and transport him, as to think *the concurrence of his reason* to the Votes of Parlament, not onely Political, but Natural, *and as necessary to the begetting,* or bringing forth of any one
25 *compleat act of public wisdom as the Suns influence is necessary to all natures productions.* So that the Parlament, it seems, is but a Female, and without his procreative reason, the Laws which they can produce are but wind-eggs. Wis-

dom, it seems, to a King is natural, to a Parlament not natural, but by conjunction with the King: Yet he professes to
hold his Kingly right by Law; and if no Law could be made
but by the great Counsel of a Nation, which we now term a
5 Parlament, then certainly it was a Parlament that first created Kings, and not onely made Laws before a King was
in being, but those Laws especially, wherby he holds his
Crown. He ought then to have so thought of a Parlament,
if he count it not Male, as of his Mother, which, to civil
10 being, created both him, and the Royalty he wore. And if
it hath bin anciently interpreted the presaging signe of a
future Tyrant, but to dream of copulation with his Mother,
what can it be less then actual Tyranny to affirme waking,
that the Parlament, which is his Mother, can neither con-
15 ceive or bring forth *any autoritative Act* without his Mas-
culine coition: Nay that his reason is as Celestial and life-
giving to the Parlament, as the Suns influence is to the
Earth: What other notions but these, or such like, could
swell up *Caligula* to think himself a God.

20 But to be ridd of these mortifying Propositions he leaves no
Tyrannical evasion unassaid; first *that they are not the joynt
and free desires of both Houses or the major part;* next, *that
the choise of many Members was carried on by Faction.* The
former of these is already discover'd to be an old device put
25 first in practice by *Charles* the fifth since Reformation. Who
when the Protestants of *Germany* for thir own defense join'd
themselves in League, in his Declarations & Remonstrances
laid the fault only upon some few (for it was dangerous to

take notice of too many Enemies) and accus'd them that under colour of Religion they had a purpose to invade his and the Churches right: by which policy he deceav'd many of the German Cities, and kept them divided from that

5 League, untill they saw themselves brought into a snare. That other cavil against the peoples chois puts us in mind rather what the Court was wont to doe, and how to tamper with Elections: neither was there at that time any Faction more potent, or more likely to doe such a business, then they them-

10 selves who complain most.

But *he must chew such Morsels as Propositions ere he let them down*. So let him; but if the Kingdom shall tast nothing but after his chewing, what does he make of the Kingdom, but a great baby. *The streitness of his conscience will*

15 *not give him leave* to *swallow down such Camels of sacrilege and injustice as others doe*. This is the Pharisee up and down, *I am not as other men are*. But what Camels of Injustice he could devoure, all his three Realms were wittness, which was the cause that they almost perish'd for want of Parlaments.

20 And he that will be unjust to man, will be sacrilegious to God; and to bereave a Christian conscience of libertie for no other reason then the narrowness of his own conscience, is the most unjust measure to man, and the worst sacrilege to God. That other, which he calls sacrilege, of taking from the

25 Clergy that superfluous wealth, which antiquitie as old as *Constantine,* from the credit of a Divine vision, counted *poyson in the Church,* hath bin ever most oppos'd by men whose righteousness in other matters hath bin least observ'd. He

concludes, as his manner is, with high commendation of his own *unbiass'd rectitude* and beleives nothing to be in them that dissent from him, but faction, innovation, and particular designes. Of these repetitions I find no end, no not in his
5 prayer; which being founded upon deceitfull principl's and a fond hope that God will bless him in those *his errors,* which he calls *honest,* finds a fitt answer of S. *James; Yee ask and receave not, because yee aske amiss.* As for the truth and sinceritie which he praies may be alwaies found in those his
10 Declarations to the people, the contrariety of his own actions will bear eternal witness how little carefull or sollicitous he was, what he promis'd, or what he utterd there.

XII. *Upon the Rebellion in* Ireland.

THE Rebellion and horrid massacher of English Prot-
15 estants in *Ireland* to the number of 154000. in the Province of *Ulster* onely, by thir own computation, which added to the other three, makes up the total summ of that slaughter in all likelyhood fowr times as great, although *so sudden, and so violent,* as at first to amaze all men that
20 were not accessory, yet from whom, and from what counsels it first sprung, neither was nor could be possibly so secret, as the contrivers therof blinded with vaine hope, or the despaire that other plots would succeed, suppos'd. For it cannot be imaginable that the Irish, guided by so many suttle and
25 *Italian* heads of the Romish party, should so farr have lost the use of reason, and indeed of common Sense, as not sup-

ported with other strength then thir own, to begin a Warr
so desperate and irreconcileable against both England and
Scotland at once. All other Nations, from whom they could
expect aid, were busied to the utmost in thir own most neces-
5 sary concernments. It remaines then that either some autoritie or som great assistance promis'd them from England, was
that wheron they cheifly trusted. And as it is not difficult to
discern from what inducing cause this insurrection first arose,
so neither was it *hard at first to have apply'd* some effectual
10 *remedy,* though not prevention. And yet prevention was not
hopeles, when *Strafford* either beleivd not, or did not care to
beleive the several warnings and discoveries therof, which
more then once by Papists and by Friers themselves were
brought him; besides what was brought by deposition, divers
15 months before that Rebellion, to the Arch-bishop of Canterbury and others of the Kings Counsel; as the Declaration of
no addresses declares. But the assurance which they had in
privat, that no remedy should be apply'd, was, it seemes, one
of the cheif reasons that drew on thir undertaking. And long
20 it was ere that assurance faild them; untill the Bishops and
Popish Lords, who while they sate and Voted, still oppos'd
the sending aid to *Ireland,* were expelld the House.

Seeing then the maine incitement and Autority for this
Rebellion must be needs deriv'd from *England,* it will be next
25 inquir'd who was the prime Author. The King heer de-
nounces a malediction temporal and eternal, not simply to
the Author, but to the *malitious Author* of this blood-shedd;
and by that limitation may exempt, not himself onely, but

perhaps the Irish Rebels themselves; who never will confess
to God or Man that any blood was shed by them malitiously;
but either in the Catholic cause, or common Liberty, or some
other specious Plea, which the conscience from grounds both
5 good and evil usually suggests to it self: thereby thinking to
elude the direct force of that imputation which lies upon
them.

Yet he acknowledges *It fell out as a most unhappy advan-*
tage of some mens malice against him: but indeed of most
10 mens just suspicion, by finding in it no such wide departure
or disagreement from the scope of his former Counsels and
proceedings. And that he himself was the Author of that
Rebelion, he denies both heer and elswhere, with many imprecations, but no solid evidence. What on the other side
15 against his denyal hath bin affirm'd in three Kingdoms being
heer briefly set in view, the Reader may so judge as he findes
cause.

This is most certain, that the King was ever friendly to the
Irish Papists, and in his third yeare, against the plain advice
20 of Parlament, like a kind of Pope, sold them many indul-
gences for Mony; and upon all occasions advancing the Popish party, and negotiating under hand by Priests who were
made his Agents, ingag'd the Irish Papists in a Warr against
the Scotch Protestants. To that end he furnish'd them, and
25 had them train'd in Arms; and kept them up, either op'nly
or under hand, the onely army in his three Kingdoms, till the
very burst of that Rebellion. The Summer before that dismal
October, a Committy of most active Papists, all since in the

head of that Rebellion, were in great favour at *White-Hall;* and admitted to many privat consultations with the King and Queen. And to make it evident that no mean matters were the subject of those Conferences, at their request he gave
5 away his peculiar right to more then five Irish Counties, for the payment of an inconsiderable Rent. They departed not home till within two Mounths before the Rebellion; and were either from the first breaking out, or soon after, found to be the cheif Rebels themselves. But what should move the King,
10 besides his own inclination to Popery, and the prevalence of his Queen over him, to hold such frequent and close meetings with a Committy of Irish Papists in his own House, while the Parlament of *England* sate unadvis'd with, is declar'd by a Scotch Author, and of it self is cleare anough. The Parla-
15 ment at the beginning of that Summer, having put *Strafford* to death, imprison'd others his chief Favorites, and driv'n the rest to fly, the K. who had in vain tempted both the Scotch and the English Army to come up against the Parlament and Citty, finding no compliance answerable to his hope from the
20 Protestant Armies, betakes himself last to the Irish; who had in readiness an Army of eight thousand Papists which he had refus'd so oft'n to disband, and a Committy heer of the same Religion. With them, who thought the time now come, which to bring about they had bin many yeares before not
25 wishing only but with much industrie complotting, to do som eminent service for the Church of *Rome* & thir own perfidious natures against a Puritan Parlmt. & the hated English thir Masters, he agrees & concludes that so soon as both

Armies in *England* were disbanded, the Irish should appeare
in Arms, maister all the Protestants, and help the King
against his Parlament. And we need not doubt that those five
Counties were giv'n to the Irish for other reason then the four
5 Northern Counties had bin a little before offerd to the Scots.
The King in *August* takes a journey into *Scotland;* and over-
taking the Scotch Army then on thir way home, attempts the
second time to pervert them, but without success. No sooner
comm into *Scotland,* but he laies a plot, so saith the Scotch
10 Author, to remove out of the way such of the Nobility there,
as were most likely to withstand, or not to furder his designes. This being discover'd, he sends from his side one
Dillon a Papist Lord, soon after a cheif Rebell, with Letters
into *Ireland;* and dispatches a Commission under the great
15 Seale of *Scotland* at that time in his own custody, command-
ing that they should forthwith, as had bin formerly agreed,
cause all the Irish to rise in Armes. Who no sooner had receiv'd such command, but obey'd; and began in Massacher;
for they knew no other way to make sure the Protestants,
20 which was commanded them expressly; and the way, it
seems, left to thir discretion. He who hath a mind to read
the Commission it self, and sound reason added why it was
not likely to be forg'd, besides the attestation of so many
Irish themselves, may have recourse to a Book intitl'd *The*
25 *Mysterie of Iniquity.* Besides what the Parlament it self in
the Declaration of *no more addresses* hath affirm'd; that they
have one copy of that Commission in thir own hands, at-
tested by the Oathes of some that were ey-witnesses, and had

seen it under the Seale. Others of the principal Rebels have confess'd that this Commission was the summer before promis'd at *London* to the Irish Commissioners, to whom the King then discoverd in plain words his great desire to be re-
5 veng'd on the Parlament of *England*.

After the Rebellion brok'n out, which in words onely he detested, but under hand favour'd and promoted by all the offices of freindship, correspondence, and what possible aide he could afford them, the particulars wherof are too many to
10 be inserted heer, I suppose no understanding Man could longer doubt who was *Author or Instigator* of that Rebellion. If there be who yet doubt, I referr them especially to that Declaration of *July* 1643. with that of *no addresses* 1647. and another full volum of examinations to be sett out speed-
15 ily concerning this matter. Against all which testimonies, likelyhoods, evidences, and apparent actions of his own, being so abundant, his bare deniall though with imprecation, can no way countervaile; and least of all in his own cause.

As for the Commission granted them, he thinkes to evade
20 that by retorting, that *some in England fight against him* and yet *pretend his authority*. But though a Parlament by the known Laws may affirme justly to have the Kings autority, inseparable from that Court, though divided from his Person, it is not credible that the Irish Rebels who so much ten-
25 derd his Person above his Autoritie, and were by him so well receavd at *Oxford,* would be so farr from all humanitie as to slander him with a particular Commission sign'd and sent them by his own hand.

And of his good affection to the Rebels this Chapter it self is not without witness. He holds them less in fault then the *Scots,* as from whom they might *allege* to have fetch'd *thir imitation;* making no difference between men that rose neces-
5 sarily to defend themselves, which no Protestant Doctrin ever disallow'd, against them who threatn'd Warr, and those who began a voluntary and causeless Rebellion with the Massacher of so many thousands who never meant them harme.

He falls next to flashes, and a multitude of words, in all
10 which is contain'd no more, then what might be the Plea of any guiltiest Offender; He was not the Author because *he hath the greatest share of loss and dishonour by what is committed.* Who is there that offends God or his Neighbour, on whom the greatest share of loss and dishonour lights not in
15 the end? But in the act of doing evil, men use not to consider the event of thir evil doing: or if they doe, have then no power to curb the sway of thir own wickedness. So that the greatest share of loss and dishonour to happ'n upon themselves, is no argument that they were not guilty. This other is
20 as weake, that *a Kings interest* above that of any other man, *lies chiefly in the common welfare of his Subjects;* therfore no King will do aught against the Common welfare. For by this evasion any tyrant might as well purge himself from the guilt of raising troubles or commotions among the people,
25 because undoubtedly his chief Interest lies in thir sitting still.

I said but now that eev'n this Chapter, if nothing els, might suffice to discover his good affection to the Rebels; which in this that follows too notoriously appeares; imputing

this insurrection to *the preposterous rigor, and unreasonable severitie, the covetous zeale and uncharitable fury of some men* (these *some men* by his continual paraphrase are meant the Parlament) and lastly, *to the feare of utter extirpation.*
5 If the whole Irishry of Rebells had fee'd som advocate to speak partially and sophistically in thir defence, he could have hardly dazl'd better: Yet never the less would have prov'd himself no other then a plausible deceiver. And per-haps, nay more then perhaps, for it is affirm'd & extant under
10 good evidence, that those fained terrors and jealousies were either by the King himself, or the Popish Preists which were sent by him, put into the head of that inquisitive people, on set purpose to engage them. For who had power *to oppress* them, or to releive them being opprest, but the King or his
15 immediat Deputy? This rather should have made them rise against the King then against the Parlament. Who threat'nd or ever thought of thir extirpation, till they themselves had begun it to the English? As for *preposterous rigor, covetous zeale, and uncharitable fury;* they had more reason to suspect
20 those evils first from his own commands, whom they saw using daily no *greater argument* to prove *the truth* of his Re-ligion then by *enduring no other but his owne* Prelatical; and to force it upon others, made Episcopal, Ceremonial, and common-Prayer-Book Warrs. But the Papists understood
25 him better then by the outside; and knew that those Warrs were their Warrs. Although if the Common-wealth should be afraid to suppress op'n Idolatry, lest the Papists thereupon should grow desperat, this were to let them grow and become

our persecuters, while we neglected what we might have don Evangelically, to be their Reformers. Or to doe as his Father *James* did, who in stead of taking heart and putting confidence in God by such a deliverance as from the Powder Plot, 5 though it went not off, yet with the meer conceit of it, as some observe, was hitt into such a *Hectic* shivering between Protestant and Papist all his life after, that he never durst from that time doe otherwise then equivocat or collogue with the Pope and his adherents.

10 He would be thought to commiserat the sad effects of that Rebellion, and to lament that *the teares and blood spilt there did not quench the sparks of our civil* discord heer. But who began these dissentions, and what can be more op'nly known then those retardings and delaies which by himself were con- 15 tinually devis'd, to hinder and put back the releif of those distressed Protestants, which undoubtedly had it not bin then put back might have sav'd many streames of those teares and that blood wherof he seems heer so sadly to bewaile the spilling. His manifold excuses, diversions and delaies are too well 20 known to be recited heer in particular, and too many.

But *he offer'd to goe himself in person upon that expedition;* and reck'ns up many surmises why he thinks they would not suffer him. But mentions not that by his underdealing to debaush Armies heer at home, and by his secret intercours 25 with the cheif Rebels, long ere that time every where known, he had brought the Parlament into so just a diffidence of him, as that they durst not leave the Public Armes to his disposal, much less an Army to his conduct.

He concludes *That next the sin of those who began that Rebellion theirs must needs be who hinder'd the suppressing, or diverted the aides.* But judgement rashly giv'n ofttimes involves the Judge himself. He findes fault with those *who* 5 *threatn'd all extremity to the Rebels,* and pleads much that mercy should be shown them. It seems he found himself not so much concern'd as those who had lost Fathers, Brothers, Wives and Children, by thir crueltie; whom in justice to re- taliat is not as he supposes *unevangelical;* so long as Magis- 10 tracy and Warr is not laid down under the Gospel. If this his Sermon of affected mercy were not too Pharisaical, how could he permit himself to cause the slaughter of so many thousands heer in *England* for meer Prerogatives, the Toys and Gewgaws of his Crown, for Copes and Surplices, the 15 Trinkets of his Priests, and not perceave his zeale, while he taxes others, to be most preposterous and unevangelical. Neither is there the same cause to destroy a whole City for the ravishing of a Sister, not don out of Villany, and recompence offer'd by Mariage; nor the same case for those Disciples to 20 summon fire from Heav'n upon the whole City where they were deny'd lodging, and for a Nation by just Warr and exe- cution to slay whole Families of them who so barbarously had slaine whole Families before. Did not all *Israel* doe as much against the *Benjamits* for one Rape committed by a few, and 25 defended by the whole Tribe? and did they not the same to *Jabesh Gilead* for not assisting them in that revenge? I speak not this that such measure should be meted rigorously to all the Irish, or as remembring that the Parlament ever so Decreed, but to shew that this his Homily hath more of craft and affectation in it, then of sound Doctrin.

But it was happy that his going into *Ireland* was not consented to: For either he had certainly turn'd his rais'd Forces against the Parlament it self, or not gon at all, or had he gon, what work he would have made there, his own following words declare.

He would have punisht some; no question; for some perhaps who were of least use, must of necessity have bin sacrific'd to his reputation, *and the conveniencie of his affaires.* Others he *would have disarm'd,* that is to say in his own time: but *all of them he would have protected from the fury of those that would have drown'd them, if they had refus'd to swim down the popular stream.* These expressions are too oft'n mett, and too well understood for any man to doubt his meaning. By the *fury of those,* he meanes no other then the Justice of Parlament, to whom yet he had committed the whole business. Those who would have refus'd to swim down the popular streame, our constant key tells us to be Papists, Prelats, and thir Faction: these, by his own confession heer, he would have protected against his Puritan Parlament: And by this who sees not that he and the Irish Rebels had but one aime, one and the same drift, and would have forthwith joyn'd in one body against us.

He goes on still in his tenderness of the Irish Rebels fearing least *our zeale should be more greedy to kill the Beare for his skin then for any harme he hath don.* This either justifies the Rebels to have don no harme at all, or inferrs his opinion

that the Parlament is more bloody and rapacious in the
prosecution of thir Justice, then those Rebels were in the execution of thir barbarous crueltie. Let men doubt now and
dispute to whom the King was a Freind most, to his English
5 Parlament, or to his Irish Rebels.

    With whom, that we may yet see furder how much he was
thir Freind, after that the Parlament had brought them every
where either to Famin, or a low condition, he, to give them
all the respit and advantages they could desire, without ad-
10 vice of Parlament, to whom he himself had committed the
mannaging of that Warr, makes a Cessation; in pretence to
releive the Protestants, *overborne there with numbers,* but as
the event prov'd, to support the Papists, by diverting and
drawing over the English Army there, to his own service
15 heer against the Parlament. For that the Protestants were
then on the winning hand, it must needs be plaine; who notwithstanding the miss of those Forces which, at thir landing
heer, maister'd without difficulty great part of Wales and
Cheshire, yet made a shift to keep thir own in *Ireland.* But
20 the plot of this Irish Truce is in good part discoverd in that
Declaration of *September* 30th. 1643. And if the Protestants
were but *handfuls* there, as he calls them, why did he stop
and waylay both by Land and Sea, to his utmost power, those
Provisions and Supplies which were sent by the Parlament?
25 How were so many *handfuls* call'd over, as for a while stood
him in no small stead, and against our main Forces heer in
England?

    Since therfore all the reasons that can be giv'n of this Ces-

sation appeare so fals and frivolous, it may be justly fear'd
that the designe it self was most wicked and pernicious. What
remaines then? He *appeales to God,* and is cast; lik'ning his
punishments to *Jobs* trials, before he saw them to have *Jobs*
5 ending. But how could Charity her self beleive ther was at
all in him any Religion, so much as but to fear ther is a God;
when as by what is noted in the Declaration of *no more ad-*
dresses, he vowd solemnly to the Parlament with imprecations upon himself and his Posterity, if ever he consented to
10 the abolishing of those Lawes which were in force against
Papists, and at the same time, as appeard plainly by the very
date of his own Letters to the Queen and *Ormond,* consented
to the abolishing of all Penal Lawes against them both in
Ireland and *England.* If these were acts of a Religious Prince,
15 what memory of man writt'n or unwritt'n can tell us newes of
any Prince that ever was irreligious? He cannot stand *to make*
prolix Apologies. Then surely those long Pamphlets set out
for Declarations and Protestations in his Name, were none of
his; and how they should be his indeed, being so repugnant
20 to the whole cours of his actions, augments the difficulty.

But he usurps a common saying, *That it is Kingly to doe*
well and heare ill. That may be sometimes true: but farr
more frequently, to doe ill and heare well; so great is the
multitude of Flatterers, and them that deifie the name of
25 King.

Yet not content with these neighbours, we have him still
a perpetual preacher of his own vertues, and of that especially
which who knows not to bee *Patience* perforce.

He *beleives it will at last appeare that they who first began to embroyle his other kingdoms, are also guilty of the blood of Ireland.* And wee beleive so too; for now the Cessation is become a Peace by publishd Articles, and Commission to
5 bring them over against *England,* first only ten thousand by the Earl of *Glamorgan,* next all of them, if possible, under *Ormond,* which was the last of all his transactions don as a public Person. And no wonder; for he lookt upon the blood spilt, whether of Subjects or of Rebels with an indifferent
10 eye, *as exhausted out of his own veines;* without distinguishing as he ought, which was good blood and which corrupt; the not letting out wherof endangers the whole body.

And what the Doctrin is ye may perceave also by the Prayer, which after a short ejaculation for the *poore Protestants,*
15 prayes at large for the Irish Rebels, that God would not give them over, *or thir Children to the covetousness, cruelty, fierce and cursed anger* of the Parlament.

He finishes with a deliberat and solemn curse *upon himself and his Fathers House.* Which how farr God hath al-
20 readie brought to pass, is to the end that men by so eminent an example should learn to tremble at his judgements; and not play with Imprecations.

XIII. *Upon the calling in of the* Scots *and thir comming.*

IT must needs seem strange, where Men accustom themselves to ponder and contemplat things in thir first original and institution, that Kings, who, as all other Officers of the Public, were at first chos'n and install'd onely by consent and suffrage of the People, to govern them as Freemen by Laws of thir own framing, and to be, in consideration of that dignity and riches bestow'd upon them, the entrusted Servants of the Common-wealth, should notwithstanding grow up to that dishonest encroachment, as to esteem themselves Maisters, both of that great trust which they serve, and of thc People that betrusted them: counting what they ought to doe both in discharge of thir public duty, and for the great reward of honour and revennue which they receave, as don all of meer grace and favour; as if thir power over us were by nature, and from themselves, or that God had sould us into thir hands. Indeed if the race of Kings were eminently the best of men, as the breed at *Tutburie* is of Horses, it would in some reason then be their part onely to command, ours always to obey. But Kings by generation no way excelling others, and most commonly not being the wisest or the worthiest by far of whom they claime to have the governing, that we should yeild them subjection to our own ruin, or hold of them the right of our common safety, and our natural freedom by meer gift, as when the Conduit pisses Wine at Coronations, from the superfluity of thir royal

grace and beneficence, we may be sure was never the intent
of God, whose ways are just and equal; never the intent of
Nature, whose works are also regular; never of any People
not wholly barbarous, whom prudence, or no more but hu-
5 man sense would have better guided when they first created
Kings, then so to nullifie and tread to durt the rest of mankind, by exalting one person and his Linage without other
merit lookt after, but the meer contingencie of a begetting,
into an absolute and unaccountable dominion over them and
10 thir posterity. Yet this ignorant or wilfull mistake of the
whole matter, had tak'n so deep root in the imagination of
this King, that whether to the English or to the Scot, men-
tioning what acts of his Regal Office, though God knows how
unwillingly, he had pass'd, he calls them, as in other places,
15 Acts of grace and bounty, so heer *special obligations, favours
to gratifie active spirits, and the desires of that party*. Words
not onely sounding pride and Lordly usurpation, but Injustice, Partiality, and Corruption. For to the Irish he so farr
condiscended, as first to tolerate in privat, then to covnant
20 op'nly the tolerating of Popery: So farr to the Scot, as to remove Bishops, establish Presbytery, and the *Militia* in thir
own hands, *preferring, as some thought, the desires of Scotland before his own interest and Honour*. But being once on
this side *Tweed,* his reason, his conscience, and his honour
25 became so streitn'd with a kind of fals Virginity, that to the
English neither one nor other of the same demands could be
granted, wherwith the Scots were gratifi'd; as if our aire and
climat on a sudden had chang'd the property and the nature

both of Conscience, Honour, and Reason, or that he found
none so fit as English to be the subjects of his arbitrary power.
Ireland was as *Ephraim,* the strength of his head, *Scotland,*
as *Judah,* was his Law-giver; but over *England* as over *Edom*
5 he meant to cast his Shoo; and yet so many sober Englishmen
not sufficiently awake to consider this, like men inchanted
with the *Circæan* cup of servitude, will not be held back from
running thir own heads into the Yoke of Bondage.

The summ of his discours is against *setling of Religion by*
10 *violent meanes;* which whether it were the Scots designe
upon *England,* they are best able to cleare themselves. But
this of all may seem strangest, that the King who, while it
was permitted him, never did thing more eagerly then to
molest and persecute the consciences of most Religious men,
15 he who had made a Warr and lost all, rather then not uphold
a Hierarchie of persecuting Bishops, should have the confidence heer to profess himself so much an Enemie of those
that force the conscience. For was it not he, who upon the
English obtruded new Ceremonies, upon the Scots a new
20 Liturgie, & with his Sword went about to score a bloody *Rub-*
ric on thir backs? Did he not forbidd and hinder all effectual
search of Truth, nay like a beseiging Enemy stopd all her
passages both by Word and Writing? Yet heer can talk of
faire and equall disputations: Where notwithstanding, if all
25 submit not to his judgement as not being *rationally con-*
victed, they must submitt (and he conceales it not) to his
penaltie as counted *obstinate.* But what if he himself and
those his *learned Churchmen,* were the convicted or the ob-

stinate part long agoe; should Reformation suffer them to
sit Lording over the Church in thir fatt Bishoprics and Pluralities, like the great Whore that sitteth upon many Waters,
till they would voutsafe to be disputed out? Or should we sit
5 disputing while they sate plotting and persecuting? Those
Clergimen were not *to be driv'n into the fold like Sheep,* as
his Simily runs, but to be driv'n out of the Fold like Wolves,
or Theeves, where they sat *Fleecing* those Flocks which they
never fed.

10 He beleeves *that Presbytery though prov'd to be the onely
Institution of Jesus Christ were not by the Sword to be set up
without his consent;* which is contrary both to the Doctrin,
and the known practice of all Protestant Churches; if his
Sword threat'n those who of thir own accord imbrace it.

15 And although *Christ* and his Apostles, being to civil affairs but privat men, contended not with Magistrats, yet
when Magistrats themselves and especially Parlaments; who
have greatest right to dispose of the civil Sword, come to
know Religion, they ought in conscience to defend all those
20 who receave it willingly, against the violence of any King or
Tyrant whatsoever. Neither is it therfore true; *That Christianity is planted or watred with Christian blood;* for there is
a large difference between forcing men by the Sword to turne
Presbyterians, and defending those who willingly are so,
25 from a furious inroad of bloody Bishops, arm'd with the
Militia of a King thir Pupil. And if *covetousness and ambition be an argument that Presbytery hath not much of Christ,*
it argues more strongly against Episcopacy; which from the

time of her first mounting to an order above the Presbyters, had no other Parents then Covetousness & Ambition. And those *Sects, Scisms, and Heresies,* which he speaks of, *if they get but strength and numbers,* need no other *pattern* then
5 Episcopacie and himself, to *set up their ways by the like method of violence.* Nor is ther any thing that hath more marks of Scism and Sectarism then English Episcopacy; whether we look at Apostolic times, or at reformed Churches; for the *universall way of Church goverment before,* may as
10 soon lead us into gross error, as thir universally corrupted Doctrin. And Goverment by reason of ambition was likeliest to be corrupted much the sooner of the two. However nothing can be to us Catholic or universal in Religion, but what the Scripture teaches; whatsoever without Scripture pleads to
15 be universal in the Church, in being universal is but the more Scismatical. Much less can *particular Laws and Constitutions* impart to the Church of *England* any power of consistory or tribunal above other Churches, to be the sole Judge of what is Sect or Scism, as with much rigor, and without
20 Scripture, they took upon them. Yet these the King resolves heer to defend and maintain to his last, pretending, after all those conferences offer'd, or had with him, *not to see more rationall and religious motives then Soldiers carry in thir Knapsacks;* with one thus resolv'd it was but folly to stand
25 disputing.

He imagins *his own judicious zeal to be most concernd in his tuition of the Church.* So thought *Saul* when he presum'd to offer Sacrifice; for which he lost his Kingdom; So

thought *Uzziah* when he went into the Temple; but was thrust out with a Leprosie for his opinion'd zeal, which he thought *judicious*. It is not the part of a King, because he ought to defend the Church, therfore to set himself supreme
5 Head over the Church, or to meddle with Ecclesial Goverment, or to defend the Church otherwise then the Church would be defended; for such defence is bondage; nor to defend abuses, and stop all Reformation under the name of *New moulds fanci'd and fashion'd to privat designes.* The
10 holy things of Church are in the power of other keys then were deliverd to his keeping. Christian libertie purchas'd with the death of our Redeemer, and establish'd by the sending of his free Spirit to inhabit in us, is not now to depend upon the doubtful consent of any earthly Monarch; nor to be
15 again fetter'd with a presumptuous negative voice, tyrannical to the Parlament, but much more tyrannical to the Church of God: which was compell'd to implore the aid of Parlament, to remove his force and heavy hands from off our consciences, who therfore complains now of that most just
20 defensive force, because onely it remov'd his violence and persecution. If this be a violation to his conscience, that it was hinderd by the Parlament from violating the more tender consciences of so many thousand good Christians, let the usurping conscience of all Tyrants be ever so violated.
25   He wonders, Fox wonder, how we could so much *distrust Gods assistance,* as to call in the Protestant aid of our Brethren in *Scotland;* why then did he, if his trust were in God and the justice of his Cause, not scruple to sollicit and invite

earnestly the assistance both of Papists and of Irish Rebels?
If the Scots were by us at length sent home, they were not
call'd to stay heer always; neither was it for the peoples ease
to feed so many Legions, longer then thir help was needfull.

5   *The Goverment of thir Kirk we despis'd not,* but thir im-
posing of that Goverment upon us; not Presbytery, but Arch-
Presbytery, *Classical, Provincial, and Diocesan* Presbytery,
claiming to it self a Lordly power and Superintendency both
over Flocks and Pastors, over Persons and Congregations no
10 way thir own. But these debates in his judgement would have
bin ended better *by the best Divines in Christ'ndom in a full
and free Synod.* A most improbable way, and such as never
yet was us'd, at least with good success, by any Protestant
Kingdom or State since the Reformation: Every true Church
15 having wherewithall from Heav'n, and the assisting Spirit of
Christ implor'd, to be complete and perfet within it self. And
the whole Nation is not easily to be thought so raw, and so perpetually a novice after all this light, as to need the help and
direction of other Nations, more then what they write in public
20 of thir opinion, in a matter so familiar as Church Goverment.

In fine he accuses *Piety* with the want of *Loyalty,* and
Religion with the breach of *Allegeance,* as if God and he
were one Maister, whose commands were so oft'n contrary to
the commands of God. He would perswade the Scots that
25 thir *chief Interest consists in thir fidelity to the Crown.* But
true policy will teach them to find a safer interest in the common friendship of *England,* then in the ruins of one ejected
Family.

XIIII. *Upon the Covnant.*

UPON this Theme his Discours is long, his Matter little but repetition; and therfore soon answerd. First after an abusive and strange apprehension of
5 Covnants, as if Men *pawn'd thir souls* to them with whom they Covnant, he digresses to plead for Bishops; first from the antiquity of thir *possession heer, since the first plantation of Christianity in this Iland,* next from *a universal prescription since the Apostles, till this last Centurie.* But what availes
10 the most Primitive Antiquity against the plain sense of Scripture; which if the last Centurie have best follow'd, it ought in our esteem to be the first. And yet it hath bin oft'n prov'd by Learned Men, from the Writings and Epistles of most ancient Christians, that Episcopacy crept not up into an order
15 above the Presbyters, till many years after that the Apostles were deceas'd.

He next *is unsatisfied with the Covnant,* not onely for *some passages in it referring to himself,* as he supposes, *with very dubious and dangerous limitations,* but for binding men
20 *by Oath and Covnant,* to the Reformation of Church Discipline. First those limitations were not more dangerous to him, then he to our Libertie and Religion; next, that which was there vow'd, to cast out of the Church an Antichristian Hierarchy which God had not planted, but ambition and
25 corruption had brought in, and fosterd to the Churches great dammage and oppression, was no point of *controversie* to be argu'd without end, but a thing of *cleer moral necessity* to be

forthwith don. Neither was the *Covnant superfluous,* though *former engagements both religious and legal bound us before:* But was the practice of all Churches heertofore intending Reformation. All *Israel,* though bound anough before
5 by the Law of *Moses, to all necessary duties;* yet with *Asa* thir King enter'd into a new Covnant at the beginning of a Reformation: And the *Jews* after Captivity, without consent demanded of that King who was thir Maister, took solemn Oath to walk in the Command'ments of God. All Protes-
10 tant Churches have don the like, notwithstanding former engagements to thir several duties. And although his aime were to sow variance between *the Protestation and the Covnant,* to reconcile them is not difficult. The Protestation was but one step, extending onely to the Doctrin of the Church
15 of *England,* as it was distinct from Church Discipline; the Covnant went furder, as it pleas'd God to dispense his light and our encouragement by degrees, and comprehended Church Goverment; Former with latter steps in the progress of well doing need not reconcilement. Nevertheless he breaks
20 through to his conclusion, *That all honest and wise men ever thought themselves sufficiently bound by former ties of Religion;* leaving *Asa, Ezra,* and the whole Church of God in sundry Ages to shift for *honestie* and wisdom from som other then his testimony. And although *after contracts absolve not*
25 till the former be made void, yet he first having don that, our duty returns back, which to him was neither *moral nor eternal;* but conditional.

Willing to perswade himself that many *good men* took

the Covnant either unwarily, or out of fear, he seems to have bestow'd som thoughts how these *good men* following his advice may keep the Covnant and not keep it. The first evasion is, presuming *that the cheif end of Covnanting in such*
5   *mens intentions was to preserve Religion in purity and the Kingdoms peace.* But the Covnant will more truly inform them that purity of Religion and the Kingdoms peace was not then in state to be preservd, but to be restor'd; and therfore binds them, not to a preservation of what was, but to a
10   Reformation of what was evil, what was Traditional, and *dangerous,* whether *novelty* or *antiquity* in Church or State. To doe this, clashes with *no former Oath* lawfully sworn either to God or the King, rightly understood.

In general he brands all *such confederations by League*
15   *and Covnant, as the common rode us'd in all Factious perturbations of State and Church.* This kinde of language reflects with the same ignominy upon all the Protestant Reformations that have bin since *Luther;* and so indeed doth his whole Book, replenish'd throughout with hardly other words
20   or arguments then Papists, and especially Popish Kings, have us'd heertofore against thir Protestant Subjects; whom he would perswade to be *every man his own Pope and to absolve himself of those ties,* by the suggestion of fals or equivocal interpretations too oft repeated to be now answer'd.
25   The Parlament, he saith, *made thir Covnant like Manna, agreeable to every mans Palat.* This is another of his glosses upon the Covnant; he is content to let it be *Manna,* but his drift is that men should loath it, or at least expound it by thir

own *relish,* and *latitude of sense;* wherin least any one of the
simpler sort should faile to be his crafts maister, he furnishes
him with two or three laxative, he termes them *general
clauses, which may serve somwhat to releeve them* against
5 the Covnant tak'n: intimating, as if *what were lawfull and
according to the Word of God,* were no otherwise so, then as
every man fansi'd to himself. From such learned explications
and resolutions as these upon the Covnant, what marvel if no
Royalist or Malignant refuse to take it, as having learnt from
10 these Princely instructions, his many *Salvo's, cautions, and
reservations,* how to be a Covnanter and Anticovnanter, how
at once to be a Scot, and an Irish Rebel.

   He returns again to disallow of *that Reformation which
the Covnant* vows, *as being the partiall advice of a few Di-*
15 *vines.* But matters of this moment, as they were not to be
decided there by those Divines, so neither are they to be
determin'd heer by Essays & curtal Aphorisms, but by solid
proofs of Scripture.

   The rest of his discourse he spends, highly accusing the
20 Parlament, *that the main Reformation by* them *intended was
to robb the Church,* and much applauding himself both for
his forwardness to all due Reformation, and his aversness
from all such kind of *Sacrilege.* All which, with his glorious
title of the *Churches Defender,* we leave him to make good,
25 by *Pharaoh's Divinity,* if he please, for to *Josephs Pietie* it
will be a task unsutable. As for *the parity and poverty of
Ministers,* which he takes to be so sad of *consequence,* the
Scripture reck'ns them for two special Legacies left by our

Saviour to his Disciples: under which two Primitive Nurses, for such they were indeed, the Church of God more truly flourisht then ever after, since the time that imparitie and Church revennue rushing in, corrupted and beleper'd all the
5 Clergie with a worse infection then *Gehezi's;* some one of whose Tribe rather then a King, I should take to be compiler of that unsalted and Simonical praier annex'd. Although the Praier it self strongly prays against them. For never such holy things as he means, were *giv'n* to more *Swine, nor the*
10 *Churches Bread* more to *Dogs,* then when it fed ambitious, irreligious and dumb Prelats.

XV. *Upon the many Jealousies,* &c.

TO wipe off jealousies and scandals, the best way, had bin by clear Actions, or till Actions could be clear'd,
15 by evident reasons; but meer words we are too well acquainted with. Had *his honour and reputation bin dearer to him* then the lust of Raigning, how could the Parlament of either Nation have laid so oft'n at his dore the breach of words, promises, acts, Oaths, and execrations, as they doe
20 avowedly in many of thir Petitions, and addresses to him: thether I remitt the Reader. And who can beleive that whole Parlaments elected by the People from all parts of the Land, should meet in one mind, and resolution not to advise him, but to conspire against him in a wors powder plot then *Cates-*
25 *bies, to blow up,* as he termes it, *the peoples affection towards him, and batter down thir loyalty by the Engins of foule as-*

persions: Water-works rather then Engines to batter with, yet those aspersions were rais'd from the foulness of his own actions. Whereof to purge himself, he uses no other argument, then a general and so oft'n iterated commendation of him-
5 self; and thinks that Court holy water hath the vertue of expiation; at least with the silly people. To whom he familiarly imputes sin where none is, to seem liberal of his *forgiveness* where none is ask'd or needed.

What wayes he hath tak'n toward the prosperitie of his
10 people, which he would seem *so earnestly to desire,* if we doe but once call to mind, it will be anough to teach us, looking on the smooth insinuations heer, that Tyrants are not more flatterd by thir Slaves, then forc'd to flatter others whom they feare.

For the peoples *tranquilitie he would willingly be the*
15 *Jonah;* but least he should be tak'n at his word, pretends to foresee within Kenn two imaginarie *windes* never heard of in the Compass, which threaten, if he be cast overboard, *to increase the storm,* but that controversy divine lot hath ended.

He had rather not rule then that his people should be ru-
20 *in'd;* and yet above these twenty yeres hath bin ruining the people about the niceties of his ruling. He is accurate *to put a difference between the plague of malice, & the ague of mistakes, the itch of noveltie, and the leprosie of disloyaltie.* But had he as wel known how to distinguish between the vener-
25 able gray haires of ancient Religion, and the old scurffe of Superstition, between the wholsome heat of well Governing, and the fevorous rage of Tyrannizing, his judgement in State-physic, had bin of more autoritie.

Much he Prophesies, *that the credit of those men who have* *have cast black scandals on him shal ere long be quite blasted* *by the same furnace of popular obloquie wherin they sought* *to cast his name and honour:* I beleive not that a Romish
5 guilded Portrature gives better Oracle then a Babylonish gold'n Image could doe, to tell us truely who heated that Furnace of obloquy, or who deserves to be thrown in, *Nebuchadnezzar* or the three Kingdoms. It *gave him great cause to* *suspect his own innocence* that he was oppos'd by *so many*
10 *who profest singular pietie.* But this qualm was soon over, and he concluded rather to suspect their Religion, then his own innocence, affirming that *many with him were both* *learned and Religious above the ordinary size.* But if his great Seal without the Parlament were not sufficient to cre-
15 ate Lords, his Parole must needs be farr more unable to create learned and religious men, and who shall authorize his unlerned judgement to point them out?

He guesses that *many well minded men were by popular* *Preachers urg'd to oppose him.* But the opposition undoubt-
20 edly proceeded and continues from heads farr wiser, and spirits of a nobler straine; those Priest-led *Herodians* with thir blind guides are in the Ditch already; travailing, as they thought, to *Sion,* but moor'd in the Ile of *Wight.*

He thanks God *for his constancy to the Protestant Religion*
25 *both abroad and at home.* Abroad, his Letter to the Pope, at home, his Innovations in the Church will speak his constancy in Religion what it was, without furder credit to this vain boast.

His *using the assistance of some Papists,* as the cause might be, could not hurt his Religion; but in the setling of Protestantism, thir aid was both unseemly & suspicious, & inferr'd that the greatest part of Protestants were against him & his
5 obtruded settlement.

But this is strange indeed, that he should appear now teaching the Parlament what no man, till this was read, thought ever he had lernt, *that difference of perswasion in religious matters may fall out where ther is the samenes of*
10 *allegeance & subjection.* If he thought so from the beginning, wherfore was there such compulsion us'd to the puritans of *England,* & the whole realm of *Scotl.* about conforming to a liturgie? Wherfore no Bishop no king? Wherfore episcopacie more agreeable to monarchie, if dif-
15 ferent perswasions in religion may agree in one duty & allegeance? Thus do court maxims like court Minions rise or fall as the king pleases.

Not to tax him for want of Elegance as a courtier, in writing *Oglio* for *Olla* the Spanish word, it might be wel affirm'd
20 that there was a greater *Medley* & disproportioning of religions to mix Papists with Protestants in a Religious cause, then to entertaine all those diversifi'd Sects, who yet were all Protestants, one Religion, though many Opinions.

Neither was it *any shame to Protestants,* that he a *declar'd*
25 Papist, if his own letter to the Pope, not yet renownc'd, bely him not, found so few protestants of his religion, as enforc'd him to call in both the counsel & the aid of papists to help establish protestancy, who were led on, not *by the sense of*

thir Allegeance, but by the hope of his Apostacy to *Rome,*
from disputing to warring; his own voluntary, and first appeale.

His hearkning to evil Counselers, charg'd upon him so
5 oft'n by the Parlament, he puts off as *a device of those men
who were so eager to give him better counsell.* That *those
men* were the Parlament, & that he ought to have us'd the
counsel of none but those, as a King, is already known. What
their civility laid upon evil Counselers, he himself most com-
10 monly own'd; but the event of those evil counsels, *the enormities, the confusions, the miseries* he transferrs from the guilt
of his own civil broiles to the just resistance made by Parlament; & imputes what miscarriages of his they could not yet
remove for his opposing, as if they were some new misde-
15 meanors of their bringing in, and not the inveterat diseases
of his own bad Goverment; which, with a disease as bad, he
falls again to magnifie and commend; and may all those who
would be govern'd by his *Retractions and concessions,* rather
then by Laws of Parlament, admire his self-*Encomiums,* and
20 be flatter'd with that *Crown of patience* to which he cunningly exhorted them, that his Monarchical foot might have
the setting it upon thir heads.

That trust which the Parlament faithfully discharg'd in
the asserting of our Liberties, he calls *another artifice to with-*
25 *draw the people from him, to their designes.* What piece of
Justice could they have demanded for the people, which the
jealousie of a King might not have miscall'd, a designe to
disparage his Goverment, and to ingratiat themselves? To

be more just, religious, wise, or magnanimous then the common sort, stirrs up in a Tyrant both feare and envy; and
streight he cries out popularitie, which in his account is little
less then Treason. The summ is, they thought to limit or take
away the *Remora* of his negative voice, which like to that
little pest at Sea, took upon it to arrest and stopp the Common-wealth stearing under full saile to a Reformation: they
thought to share with him in the *Militia,* both or either of
which he could not possibly hold without consent of the
people, and not be absolutely a Tyrant. He professes *to desire*
no other liberty then what he envies not his Subjects accord-
ing to Law; yet fought with might and maine against his Subjects to have a sole power over them in his hand, both against
and beyond Law. As for the Philosophical Libertie which in
vaine he talks of, we may conclude him very ill train'd up in
those free notions, who to civil Libertie was so injurious.

He calls the conscience *Gods sovrantie,* why then doth he
contest with God about that supreme title? Why did he *lay*
restraints, and force enlargements upon our consciences in
things for which we were to answer God onely and the
Church? God bids us *Be subject for conscience sake,* that is,
as to a Magistrat, and in the Laws; not usurping over spiritual things, as *Lucifer* beyond his sphere. And the same Precept bids him likewise for conscience sake be subject to the
Parlament, both his natural and his legal superior.

Finally, having layd the fault of these Commotions, not
upon his own mis-goverment, but upon *the ambition of oth-*
ers, the necessity of some mens fortune, and thirst after nov-

eltie, he bodes himself *much honour and reputation that like the Sun shall rise and recover it self to such a Splendour, as Owles, Batts, and such fatal Birds shall be unable to beare.* Poets indeed use to vapor much after this manner. But to 5 bad Kings, who without cause expect future glory from thir actions, it happ'ns as to bad Poets; who sit and starve themselves with a delusive hope to win immortality by thir bad lines. For though men ought not to *speak evil of Dignities* which are just, yet nothing hinders us to speak evil, as oft as 10 it is the truth, of those who in thir Dignities doe evil; thus did our Saviour himself, *John* the Baptist, and *Steev'n* the Martyr. And those *black vailes* of his own misdeeds he might be sure would ever keep *his face from shining,* til he could *refute evil speaking with wel doing,* which grace he seems heer 15 to pray for; and his prayer doubtless as it was prayd, so it was heard. But eev'n his prayer is so ambitious of Prerogative, that it dares ask away the Prerogative of Christ himself, *To become the head stone of the Corner.*

XVI. *Upon the Ordinance against the* 20 *Common-Prayer Book.*

WHAT to think of Liturgies, both the sense of Scripture, and Apostolicall practice would have taught him better, then his human reasonings and conjectures: Nevertheless what weight they have, let us 25 consider. If it be *no newes to have all innovations usherd in with the name of Reformation,* sure it is less news to have all

reformation censur'd and oppos'd under the name of innovation; *by those* who beeing exalted in high place above thir
merit, fear all change though of things *never so* ill or so *un-
wisely settl'd. So hardly can the* dotage of those that dwell
5 upon Antiquitie *allow* present *times any share of godliness
or wisdom.*

The removing of Liturgie he traduces to be don onely as a
thing plausible to the People; whose rejection of it he lik'ns
with small reverence to the *crucifying* of our Saviour; next
10 that it was don *to please these men who gloried in their ex-
temporary vein,* meaning the Ministers. For whom it will be
best to answer, as was answer'd for the man born blind, *They
are of age let them speak for themselves;* not how they came
blind, but whether it were Liturgie that held them tongue-
15 ti'd.

For the matter contain'd in that Book we need no better
witness then King *Edward* the sixth, who to the Cornish
Rebels confesses it was no other then the old Mass-Book don
into English, all but some few words that were expung'd.
20 And by this argument which King *Edward* so promptly had
to use against that irreligious Rabble, we may be assur'd it
was the carnal fear of those Divines and Polititians that model'd the Liturgie no furder off from the old Mass, least by too
great an alteration they should incense the people, and be
25 destitute of the same shifts to fly to, which they had taught
the young King.

*For the manner of using sett formes, there is no doubt but
that, wholesom* matter, and good desires rightly conceav'd in

the heart, wholesom words will follow of themselves. Neither
can any true Christian find a reason why Liturgie should be
at all admitted, a prescription not impos'd or practis'd by
those first Founders of the Church, who alone had that au-
5 tority: Without whose precept or example, how constantly
the Priest puts on his Gown and Surplice, so constantly doth
his praier put on a servile yoak of Liturgie. This is evident,
that they *who use no set formes of prayer,* have words from
thir affections; while others are to seek affections fit and pro-
10 portionable to a certain doss of prepar'd words; which as they
are not rigorously forbidd to any mans privat infirmity, so to
imprison and confine by force, into a Pinfold of sett words,
those two most unimprisonable things, our Prayers and that
Divine Spirit of utterance that moves them, is a tyranny that
15 would have longer hands then those Giants who threatn'd
bondage to Heav'n. What *we may doe* in the same forme of
words is not so much the question, as whether Liturgie may
be forc'd, as he forc'd it. It is true that we *pray to the same
God,* must we therfore always use the same words? Let us
20 then use but one word, because we pray to one God. *We
profess the same truths,* but the Liturgie comprehends not all
truths: *wee read the same Scriptures;* but never read that all
those Sacred expressions, all benefit and use of Scripture, as
to public prayer, should be deny'd us, except what was bar-
25 reld up in a Common-praier Book with many mixtures of thir
own, and which is worse, without salt. But suppose them
savoury words and unmix'd, suppose them *Manna* it self, yet
if they shall be hoarded up and enjoynd us, while God every

morning raines down new expressions into our hearts, in
stead of being fit to use, they will be found like reserv'd
Manna, rather *to breed wormes and stink. Wee have the same
duties upon us and feele the same wants;* yet not alwayes the
5 same, nor at all times alike; but with variety of Circumstances, which ask varietie of words. Wherof God hath giv'n
us plenty; not to use so copiously upon all other occasions,
and so niggardly to him alone in our devotions. As if Christians were now in a wors famin of words fitt for praier, then
10 was of food at the seige of Jerusalem, when perhaps the
Priests being to remove the shew bread, as was accustom'd,
were compell'd every Sabbath day, for want of other Loaves,
to bring again still the same. If *the Lords Prayer* had bin the
warrant or the pattern of set Liturgies, as is heer affirm'd,
15 why was neither that Prayer, nor any other sett forme ever
after us'd, or so much as mention'd by the Apostles, much
less commended to our use? Why was thir care wanting in a
thing so usefull to the Church? So full of danger and con-
tention to be left undon by them to other mens Penning, of
20 whose autority we could not be so certain? Why was this
forgott'n by them who declare that they have reveal'd to us
the whole Counsel of God; who as he left our affections to be
guided by his sanctifying spirit, so did he likewise our words
to be put into us without our premeditation; not onely those
25 cautious words to be us'd before Gentiles and Tyrants, but
much more those filial words, of which we have so frequent
use in our access with freedom of speech to the Throne of
Grace. Which to lay aside for other outward dictates of men,

were to injure him and his perfet Gift, who is the spirit, and
the giver of our abilitie to pray; as if his ministration were in-
complete, and that to whom he gave affections, he did not
also afford utterance to make his Gift of prayer a perfet Gift,
5 to them especially whose office in the Church is to pray publicly.

And although the gift were onely natural, yet voluntary
prayers *are less subject to formal and superficial tempers then
sett formes:* For in those, at least for words & matter, he who
10 prays, must consult first with his heart; which in likelyhood
may stirr up his affections; in these, having both words and
matter readie made to his lips, which is anough to make up
the outward act of prayer, his affections grow lazy, and com
not up easilie at the call of words not thir own; the prayer also
15 having less intercours and sympathy with a heart wherin it
was not conceav'd, saves it self the labour of so long a journey
downward, and flying up in hast on the specious wings of
formalitie, if it fall not back again headlong, in stead of a
prayer which was expected, presents God with a sett of stale
20 and empty words.

No doubt but *ostentation and formalitie* may taint the
best duties: we are not therfore to leave duties for no duties,
and to turne prayer into a kind of Lurrey. Cannot unpre-
meditated babling be rebuk'd, and restraind in whom we
25 find they are, but the spirit of God must be forbidd'n in all
men? But it is the custom of bad men and Hypocrits to take
advantage at the least abuse of good things, that under that
covert they may remove the goodness of those things, rather

then the abuse. And how unknowingly, how weakly is the using of sett forms attributed here to *constancy*, as if it were constancie in the Cuckoo to be alwaies in the same liturgie.

Much less can it be lawfull that an Englisht Mass-Book,
5 compos'd for ought we know, by men neither *lerned,* nor *godly, should justle out,* or at any time *deprive* us the exercise of that Heav'nly gift, which God by special promise powrs out daily upon his Church, that is to say, the spirit of Prayer. Wherof to help those many infirmities, which he
10 reck'ns up, *rudeness, impertinencie, flatness,* and the like, we have a remedy of Gods finding out, which is not Liturgie, but his own free spirit. Though we know not what to pray as we ought, yet he with sighs unutterable by any words, much less by a stinted Liturgie, dwelling in us makes intercession
15 for us, according to the mind and will of God, both in privat, and in the performance of all Ecclesiastical duties. For it is his promise also, that where two or three gather'd together in his name shall agree to ask him any thing, it shall be granted; for he is there in the midst of them. If then ancient
20 Churches to remedie the infirmities of prayer, or rather the infections of Arian and Pelagian Heresies, neglecting that ordain'd and promis'd help of the spirit, betook them, almost four hundred yeares after Christ, to Liturgie thir own invention, wee are not to imitate them, nor to distrust God in the
25 removal of that Truant help to our Devotion, which by him never was appointed. And what is said of Liturgie is said also of Directory, if it be impos'd: although to forbidd the Service Book there be much more reason, as being of it self super-

stitious, offensive, and indeed, though Englisht, yet still the
Mass-Book: and public places ought to be provided of such
as need not the help of Liturgies or Directories continually,
but are supported with Ministerial gifts answerable to thir
5 Calling.

   Lastly that the Common-Prayer Book was rejected because
it *prayd so oft for him,* he had no reason to Object: for what
large and laborious Prayers were made for him in the Pulpits,
if he never heard, tis doubtful they were never heard in
10 Heav'n. Wee might now have expected that his own following Prayer should add much credit to sett Forms; but on the
contrary we find the same imperfections in it, as in most before, which he lays heer upon Extemporal. Nor doth he ask
of God to be directed whether Liturgies be lawful, but pre-
15 sumes, and in a manner would perswade him that they be so;
praying *that the Church and he may never want them.* What
could be prayd wors extempore? unless he mean by wanting,
that they may never need them.

XVII. *Of the differences in point of*
20 *Church-Goverment.*

THE Goverment of Church by Bishops hath bin so
fully prov'd from the Scriptures to be vitious and
usurp'd, that whether *out of Piety or Policy* maintain'd, it is not much material. For Pietie grounded upon
25 error can no more justifie King *Charles,* then it did Queen
Mary, in the sight of God or Man. This however must not be

let pass without a serious observation; God having so dispos'd the Author in this Chapter as to confess and discover
more of Mysterie and combination between Tyranny and fals
Religion, then from any other hand would have bin credible.
5 Heer we may see the very dark roots of them both turn'd up,
and how they twine and interweave one another in the Earth,
though above ground shooting up in two sever'd Branches.
We may have learnt both from sacred History, and times of
Reformation, that the Kings of this World have both ever
10 hated, and instinctively fear'd the Church of God. Whether it
be for that thir Doctrin seems much to favour two things to
them so dreadful, Liberty and Equality, or because they are
the Children of that Kingdom, which, as ancient Prophesies
have foretold, shall in the end break to peeces and dissolve
15 all thir great power and Dominion. And those Kings and
Potentates who have strove most to ridd themselves of this
feare, by cutting off or suppressing the true Church, have
drawn upon themselves the occasion of thir own ruin, while
they thought with most policy to prevent it. Thus *Pharaoh,*
20 when once he began to feare and wax jealous of the Israelites,
least they should multiply and fight against him, and that his
feare stirr'd him up to afflict and keep them under, as the
onely remedy of what he feard, soon found that the evil which
before slept, came suddenly upon him, by the preposterous
25 way he took to shun it. Passing by examples between, & not
shutting wilfully our eyes, we may see the like story brought
to pass in our own Land. This King more then any before
him, except perhapps his Father, from his first entrance to

the Crown, harbouring in his mind a strange feare and suspicion of men most religious, and thir Doctrin, which in his
own language he heer acknowledges, terming *it the seditious
exorbitancie* of Ministers tongues, and doubting *least they,*
5 as he not Christianly expresses it, *should with the Keys of
Heav'n let out Peace and Loyaltie from the peoples hearts,*
though they never preacht or attempted aught that might
justly raise in him such apprehensions, he could not rest, or
think himself secure, so long as they remain'd in any of his
10 three Kingdoms unrooted out. But outwardly professing the
same Religion with them, he could not presently use violence
as *Pharaoh* did, and that course had with others before but ill
succeeded. He chooses therfore a more mystical way, a newer
method of Antichristian fraud, to the Church more danger-
15 ous: and like to *Balac* the Son of *Zippor,* against a Nation of
Prophets thinks it best to hire other esteemed Prophets, and
to undermine and weare out the true Church by a fals Ecclesiastical policy. To this drift he found the Goverment of Bishops most serviceable; an order in the Church, as by men first
20 corrupted, so mutually corrupting them who receave it, both
in judgement and manners. He, by conferring Bishoprics
and great Livings on whom he thought most pliant to his
will, against the known Canons and universal practice of the
ancient Church, wherby those elections were the peoples
25 right, sought, as he confesses, to have *greatest influence upon
Church-men.* They on the other side finding themselves in a
high Dignity, neither founded by Scripture, nor allow'd by
Reformation, nor supported by any spiritual gift or grace of

thir own, knew it thir best cours to have dependence onely
upon him: and wrought his fansie by degrees to that degenerat, and unkingly perswasion of *No Bishop, no King*. When
as on the contrary all Prelats in thir own suttle sense are of
5 another mind; according to that of *Pius* the fourth, rememberd in the *Trentine* storie, that Bishops then grow to be most
vigorous and potent, when Princes happ'n to be most weak,
and impotent. Thus when both Interests of Tyrannie and
Episcopacie were incorporat into each other, the King whose
10 principal safety and establishment consisted in the righteous
execution of his civil power, and not in Bishops and thir
wicked counsels, fatally driv'n on, set himself to the extir-
pating of those men whose Doctrin, and desire of Church
Discipline he so fear'd would bee the undoing of his Mon-
15 archie. And because no temporal Law could touch the innocence of thir lives, he begins with the persecution of thir
consciences, laying scandals before them: and makes that the
argument to inflict his unjust penalties both on thir bodies
and Estates. In this Warr against the Church if he hath sped
20 so, as other haughty Monarchs whom God heertofore hath
hard'nd to the like enterprize, we ought to look up with
praises and thanksgiving to the Author of our deliverance, to
whom victorie and power, Majestie, Honour, and Dominion
belongs for ever.

25   In the mean while from his own words we may perceave
easily, that the special motives which he had to endeere and
deprave his judgement to the favouring and utmost defending of Episcopacie, are such as heer wee represent them: and

how unwillingly and with what mental reservation he condescended against his interest to remove it out of the Peers
house, hath bin shown alreadie. The reasons, which he affirmes wrought so much upon his judgement, shall be so farr
5 answerd as they be urg'd.

Scripture, he reports, but distinctly produces none; and
next the *constant practice of all Christian Churches, till of
late years tumult, faction, pride, and covetousness, invented
new models under the Title of Christs Goverment.* Could
10 any Papist have spoke more scandalously against all Reformation? Well may the Parlament and best-affected People
not now be troubl'd at his calumnies and reproaches, since he
binds them in the same bundle with all other the reformed
Churches; who also may now furder see, besides thir own
15 bitter experience, what a Cordial and well meaning helper
they had of him abroad, and how true to the Protestant cause.

As for *Histories* to prove Bishops, the Bible, if we mean
not to run into errors, vanities, and uncertainties, must be our
onely Historie. Which informs us that the Apostles were not
20 properly Bishops; next, that Bishops were not successors of
Apostles, in the function of Apostleship: And that if they
were Apostles, they could not be preciselie Bishops; if Bishops, they could not be Apostles; this being Universal, extraor-
dinarie, and immediat from God; that being an ordinarie,
25 fixt, & particular charge, the continual inspection over a certain Flock. And although an *ignorance and deviation* of the
ancient Churches afterward, may with as much *reason and
charity* be suppos'd as *sudden* in point of Prelatie, as in other

manifest corruptions, yet that *no example since the first age for* 1500 *yeares can be produc'd of any setled Church, wherin were many Ministers and Congregations, which had not some Bishops above them,* the Ecclesiastical storie, to which
5 he appeals for want of Scripture, proves cleerly to be a fals and over-confident assertion. *Sozomenus* who wrote above Twelve hundred years agoe, in his seventh Book relates from his own knowledge, that in the Churches of *Cyprus* and *Arabia,* (places neer to Jerusalem, and with the first frequented
10 by Apostles) they had Bishops in every Village; and what could those be more then Presbyters? The like he tells of other Nations; and that Episcopal Churches in those daies did not condemn them. I add that many Western Churches eminent for thir Faith and good Works, and settl'd above four
15 hundred years agoe in *France,* in *Piemont* and *Bohemia,* have both taught and practis'd the same Doctrin, and not admitted of Episcopacie among them. And if we may beleeve what the Papists themselves have writt'n of these Churches, which they call *Waldenses,* I find it in a Book writt'n almost four
20 hundred years since, and set forth in the *Bohemian* Historie, that those Churches in *Piemont* have held the same Doctrin and Goverment, since the time that *Constantine* with his mischeivous donations poyson'd *Silvester* and the whole Church. Others affirme they have so continu'd there since the Apos-
25 tles: and *Theodorus Belvederensis* in his relation of them, confesseth that those Heresies, as he names them, were, from the first times of Christianity, in that place. For the rest I referr me to that famous testimonie of *Jerom,* who upon this

very place which he onely roaves at heer, the Epistle to *Titus,*
declares op'nly that Bishop and Presbyter were one and the
same thing, till by the instigation of Satan, partialities grew
up in the Church; and that Bishops rather by custom, then
5 any ordainment of Christ, were exalted above Presbyters:
whose interpretation we trust shall be receav'd before this in-
tricate stuffe tattl'd heer of *Timothy* and *Titus,* and I know
not whom thir Successors, farr beyond Court Element, and
as farr beneath true edification. These are his *fair grounds*
10 *both from Scripture-Canons and Ecclesiastical examples;* how
undivinelike writt'n, and how like a worldly Gospeller that
understands nothing of these matters, posteritie no doubt will
be able to judge: and will but little regard what he calls *Apos-*
tolical, who in his Letter to the Pope calls Apostolical the Ro-
15 man Religion.

Nor let him think to plead, that therfore *it was not policy*
of State, or obstinacie in him which upheld Episcopacie, because the injuries and losses which he sustain'd by so doing,
were to him *more considerable* then Episcopacie it self; for
20 all this might *Pharaoh* have had to say in his excuse of detaining the *Israelites;* that his own and his Kingdoms safety
so much endanger'd by his denial, was to him more deer,
then all thir building labours could be worth to *Ægypt.* But
whom God hard'ns, them also he blinds.

25 He endeavours to make good Episcopacie not only in *Re-*
ligion, but from the nature of all civil Goverment, where
parity breeds confusion and faction. But of faction and confusion, to take no other then his own testimony, where hath

more bin ever bred then under the imparitie of his own Monarchical Goverment? Of which to make at this time longer
dispute, and from civil constitutions, and human conceits to
debate and question the convenience of Divine Ordinations,
5 is neither wisdom nor sobrietie: and to confound *Mosaic
Preisthood* with Evangelic Presbyterie against express institution, is as far from warrantable. As little to purpose is it,
that we should stand powling the Reformed Churches,
whether they *equalize* in number *those of his three King-
10 doms;* of whom so lately the far greater part, what they have
long desir'd to doe, have now quite thrown off Episcopacie.

Neither may we count it the language or Religion of a
Protestant, so to vilifie the best Reformed Churches (for none
of them but Lutherans retain Bishops) as to feare more the
15 *scandalizing* of Papists, because more numerous, then of our
Protestant Brethren because a *handful.* It will not be worth
the while to say what *Scismatics or Heretics* have had no
Bishops; yet least he should be tak'n for a great Reader, he
who prompted him, if he were a Doctor, might have remem-
20 berd the foremention'd place in *Sozomenus;* which affirmes
that besides the *Cyprians and Arabians* who were counted
Orthodoxal, the *Novatians* also, and *Montanists* in *Phrygia*
had no other Bishops then such as were in every Village: and
what Presbyter hath a narrower Diocess? As for the *Aërians*
25 we know of no Heretical opinion justly father'd upon them,
but that they held Bishops & Presbyters to be the same. Which
he in this place not obscurely seems to hold a Heresie in all the
Reformed Churches: with whom why the Church of *Eng-*

land desir'd conformitie, he can find no reason with all his *charity, but the comming in of the Scots Army;* Such a high esteem he had of the English.

He tempts the Clergie to return back again to Bishops, 5 from the feare of *tenuity and contempt,* and the assurance of better *thriving under the favour of Princes;* against which temptations if the Clergie cannot arm themselves with thir own spiritual armour, they are indeed as *poor a Carkass* as he terms them.

10 Of Secular honours and great Revenues added to the dignitie of Prelats, since the subject of that question is now remov'd, we need not spend time: But this perhaps will never bee unseasonable to beare in minde out of *Chrysostome,* that when Ministers came to have Lands, Houses, Farmes, 15 Coaches, Horses, and the like Lumber, then Religion brought forth riches in the Church, and the Daughter devour'd the Mother.

But if his judgement in Episcopacie may be judg'd by the goodly chois he made of Bishops, we need not much amuse 20 our selves with the consideration of those evils which, by his foretelling, will *necessarily follow* thir pulling down, untill he prove that the Apostles having no certain Diocess or appointed place of residence, were properly *Bishops over those Presbyters whom they ordain'd, or Churches they planted;* 25 wherein ofttimes thir labours were both joint and promiscuous: Or that the Apostolic power must *necessarily descend to Bishops, the use and end* of either function being so different. And how the Church hath flourisht under Episco-

pacie, let the multitude of thir ancient and gross errors testifie; and the words of some learnedest and most zealous
Bishops among them; *Nazianzen* in a devout passion wishing Prelaty had never bin; *Basil* terming them the Slaves of
5 Slaves; Saint *Martin,* the enemies of Saints, and confessing
that after he was made a Bishop, he found much of that grace
decay in him which he had before.

Concerning his *Coronation Oath* what it was, and how
farr it bound him, already hath bin spok'n. This we may
10 take for certain, that he was never sworn to his own particular conscience and reason, but to our conditions as a free
people; which requir'd him to give us such Laws as our
selves shall choose. This the Scots could bring him to, and
would not be baffl'd with the pretence of a Coronation Oath,
15 after that Episcopacy had for many years bin settl'd there.
Which concession of his to them, and not to us, he seeks heer
to put off with evasions that are ridiculous. And to omit no
shifts, he alleges that the Presbyterian manners gave him no
encouragement to like thir *modes* of Goverment. If that were
20 so, yet certainly those men are in most likelihood neerer to
amendment, who seek a stricter Church Discipline then that
of Episcopacy; under which the most of them learnt thir
manners. If estimation were to be made of Gods Law by their
manners, who leaving *Ægypt,* receav'd it in the Wilderness,
25 it could reap from such an inference as this, nothing but rejection and disesteem.

For the Prayer wherwith he closes, it had bin good som
safe Liturgie, which he so commends, had rather bin in his

way; it would perhaps in som measure have perform'd the
end for which they say Liturgie was first invented; and have
hinder'd him, both heer and at other times, from turning his
notorious errors into his Praiers.

---

5   XVIII. *Upon the* Uxbridge *Treaty*, &c.

IF the way of Treaties be look'd upon *in general, as a
retiring* from bestial force to human reason, his first
Aphorism heer is in part deceav'd. For men may Treat
like Beasts as well as fight. If som fighting were not man-
10 like, then either fortitude were no vertue, or no fortitude in
fighting: And as Politicians ofttimes through dilatory purposes, and emulations handle the matter, there hath bin no
where found more bestialitie then in treating: which hath
no more commendation in it then from fighting to come to
15 undermining, from violence to craft, and when they can no
longer doe as Lions, to doe as Foxes.

The sincerest end of Treating after War once Proclaim'd,
is either to part with more, or to demand less then was at first
fought for, rather then to hazzard more lives, or wors mis-
20 chiefs. What the Parlament in that point were willing to have
don, when first after the Warr begun, they Petition'd him at
Colebrook to voutsafe a Treaty, is unknown. For after he
had tak'n God to witness of his continual readiness to Treat,
or to offer Treaties to the avoiding of bloodshed, had nam'd
25 *Windsor* the place of Treaty, and pass'd his royal word not
to advance furder, till Commissioners by such a time were

speeded towards him, taking the advantage of a thick Mist, which fell that evening, weather that soon invited him to a designe no less treacherous and obscure; he follows at the heels those Messengers of Peace with a traine of covert Warr:

5 and with a bloody surprise falls on our secure Forces which lay quartering at *Brentford* in the thoughts and expectation of a Treaty. And although in them who make a Trade of Warr, and against a natural Enemy, such an onset might in the rigor of Military Law have bin excus'd, while Armes

10 were not yet by agreement suspended, yet by a King, who seem'd so heartily to accept of treating with his subjects, and professes heer, *He never wanted either desire or disposition to it,* professes *to have greater confidence in his Reason, then in his Sword, and as a Christian to seek Peace and ensue it,*

15 such bloody and deceitful advantages would have bin forborn one day at least, if not much longer; in whom there had not bin a thirst rather then a detestation of civil Warr and blood, and a desire to subdue rather then to treat.

In the midst of a second Treaty not long after, sought by

20 the Parlament, and after much adoe obtain'd with him at *Oxford,* what suttle and unpeaceable designes he then had in chace, his own Letters discover'd: What attempts of treacherous hostility successful and unsuccessful he made against *Bristow, Scarborow,* and other places, the proceedings of that

25 Treaty will soon put us in mind: and how he was so far from granting more of reason, after so much of blood, that he deny'd then to grant, what before he had offerd; making no other use of Treaties pretending Peace, then to gaine advan-

tages that might enable him to continue Warr. What marvel
then if *he thought it no diminution of himself,* as oft as he
saw his time, *to be importunate for Treaties,* when hee sought
them onely, as by the upshot appeard, *to get opportunities:*
5 and once to a most cruel purpose, if we remember *May* 1643.
and that Messenger of Peace from *Oxford,* whose secret Message and Commission, had it bin effected, would have
drownd the innocence of our Treating, in the blood of a de-
signed Massacher. Nay, when treaties from the Parlament
10 sought out him, no less then seven times, oft anough to testifie the willingness of thir obedience, and too oft for the
Majesty of a Parlament to court thir Subjection, he in the
confidence of his own strength, or of our divisions, returnd
us nothing back but denials, or delaies, to thir most necessary
15 demands; and being at lowest kept up still and sustain'd his
almost famishd hopes with the howrly expectation of raising
up himself the higher, by the greater heap which he sate
promising himself of our sudden ruin through dissention.

But he inferrs, as if the Parlament would have compell'd
20 him *to part with* somthing of *his honour as a King.* What
honour could he have, or call his, joyn'd, not onely with the
offence or disturbance, but with the bondage and destruction
of three Nations; wherof though he be careless and improvident, yet the Parlament, by our Laws and freedom, ought to
25 judge and use prevention; our Laws els were but cobweb
Laws. And what were all his most rightful honours, but the
peoples gift, and the investment of that lustre, Majesty, and
honour, which for the public good & no otherwise, redounds

from a whole Nation into one person? So far is any honour
from being his to a common mischeif and calamity. Yet still
he talks on equal termes with the grand Representative of that
people, for whose sake he was a King; as if the general wel-
5 fare, and his subservient Rights were of equal moment, or
consideration. His aime indeed hath ever bin to magnifie
and exalt his borrowd Rights and Prerogatives, above the
Parlament and Kingdom of whom he holds them. But when
a King setts himself to bandy against the highest Court and
10 residence of all his Regal power, he then, in the single person
of a Man, fights against his own Majesty and Kingship, and
then indeed sets the first hand to his own deposing.

   The Treaty at Uxbridge, he saith, *gave the fairest hopes of
a happy composure,* fairest indeed, if his instructions to bribe
15 our Commissioners with the promise of *Security, rewards,*
and *places,* were faire: What other hopes it gave no man can
tell. There being but three maine heads whereon to be treated,
Ireland, Episcopacy, and the Militia, the first was anticipated
and forestall'd by a Peace at any rate to be hast'nd with the
20 Irish Rebels, ere the Treaty could begin; that he might pretend his word and honour past against *the specious and popular arguments* (he calls them no better) which the Parlament would urge upon him for the continuance of that just
Warr. Episcopacy he bids the Queen be confident he will
25 never quitt: which informes us by what Patronage it stood;
and the Sword he resolves to clutch as fast, as if God with his
own hand had put it into his. This was the *moderation which
he brought;* this was *as farr as Reason, Honour, Conscience,*

and the Queen who was his Regent in all these, *would give him leave*. Lastly for *composure,* in stead of *happy,* how miserable it was more likely to have bin, wise men could then judge; when the English, during Treaty, were call'd Rebels, the Irish, good and Catholic Subjects; and the Parlament before hand, though for fashions sake call'd a Parlament, yet by a Jesuitical slight not acknowledg'd though call'd so; but privatly in the Counsel Books inroull'd no Parlament: that if accommodation had succeeded upon what termes soever, such a devilish fraud was prepar'd, that the King in his own esteem had bin absolv'd from all performance, as having treated with Rebels and no Parlament; and they on the other side in stead of an expected happines, had bin brought under the Hatchet. Then no doubt *Warr had ended,* that Massacher and Tyranny might begin. These *jealousies* however *rais'd,* let all men see whether they be diminish'd or *allay'd,* by the Letters of his own Cabinet open'd. And yet the breach of this Treaty is lay'd all upon the Parlament and thir Commissioners, with odious Names of *Pertinacy, hatred of Peace, Faction, and Covetousness,* nay his own Bratt *Superstition* is layd to their charge; notwithstanding his heer profess'd resolution to continue both *the Order, Maintenance, and Authority* of Prelats, as a truth of God.

And who *were most to blame in the unsuccessfullness of that Treaty,* his appeale is to Gods decision: *beleeving* to be *very excusable* at that Tribunal. But if ever man *gloried in an unflexible stifness,* he came not behind any: and that *grand Maxim,* always to put somthing into his Treaties,

which might give *colour* to refuse all that was in other things granted, and to make them *signifie nothing,* was his own Principal Maxim, and particular instructions to his Commissioners. Yet all, by his own verdit, must be consterd *Reason*
5 in the King, and *depraved temper* in the Parlament.

That the *highest Tide of success,* with these principles and designes, *set him not above a Treaty,* no great wonder. And yet if that be spok'n to his praise, the Parlament therin surpass'd him; who, when he was thir vanquish'd and thir cap-
10 tive, his forces utterly brok'n and disbanded, yet offerd him three several times no wors proposals or demands, then when he stood fair to be thir Conqueror. But that imprudent surmise that his lowest *Ebb* could not set him *below a Fight,* was a presumption that ruin'd him.

15 He presag'd the future *unsuccessfulness of Treaties by the unwillingness of som men to treat:* and could not see what was present, that thir unwillingness had good cause to proceed from the continual experience of his own obstinacy and breach of word.

20 His prayer therfore of *forgiveness* to the guilty of *that treaties breaking,* he had good reason to say heartily over; as including no man in that guilt sooner then himself.

As for that Protestation following in his Prayer, *How oft have I entreated for peace, but when I speak therof, they*
25 *make them ready to Warr,* unless he thought himself still in that perfidious mist, between *Colebrook* and *Houndslow,* and thought that mist could hide him from the eye of Heav'n as well as of Man, after such a bloody recompence giv'n to

our first offers of Peace, how could this in the sight of Heav'n without horrours of conscience be utter'd?

XIX. *Upon the various events of the Warr.*

IT is no new, or unwonted thing for bad men to claim as much part in God as his best servants; to usurp and imitate thir words, and appropriate to themselves those properties which belong onely to the good and righteous. This not onely in Scripture is familiarly to be found, but heer also in this Chapter of *Apocrypha*. He tells us much, why *it pleas'd God* to send him Victory or Loss (although what in so doing was the intent of God, he might be much mistak'n as to his own particular) but we are yet to learn what real good use he made therof in his practice.

Those numbers which he grew to *from small beginnings,* were not such as out of love came to protect him, for none approv'd his actions as a King, except Courtiers and Prelats, but were such as fled to be protected by him from the fear of that Reformation which the pravity of thir lives would not bear. Such a Snowball he might easily gather by rowling through those cold and dark provinces of ignorance and leudness, where on a sudden he became so numerous. He imputes that to Gods *protection,* which, to them who persist in a bad cause, is either his long-suffering, or his hard'ning; and that to wholesom *chastisement,* which were the gradual beginnings of a severe punishment. For if neither God nor nature

put civil power in the hands of any whomsoever, but to a lawfull end, and commands our obedience to the autority of Law
onely, not to the Tyrannical force of any person, and if the
Laws of our Land have plac'd the Sword in no mans single
5 hand, so much as to unsheath against a forren enemie, much
less upon the native people, but have plac'd it in that elective
body of the Parlament, to whom the making, repealing, judging, and interpreting of Law it self was also committed, as
was fittest, so long as wee intended to bee a free Nation, and
10 not the Slaves of one mans will, then was the King himself
disobedient and rebellious to that Law by which he raign'd;
any by autority of Parlament to raise armes against him in
defence of Law and Libertie, we doe not onely *think,* but beleeve and know was justifiable both *by the Word of God, the*
15 *Laws of the Land, and all* lawfull *Oaths;* and they who sided
with him fought against all these.

The same Allegations, which he uses for himself and his
Party, may as well fitt any Tyrant in the world: for let the
Parlament bee call'd a Faction when the King pleases, and
20 that no Law must bee made or chang'd either civil or religious, because no Law will content *all sides,* then must be
made or chang'd no Law at all; but what a Tyrant, be he
Protestant or Papist, thinks fitt. Which tyrannous assertion
forc'd upon us by the Sword, he who fights against, and dyes
25 fighting, if his other sins overweigh not, dyes a *Martyr* undoubtedly both of the Faith and of the Common-wealth: and
I hold it not as the opinion, but as the full beleef and persua-
sion of farr holier and wiser men then *Parasitic Preachers.*

Who, without their dinner-Doctrin, know that neither *King, Law, civil Oaths, or Religion,* was ever *establish'd* without the Parlament: and thir power is the same to abrogate as to establish: neither is any thing to bee thought *establish'd*

5 which that House declares to be abolisht. Where the Parlament sitts, there inseparably sitts the King, there the Laws, there our Oaths, and whatsoever can be civil in Religion. They who fought for the Parlament, in the truest sense fought for all these; who fought for the King divided from his Par-

10 lament, fought for the shadow of a King against all these; and for things that were not, as if they were *establisht.* It were a thing monstrously absurd and contradictory to give the Parlament a Legislative power, and then to upbraid them for transgressing old Establishments.

15 But the King and his Party having lost in this Quarrel thir Heav'n upon Earth, beginn to make great reckning of *Eternal Life,* and at an easie rate *in forma Pauperis* Canonize one another into Heav'n; he them in his Book, they him in the Portrature before his Book: but as was said before, Stage-

20 work will not doe it; much less *the justness of thir Cause:* wherin most frequently they dy'd *in a brutish fierceness,* with Oaths and other damning words in thir mouths; as if such had bin *all the Oaths* they fought for: which undoubtedly sent them full Sail on another Voyage then to Heav'n.

25 In the mean while they to whom God gave Victory, never brought to the King at *Oxford* the state of thir *consciences,* that he should presume without confession, more then a Pope presumes, to tell abroad what *conflicts and accusations,* men

whom he never spoke with, have *in thir own thoughts.* We
never read of any English King but one that was a Confessor;
and his name was *Edward:* yet sure it pass'd his skill to know
thoughts, as this King takes upon him. But they who will
5 not stick to slander mens inward consciences, which they can
neither see nor know, much less will care to slander outward
actions, which they pretend to see, though with senses never
so vitiated.

To judge of *his conditions conquerd,* and the manner of
10 *dying* on that side, by the *sober men* that *chose* it, would be
his small advantage: it being most notorious, that they who
were hottest in his Cause, the most of them were men oftner
drunk, then by thir good will sober, and very many of them
so fought and so dy'd.

15 And that *the conscience* of any man should grow *suspicious,* or *be now convicted* by any *pretentions* in the Parlament, which are now prov'd *fals, and unintended,* there can
be no just cause. For neither did they ever pretend to establish his Throne without our Liberty and Religion, nor Re-
20 ligion without the Word of God, nor to judge of Laws by thir
being *establisht,* but to establish them by thir being good and
necessary.

He tells the World *He oft'n prayd that all on his side
might be as faithfull to God and thir own souls, as to him.*
25 But Kings, above all other men, have in thir hands not to
pray onely but to doe. To make that prayer effectual, he
should have govern'd as well as pray'd. To pray and not to
govern is For a Monk and not a King. Till then he might be

well assur'd they were more *faithfull* to thir lust and rapine then to him.

In the wonted predication of his own vertues he goes on to tell us, that to *Conquer he never desir'd, but onely to re-*
5 *store the Laws and Liberties of his people.* It had bin happy then he had known at last, that by force to restore Laws abrogated by the Legislative Parlament; is to conquer absolutely both them, and Law it self. And for our Liberties, none ever oppress'd them more, both in Peace and Warr; first like a
10 maister by his arbitrary power; next as an enemy by hostile invasion.

And if his best freinds fear'd him, and *he himself, in the temptation of an absolute Conquest,* it was not only pious, but freindly in the Parlament, both to fear him and resist him;
15 since their not yeelding, was the onely meanes to keep him out of that *temptation* wherin he doubted his own strength.

He takes himself to be *guilty in this Warr of nothing* els, *but of confirming the power of some Men:* Thus all along he signifies the Parlament, whom to have settl'd by an Act he
20 counts to be his onely guiltiness. So well he knew that to continue a Parlament, was to raise a War against himself; what were his actions then and his Goverment the while? For never was it heard in all our Story, that Parlaments made Warr on thir Kings, but on thir Tyrants; whose *modesty and*
25 *gratitude* was more wanting to the Parlament, then theirs to any of such Kings.

What he *yeelded* was his feare; what he *deny'd* was his obstinacy; *had he yeelded more,* fear might perchance have sav'd him; had he granted *less,* his obstinacy had perhaps the sooner deliverd us.

To review the occasions of this Warr will be to them never *too late,* who would be warn'd by his example from the like evils: but *to wish onely a happy conclusion,* will never expiate the fault of his *unhappy beginnings.* Tis true on our side the sins of our lives not seldom fought against us: but on their side, besides those, the grand sin of thir Cause.

How can it be otherwise when *he desires* heer most unreasonably, and indeed sacrilegiously, that we should be *subject to him,* though not *furder,* yet as farr as *all of us may be subject to God;* to whom this expression leaves no precedency. Hee who *desires* from men as much obedience and subjection, as we may all pay to God, desires not less then to be a God; a sacrilege farr wors then medling with the Bishops Lands, as he esteems it.

His Praier is a good Praier and a glorious; but glorying is not good, if it know not that a little leven levens the whole lump. It should have purg'd out the leven of untruth in telling God that the *blood of his Subjects by him shedd* was *in his just and necessary defence.* Yet this is remarkable; God hath heer so orderd his Prayer, that as his own lipps acquitted the Parlament, not long before his death, of all the blood spilt in this Warr, so now his prayer unwittingly drawes it upon himself. For God *imputes* not to any man the blood he spills in a just cause: and no man ever begg'd his *not imputing* of that which he in his justice could not impute. So that now whether purposely, or unaware he hath confess'd both to God and Man the bloodguiltiness of all this Warr to lie upon his own head.

XX. *Upon the Reformation of the times.*

THIS Chapter cannot punctually be answer'd without more repetitions then now can be excusable: Which perhaps have already bin more humour'd then was needfull. As it presents us with nothing new, so with his exceptions against Reformation pittifully old, and tatter'd with continual using; not onely in his Book, but in the words and Writings of every Papist and Popish King. On the Scene he thrusts out first an Antimasque of two bugbeares, *Noveltie* and *Perturbation;* that the ill looks and noise of those two, may as long as possible, drive off all endeavours of a Reformation. Thus sought Pope *Adrian* by representing the like vain terrors, to divert and dissipate the zeal of those reforming Princes of the age before in *Germany.* And if we credit *Latimers* Sermons, our Papists heer in *England* pleaded the same dangers and inconveniencies against that which was reform'd by *Edward* the sixth. Whereas if those fears had bin available, Christianity it self had never bin receav'd. Which Christ foretold us, would not be admitted without the censure of noveltie and many great commotions. These therfore are not to deterr us.

He grants Reformation to be *a good work,* and confesses *What the indulgence of times and corruption of manners might have deprav'd.* So did the foremention'd Pope and our

Gransire Papists in this Realm. Yet all of them agree in one song with this heer, that *they are sorry to see so little regard had to Laws establisht, and the Religion settl'd.*

Popular compliance, dissolution of all order and gover-
5 *ment in the Church, Scisms, Opinions, Undecencies, Con-fusions, Sacrilegious invasions, contempt of the Clergie, and thir Liturgie, Diminution of Princes:* all these complaints are to be read in the Messages and Speeches almost of every Legat from the Pope to those States and Citties which began
10 Reformation. From whence he either learnt the same pre-tences, or had them naturally in him from the same spirit. Neither was there ever so sincere a Reformation that hath es-cap'd these clamours.

He offer'd a *Synod or Convocation rightly chosen.* So
15 offerd all those Popish Kings heertofore; a cours the most unsatisfactory, as matters have been long carried, and found by experience in the Church liable to the greatest fraud and packing: no solution, or redress of evil, but an increase rather; detested therfor by *Nazianzen* and som other of the Fath-
20 ers. And let it bee produc'd what good hath bin don by Syn-ods from the first times of Reformation.

Not to justifie what enormities the Vulgar may committ in the rudeness of thir zeal, we need but onely instance how he bemoanes *the pulling down of Crosses* and other supersti-
25 tious Monuments, as the effect *of a popular and deceitful Reformation.* How little this savours of a Protestant, is too easily perceav'd.

What he charges in defect of *Piety, Charity, and Morality,*

hath bin also charg'd by Papists upon the best reformed
Churches: not as if they the accusers were not tenfold more
to be accus'd, but out of thir Malignity to all endeavour of
amendment; as we know who accus'd to God the sincerity of
5 *Job;* an accusation of all others the most easie, when as there
livs not any mortal man so excellent, who in these things is not
alwaies deficient. But the infirmities of best men, and the scandals of mixt Hypocrits in all times of reforming, whose bold
intrusion covets to bee ever seen in things most sacred as they
10 are most specious, can lay no just blemish upon the integritie
of others, much less upon the purpose of Reformation it self.
Neither can the evil doings of som be the excuse of our delay-
ing or deserting that duty to the Church, which for no respect
of times or carnal policies can be at any time unseasonable.

15   He tells with great shew of piety what kinde of persons
public Reformers ought to be, and what they ought to doe.
Tis strange that in above twenty years, the Church growing
still wors and wors under him, he could neither be as he bids
others be, nor doe, as he pretends heer so well to know; nay,
20 which is worst of all, after the greatest part of his Raign spent
in neither knowing, nor doing aught toward a Reformation
either in Church or State, should spend the residue in hin-
dring those by a seven years Warr, whom it concernd, with
his consent or without it, to doe thir parts in that great per-
25 formance.

     Tis true that the *method of reforming* may well subsist
without *perturbation of the State;* but that it falls out otherwise for the most part, is the plaine Text of Scripture. And

if by his own rule hee had allow'd us *to feare God first,* and the King in due order, our Allegeance might have still follow'd our Religion in a fit subordination. But if *Christs Kingdom* be tak'n for the true Discipline of the Church, and by *his Kingdom* be meant the violence he us'd against it, and to uphold an Antichristian Hierarchie, then sure anough it is, that Christs Kingdom could *not be sett up* without *pulling down his:* And they were best Christians who were least subject to him. *Christs Goverment,* out of question meaning it Prelatical, hee thought would *confirm his:* and this was that which *overthrew it.*

He professes *to own his Kingdom from Christ, and to desire to rule for his glory, and the Churches good:* The Pope and the King of *Spain* profess every where as much; and both his practice and all his reasonings, all his enmitie against the true Church we see hath bin the same with theirs, since the time that in his Letter to the Pope he assur'd them both of his full compliance. *But evil beginnings never bring forth good conclusions:* they are his own words, and he ratifi'd them by his own ending. To the Pope he ingag'd himself to hazard life and estate for the Roman Religion, whether in complement he did it, or in earnest; and God, who stood neerer then he for complementing minded, writ down those words; that according to his resolution, so it should come to pass. He praies against *his hypocrisie and Pharisaical washings,* a Prayer to him most pertinent, but choaks it straight with other words which pray him deeper into his old errors and delusions.

XXI. *Upon His Letters tak'n and di-vulg'd.*

THE Kings Letters taken at the Battell of *Naesby,*
being of greatest importance to let the people see
what Faith there was in all his promises and solemn
Protestations, were transmitted to public view by special
Order of the Parlament. They discover'd his good affection
to Papists and Irish Rebels, the straight intelligence he held,
the pernitious & dishonorable peace he made with them, not
solicited but rather soliciting, which by all invocations that
were holy he had in public abjur'd. They reveal'd his endeavours to bring in forren Forces, Irish, French, Dutch, Lor-
rainers, and our old Invaders the Danes upon us, besides his
suttleties and mysterious arts in treating: to summ up all,
they shewd him govern'd by a Woman. All which though
suspected vehemently before, and from good grounds beleev'd, yet by him and his adherents peremptorily deny'd,
were, by the op'ning of that Cabinet, visible to all men under
his own hand.

The Parlament therfore to cleer themselves of aspersing
him without cause, and that the people might no longer be
abus'd and cajol'd, as they call it, by falsities and Court im-
pudence, in matters of so high concernment, to let them know
on what termes thir duty stood, and the Kingdoms peace,
conceavd it most expedient and necessary, that those Letters
should be made public. This the King affirmes was by them
don without *honour and civilitie:* words, which if they con-

tain not in them, as in the language of a Courtier most commonly they do not, more of substance and realitie then complement, Ceremony, Court fauning and dissembling, enter not I suppose furder then the eare into any wise mans con-
5 sideration. Matters were not then between the Parlament and a King thir enemie in that state of trifling, as to observ those superficial vanities. But if honour and civilitie mean, as they did of old, discretion, honesty, prudence, and plaine truth, it will be then maintain'd against any Sect of those *Cabalists,*
10 that the Parlament in doing what they did with those Letters, could suffer in thir honour and civilitie no diminution. The reasons are already heard.

And that it is with none more familiar then with Kings, to transgress the bounds of all honour and civility, there
15 should not want examples good store, if brevity would permitt; In poynt of Letters this one shall suffice. The *Duchess* of *Burgundie* and heire of *Duke Charles,* had promis'd to her Subjects that shee intended no otherwise to Govern, then by advise of the three Estates, but to *Lewis* the French King had
20 writt'n Letters, that shee had resolv'd to committ wholly the managing of her affaires to foure Persons, whom shee nam'd. The three Estates not doubting the sincerity of her Princely word, send Embassadors to *Lewis,* who then beseig'd *Arras* belonging to the Duke of *Burgondy.* The King taking hold
25 of this occasion to set them at division among themselves, question'd thir Credence; which when they offerd to produce with thir instructions, he not only shewes them the privat Letter of thir Duchess, but gives it them to carry home, wher-

with to affront her; which they did, shee denying it stoutly;
till they, spredding it before her face in a full assembly, convicted her of an op'n lye. Which although *Commines* the his-
torian much blames, as a deed too harsh and dishonourable in
5 them who were Subjects, and not at Warr with thir Princess,
yet to his Maister *Lewis,* who first divulg'd those Letters, to
the op'n shaming of that young Governess, he imputes no
incivilitie or dishonour at all, although betraying a certaine
confidence repos'd by that Letter in his royal secrecie.

10   With much more reason then may letters not intercepted
only, but won in battell from an enemie, be made public to
the best advantages of them that win them, to the discovery
of such important truth or falshood. Was it not more dishonourable in himself to faine suspicions and jealousies, which
15 we first found among those Letters, touching the chastitie
of his Mother, thereby to gaine assistance from the King of
Denmark, as in vindication of his Sister? The Damsell of
Burgundie, at sight of her own letter, was soon blank, and
more ingenuous then to stand out-facing; but this man whom
20 nothing will convince, thinks by talking world without end,
to make good his integrity and faire dealing contradicted by
his own hand and seale. They who can pick nothing out of
them but phrases shall be counted *Bees:* they that discern
furder both there and here, that *constancy to his Wife* is set
25 in place before Laws and Religion, are in his naturalities no
better then *Spiders.*

He would work the people to a perswasion, that *if he be
miserable they cannot be happy.* What should hinder them?

Were they all born Twins of *Hippocrates* with him and his
fortune, one birth one burial? It were a Nation miserable indeed, not worth the name of a Nation, but a race of Idiots,
whose happiness and welfare depended upon one Man. The
5 happiness of a Nation consists in true Religion, Piety, Justice,
Prudence, Temperance, Fortitude, and the contempt of Avarice and Ambition. They in whomsoever these vertues dwell
eminently, need not Kings to make them happy, but are the
architects of thir own happiness; and whether to themselves
10 or others are not less then Kings. But in him, which of these
vertues were to be found, that might extend to the making
happy, or the well-governing of somuch as his own houshold,
which was the most licentious and ill govern'd in the whole
Land.

15   But the op'ning of his Letters was design'd by the Parlament to make *all reconciliation desperate.* Are the lives of
so many good and faithfull men, that dy'd for the freedom of
thir Country, to be so slighted, as to be forgott'n in a stupid
reconcilement without Justice don them? What he feares not
20 by Warr and slaughter, should we feare *to make desperate* by
op'ning his Letters? Which fact he would parallell with
Chams revealing of his Fathers nakedness: When he at that
time could be no way esteem'd *the Father of his Countrey,*
but the destroyer; nor had he ever before merited that former
25 title.

He thanks God he cannot onely beare this with patience,
but with charity forgive the doers. Is not this meer mockery
to thank God for what he can doe, but will not? For is it pa-

tience to impute *Barbarism* and *inhumanity* to the op'ning
of an Enemies Letter, or is it Charity to cloth them with
curses in his Prayer whom he hath forgiv'n in his Discours?
In which Prayer to shew how readily he can return good
5 for evil to the Parlament, and that if they take away his
Coat, he can let them have his Cloak also, for the dismantling
of his Letters he wishes *They may be cover'd with the Cloak
of confusion.* Which I suppose they do resigne with much
willingness, both Livery, Badge, and Cognizance, to them
10 who chose rather to be the Slaves and Vassals of his will, then
to stand against him, as men by nature free; born and created with a better title to thir freedom, then any King hath
to his Crown.

XXII. *Upon His going to the Scots.*

15 THE Kings comming in, whether to the Scots or English, deserv'd no thanks: for *necessitie was his Coun-
selor:* and that he hated them both alike, his expressions every where manifest. Som say his purpose was to have
come to *London,* till hearing how strictly it was proclaim'd
20 that no man should conceal him, he diverted his course. But
that had bin a frivolous excuse: and besides he himself re-
hearsing the consultations had, before he took his journey,
shewes us cleerly that he was determin'd to adventure *upon
their Loyalty who first began his troubles.* And that the Scots
25 had notice of it before, hath bin long since brought to light.
What prudence there could be in it, no man can imagin;

Malice there might be, by raising new jealousies to divide
Freinds. For besides his diffidence of the English, it was no
small dishonour that he put upon them, when rather then
yeild himself to the Parlament of *England,* he yeelded to an
5 hireling Army of Scots in *England,* payd for thir Service
heer, not in Scotch coyn, but in English Silver; nay who
from the first beginning of these troubles, what with brotherly assistance, and what with mounthly pay, have defended
thir own Liberty and consciences at our charge. However it
10 was a hazardous and rash journey taken, *to resolve riddles in
mens Loyaltie,* who had more reason to mistrust the Riddle
of such a disguised yeelding; and to put himself in their hands
whose Loyalty was a Riddle to him, was not the cours to be
resolv'd of it, but to tempt it. *What providence deny'd to
15 force,* he thought *it might grant* to fraud, which he stiles
Prudence: But Providence was not couzen'd with disguises,
neither outward nor inward.

To have known *his greatest danger in his supposed safety,
and his greatest safety in his supposed danger* was to him a
20 fatal Riddle never yet resolv'd; wherin rather to have imployd his main skill, had bin much more to his preservation.

Had he *known when the Game was lost,* it might have
sav'd much *contest:* but the way *to give over fairely,* was not
to slip out of op'n Warr into a new disguise. He layes down
25 his Armes, but not his Wiles; nor all his Armes, for in obstinacy he comes no less arm'd then ever, *Cap a pè.* And
what were they but wiles, continually to move for Treaties,
and yet to persist the same man, and to *fortifie his mind* be-

fore hand, still purposing to grant no more then what seem'd good to that violent and lawless Triumvirate within him, under the falsifi'd names of his Reason, Honour, and Conscience, the old circulating dance of his shifts and evasions.

5   *The words of a King,* as they are *full of power,* in the autority and strength of Law, so like *Sampson,* without the strength of that *Nazarites* lock, they have no more power in them then the words of another man.

He adores Reason as *Domitian* did *Minerva,* and calls her 10 the *Divinest power,* thereby to intimate as if at reasoning, as at his own weapon, no man were so able as himself. Might we be so happy as to know where these monuments of his Reason may be seen, for in his actions & his writing they appeare as thinly as could be expected from the meanest parts, bredd up 15 in the midst of so many wayes extraordinary to know somthing. He who reads his talk, would think he had left *Oxford* not without mature deliberation: Yet his Prayer confesses that *he knew not what to doe.* Thus is verifi'd that Psalme; *He powreth contempt upon Princes and causeth them to wander* 20 *in the Wilderness where there is no way, Psal.* 107.

XXIII. *Upon the Scots delivering the King to the English.*

THAT the Scots in *England* should *sell thir King,* as he himself here affirmes, and for a *price so much* 25 *above that,* which the covetousness of *Judas* was contented with to sell *our Saviour,* is so foule an infamy and

dishonour cast upon them, as befitts none to vindicate but
themselves. And it were but friendly Counsel to wish them
beware the Son, who comes among them with a firme beleif
that they sould his Father. The rest of this Chapter he Sacri-
5 fices to the Echo of his Conscience, out-babling Creeds and
Ave's; glorying in his resolute obstinacy, and as it were tri-
umphing how *evident it is now,* that *not evill Counselors,* but
he himself hath been the Author of all our troubles. Herein
onely we shall disagree to the worlds end, while he who
10 sought so manifestly to have annihilated all our Laws and
Liberties, hath the confidence to perswade us that he hath
fought and *suffer'd* all this while in thir defence.

But he who neither by his own Letters and Commissions
under hand and Seale, nor by his own actions held as in a
15 Mirror before his face, will be convinc'd to see his faults, can
much less be won upon by any force of words, neither he, nor
any that take after him; who in that respect are no more to
be disputed with, then they who deny Principles. No question then, but the Parlament did wisely in thir decree at last,
20 to make no more addresses. For how unalterable his will was,
that would have bin our Lord, how utterly averse from the
Parlament, and Reformation, during his confinement, we
may behold in this Chapter. But to be ever answering fruitless Repetitions, I should become liable to answer for the
25 same my self. He borrows *Davids* Psalmes, as he charges the
Assembly of Divines in his twentith Discourse, *To have set
forth old Catechisms and confessions of faith new drest.* Had
he borrow'd *Davids* heart, it had bin much the holier theft.

For such kind of borrowing as this, if it be not better'd by the borrower, among good Authors is accounted *Plagiarie*. However, this was more tolerable then *Pammela's* Praier, stol'n out of Sir *Philip*.

XXIV. *Upon the denying him the attendance of his Chaplains.*

ACHAPLAIN is a thing so diminutive, and inconsiderable, that how he should come heer among matters of so great concernment, to take such room up in the Discourses of a Prince, if it be not wonderd, is to be smil'd at. Certainly by me, so mean an argument shall not be writt'n; but I shall huddle him as he does Prayers. The Scripture ownes no such order, no such function in the Church; and the Church not owning them, they are left, for ought I know, to such a furder examining as the Sons of *Sceva* the Jew met with; Bishops or Presbyters we know, and Deacons we know, but what are Chaplains? In State perhaps they may be listed among the upper Servingmen of som great houshold, and be admitted to som such place, as may stile them the Sewers, or the Yeomen-Ushers of Devotion, where the Maister is too restie, or too rich to say his own prayers, or to bless his own Table. Wherfore should the Parlament then take such implements of the Court Cupbord into thir consideration? They knew them to have bin the main corrupters at the kings elbow: they knew the king to have bin always thir most attentive Scholar, & Imitator, & of a child to have

suckt from them & thir closetwork all his impotent principles
of tyranny & superstition. While therfore they had any hope
left of his reclaiming, these sowers of Malignant Tares they
kept asunder from him: and sent to him such of the Ministers
5 and other zealous persons, as they thought were best able to
instruct him, and to convert him. What could religion her
self have don more to the saving of a soule? But when they
found him past cure, & that he to himself was grown the most
evil Counseler of all, they deny'd him not his Chaplains, as
10 many as were fitting, and som of them attended him, or els
were at his call to the very last. Yet heer he makes more
Lamentation for the want of his Chaplains, then superstitious *Micah* did to the *Danites,* who had tak'n away his houshold Priest. *Yee have tak'n away my Gods which I made,*
15 *and the Priest, and what have I more?* And perhaps the
whole Story of *Micah* might square not unfitly to this Argument: *Now know I,* saith he, *that the Lord will doe me good,*
seeing I have a Levite to my Priest. Micah had as great a care
that his Priest should be Mosaical, as the King had that his
20 should be *Apostolical;* yet both in an error touching thir
Priests. Houshold and privat Orisons were not to be offici-
ated by Priests; for neither did public Prayer appertain onely
to their Office. Kings heertofore, *David, Salomon,* and *Je-*
hosaphat, who might not touch the Priesthood, yet might
25 pray in public, yea in the Temple, while the Priests themselves stood and heard. What aild this King then that he
could not chew his own Mattins without the Priests *Oretenus?*
Yet is it like he could not pray at home, who can heer pub-

lish a whole Prayer-book of his own, and signifies in some
part of this Chapter, almost as good a mind to be a Priest
himself, as *Micah* had to let his Son be. There was doubtless
therfore some other matter in it, which made him so desirous
5 to have his Chaplaines about him, who were not onely the
contrivers, but very oft the instruments also of his designes.

The Ministers which were sent him no marvel he indur'd
not; for they Preacht repentance to him: the others gave him
easie confession, easie absolution, nay *strength'nd his hands*
10 *and hard'nd his heart* by applauding him in his wilfull wayes.
To them he was an *Ahab,* to these a *Constantine;* it must follow then that they to him were as unwelcome as *Eliah* was to
Ahab, these as deer, and pleasing as *Amaziah* the Priest of
Bethel was to *Jeroboam.* These had learnt well the lesson that
15 would please; *Prophesie not against Bethel, for it is the Kings*
Chappel, the Kings Court; and had taught the King to say
of those Ministers which the Parlament had sent, *Amos hath*
conspir'd against me; the Land is not able to beare all his
words.
20 Returning to our first Parallel, this King lookt upon his
Prelats *as Orphans under the sacrilegious eyes of many rapa-*
cious Reformers: and there was as great feare of Sacrilege between *Micah* and his Mother, till with thir holy treasure,
about the loss whereof there was such cursing, they made a
25 grav'n and a molt'n *Image,* and got a Priest of thir own. To
let go his Criticizing about the *sound of Prayers, imperious,*
rude, or passionat, modes of his own divising, we are in danger to fall again upon the flats and shallows of Liturgie.

Which if I should repeat again, would turn my answers into *Responsories,* and begett another Liturgie, having too much of one already.

This onely I shall add, that if the heart, as he alleges, can-
5 not safely *joyn with another mans extemporal sufficiency,* because we know not so exactly what they mean to say, then those public Prayers made in the Temple by those forenamed Kings, and by the Apostles in the Congregation, and by the ancient Christians for above three hundred yeares before Lit-
10 urgies came in, were with the People made in vain.

After he hath acknowledg'd that kings heertofore prayd without Chaplains, eev'n publicly in the Temple it self, and that every *privat Beleever is invested with a royall Priesthood,* yet like one that relisht not what he *tasted of the heav'nly*
15 *gift, and the good word of God* whose name he so confidently takes into his mouth, he frames to himself impertinent and vain reasons, why he should rather pray by the officiating mouth of a Closet Chaplain. *Their prayers,* saith he, *are more prevalent, they flow from minds more enlightn'd,*
20 *from affections less distracted.* Admitt this true, which is not; this might be somthing said as to thir prayers for him, but what availes it to thir praying with him? If his own minde *be incumbred with secular affaires,* what helps it his particular prayer, though the mind of his Chaplain be not wandring,
25 either after new preferment, or his Dinner? The fervencie of one man in prayer, cannot supererogate for the coldness of another; neither can *his spiritual defects* in that duty be made out, in the acceptance of God, by another mans abilities. Let

him endeavour to have more light in himself: And not to
walk by another mans Lamp, but to get Oyle into his own.
Let him cast from him, as in a Christian warrfare, that secular incumbrance which either distracts, or overloads him; his
5 load els will never be the less heavie, because another mans is
light. Thus these pious flourishes and colours examin'd
throughly, are like the Apples of *Asphaltis,* appearing goodly
to the sudden eye, but look well upon them, or at least but
touch them, and they turne into Cinders.

10   In his Prayer he remembers what *voices of joy and glad-*
ness there were in his Chappell, *Gods house,* in his opinion,
between the Singing men and the Organs; and this was *unity*
of spirit in the bond of peace; the vanity, superstition, and
misdevotion of which place was a scandall farr and neer:
15 Wherin so many things were sung, and pray'd in those Songs,
which were not understood: and yet he who makes a difficulty how the people can joyne thir hearts to extemporal
prayers, though distinctly heard and understood, makes no
question how they should joyn thir hearts in unitie to songs
20 not understood.

      I beleeve that God is no more mov'd with a prayer elabo-
ratly pend, then men truely charitable are mov'd with the
pen'd speech of a Begger.

      Finally O yee Ministers, ye pluralists, whose lips preserve
25 not knowledge, but the way ever op'n to your bellies, read
heer what work he makes among your wares, your Gally pots,
your *Balmes* and *Cordials* in print, & not onely your *sweet*
Sippets in widows houses, but the huge gobbets wherewith he

charges you to have devourd houses and all; the *houses of your Brethren, your King, and your God.* Crie him up for a Saint in your Pulpits, while he cries you down for Atheists into Hell.

---

5 ## XXV. *Upon His penitentiall Meditations and Vowes at* Holmby.

IT is not hard for any man, who hath a Bible in his hands, to borrow good words and holy sayings in abundance; but to make them his own, is a work of grace onely from 10 above. He borrows heer many penitential Verses out of *Davids* Psalmes. So did many among those Israelites, who had revolted from the true worship of God, *invent to themselves instruments of music like David,* and probably Psalmes also like his, and yet the Profet *Amos* complaines heavily against 15 them. But to prove how short this is of true repentance, I will recite the penitence of others, who have repented in words not borrowd, but thir own and yet by the doom of Scripture it self are judg'd reprobates.

Cain said unto the Lord, *My iniquity is greater then I can* 20 *beare, behold thou hast driv'n me this day from the face of the earth, and from thy face shall I be hid.*

And when Esau *heard the words of his Father he cry'd with an exceeding bitter cry, and said, Bless me eev'n me also O my Father;* yet *found no place of repentance though he* 25 *sought it carefully with teares, Heb.* 12.

And *Pharaoh* said to *Moses, The Lord is righteous, I and*

*my people are wicked; I have sind against the Lord your God
and against you.*

And *Balaam* said, *Let me die the death of the righteous
and let my last end be like his.*

5   And *Saul* said to *Samuel, I have sin'd, for I have transgress'd the commandment of the Lord; yet honour me now
I pray thee before the Elders of my People.*

And when Ahab *heard the words of* Eliah, *he rent his
cloaths and put sackcloth upon his flesh, and fasted, and lay
10 in sackcloth, and went softly.*

Jehoram also *rent his cloaths, and the people look'd, and
behold he had Sackcloth upon his flesh,* yet in the very act of
his humiliation he could say, *God doe so, and more also to
me, if the head of* Elishah *shall stand on him this day.*

15   Therfore *saith the Lord, They have not cri'd unto me
with thir heart, when they howl'd upon thir beds. They returne, but not to the most High. Hosea* 7.

And *Judas* said, *I have sind, in that I have betray'd innocent blood.*

20 And *Symon Magus* sayd, *Pray yee to the Lord for me that
none of these things come upon me.*

All these took the paines both to confess and to repent in
thir own words, and many of them in thir own tears, not in
Davids. But transported with the vain ostentation of imi-
25 tating *Davids* language, not his life, observe how he brings a
curse upon himself and his Fathers house (God so disposing
it) by his usurp'd and ill imitated prayer: *Let thy anger I beseech thee be against me and my Fathers house, as for these*

Sheep what have they don. For if *David* indeed sind in num-
bring the people, of which fault he in earnest made that confession, & acquitted the whole people from the guilt of that
sin, then doth this King, using the same words, bear witness
5 against himself to be the guilty person; and either in his soule
and conscience heer acquitts the Parlament and the people,
or els abuses the words of *David,* and dissembles grossly to
the very face of God, which is apparent in the next line;
wherein he accuses eev'n the Church it self to God, as if she
10 were *the Churches enemie,* for having overcom his Tyranny
by the powerfull and miraculous might of Gods manifest
arme: For to other strength in the midst of our divisions and
disorders, who can attribute our Victories? Thus had this miserable Man no worse enemies to sollicit and mature his own
15 destruction from the hast'nd sentence of Divine Justice, then
the obdurat curses which proceeded against himself out of his
own mouth.

Hitherto his Meditations, now his Vowes; which as the
Vowes of hypocrits use to be, are most commonly absurd, and
20 som wicked. *Jacob* Vow'd that God should be his God, if he
granted him but what was necessary to perform that Vow,
life and subsistence: but the obedience profferd heer is nothing so cheap. He who took so hainously to be offer'd nineteen Propositions from the Parlament, capitulates heer with
25 God almost in as many Articles.

If he will continue that light or rather that darkness of the
Gospel, which is among his Prelats, settle thir luxuries, and
make them gorgeous Bishops,

If he will *restore* the greevances and mischeifs of those obsolete and Popish Laws, which the Parlament without his consent hath abrogated, and will suffer Justice to be executed according to his sense,

5   *If he will suppress the many Scisms in Church,* to contradict himself in that which he hath foretold must and shall come to pass, and will remove Reformation as the greatest Scism of all, and Factions in State, by which he meanes in every leafe the Parlament,

10   If he will *restore him* to his negative voice and the Militia, as much to say as arbitrary power, which he wrongfully averrs to be the *right of his Predecessors,*

If he will turne the hearts of his people to thir old Cathedral and Parochial service in the Liturgie, and thir passive
15 obedience to the King,

If he will quench the Army, and withdraw our Forces from withstanding the Piracy of *Rupert,* and the plotted Irish invasion,

If he will bless him with the freedom of Bishops again in
20 the House of Peers, and of fugitive Delinquents in the House of Commons, *and deliver the honour of Parlament* into his hands, from the most natural and due protection of the people, that entrusted them with the dangerous enterprize of being faithfull to thir Country against the rage and malice of
25 his tyrannous opposition,

If he will keep him from that great offence of following the counsel of his Parlament, and *enacting* what they advise him to, which in all reason, and by the known Law, and Oath

of his Coronation he ought to doe, and not to call that *Sacri-lege* which necessity through the continuance of his own civil Warr hath compelld them to, necessity, which made *David* eat the Shewbread, made *Ezechiah* take all the Silver which
5 was found in Gods House, and cut off the Gold which over-layd those dores and Pillars, and give it to *Sennacherib;* ne-cessity, which oft times made the Primitive Church to sell her sacred utensils, eev'n to the Communion Chalice,

If he will restore him to a capacity of glorifying him by
10 *doing* that both in Church and State, which must needs dis-honour and pollute his name,

If he will bring him again with peace, honour and safety to his cheife Citty, without repenting, without satisfying for the blood spilt, onely for a few politic concessions which are
15 as good as nothing,

If *he will put again the Sword into his hand, to punish* those that have deliverd us, and to *protect* Delinquents against the Justice of Parlament,

Then, if it be possible to reconcile contradictions, he will
20 praise him by displeasing him, and serve him by disserving him.

His glory, in the gaudy Copes, and painted Windows, Miters, Rochets, Altars, and the chanted Service-Book *shall be dearer to him* then the establishing his *Crowne* in right-
25 eousness, and the spiritual power of Religion.

He will pardon those that have offended him in particular, but there shall want no suttle wayes to be eev'n with them upon another score of thir suppos'd offences against the Com-

mon-wealth; wherby he may at once affect the glory of a
seeming justice, and destroy them pleasantly, while he faines
to forgive them as to his own particular, and outwardly bewailes them.

5 These are the conditions of his treating with God, to whom
he bates nothing of what he stood upon with the Parlament:
as if Commissions of Array could deale with him also. But
of all these conditions, as it is now evident in our eyes, God
accepted none, but that final Petition which he so oft, no
10 doubt but by the secret judgement of God, importunes against
his own head; praying God *That his mercies might be so
toward him, as his resolutions of Truth and Peace were toward his People.* It follows then, God having cutt him off
without granting any of these mercies, that his resolutions
15 were as fained as his Vows were frustrat.

XXVI. *Upon the Armies surprisall of the King at* Holmeby.

TO give account to Royalists what was don with thir
vanquisht King, yeilded up into our hands, is not to
20 be expected from them whom God hath made his
Conquerors. And for brethren to debate & rippe up thir falling out, in the eare of a common enemy, thereby making him
the judge or at least the wel pleas'd auditor of thir disagreement, is neither wise nor comely. To the King therfore, were
25 he living, or to his Party yet remaining, as to this action, there
belongs no answer. Æmulations, all men know, are incident

among Military men, and are, if they exceed not, pardonable.
But som of the former Army, eminent anough for thir own
martial deeds, and prevalent in the House of Commons,
touch'd with envy to be so farr outdon by a new modell which
5 they contemn'd, took advantage of Presbyterian and Independent names, and the virulence of som Ministers to raise
disturbance. And the Warr being then ended, thought slightly to have discarded them who had faithfully don the work,
without thir due pay, and the reward of thir invincible val-
10 our. But they who had the Sword yet in thir hands, disdain-
ing to be made the first objects of ingratitude and oppression,
after all that expens of thir blood for Justice and the common
Liberty, seiz'd upon the King thir pris'ner, whom nothing
but their matchles deeds had brought so low as to surrender
15 up his Person: though he, to stirr up new discord, chose rather
to give up himself a captive to his own Countrymen, who less
had won him. This in likelihood might have grown to som
hight of mischeif; partly through the strife which was kin-
dling between our elder and our younger Warriors, but chiefly
20 through the seditious tongues of some fals Ministers, more
zealous against Scisms, then against thir own Simony and
Pluralities, or watchfull of the common enemy, whose suttle
insinuations had got so farr in among them, as with all diligence to blow the coles. But it pleas'd God not to embroile
25 and put to confusion his whole people for the perversness of
a few. The growth of our dissention was either prevented or
soon quieted; the Enemy soon deceav'd of his rejoycing, and
the King especially disappointed of not the meanest morsel

that his hope presented him, to ruin us by our division. And being now so nigh the end, we may the better be at leasure to stay a while, and hear him commenting upon his own Captivity.

5   He saith of his surprisal that it was a *motion eccentric and irregular*. What then? his own allusion, from the Celestial bodies, puts us in minde, that irregular motions may be necessary on earth somtimes, as well as constantly in Heav'n. That is not always best, which is most regular to writt'n Law.

10 Great Worthies heertofore by disobeying Law, ofttimes have sav'd the Common-wealth: and the Law afterward by firme Decree hath approv'd that planetary motion, that unblamable exorbitancy in them.

   He meanes no good to either Independent or Presbyterian,

15 and yet his parable, like that of *Balaam,* is overul'd to portend them good, farr beside his intention. *Those twins* that strove *enclos'd in the womb* of *Rebeccah,* were the seed of *Abraham;* the younger undoubtedly gain'd the heav'nly birthright; the elder though supplanted in his Similie, shall yet no

20 question find a better portion then *Esau* found, and farr above his uncircumcis'd Prelats.

   He censures, and in censuring seems to hope *it will be an ill Omen* that they *who build Jerusalem divide thir tongues and hands.* But his hope fail'd him with his example; for

25 that there were divisions both of tongues and hands at the building of *Jerusalem,* the Story would have certifi'd him; and yet the work prosper'd; and if God will, so may this; notwithstanding all the craft and malignant wiles of *Sanbal-*

lat and *Tobiah,* adding what fuell they can to our dissentions; or the indignity of his comparison that lik'ns us to those seditious *Zelots* whose *intestine fury* brought destruction to the last *Jerusalem.*

5   It being now no more in his hand to be reveng'd on his opposers, he seeks to satiat his fansie with the imagination of som revenge upon them from above; and like one who in a drowth observes the Skie, he sits and watches when any thing will dropp, that might solace him with the likeness of
10 a punishment from Heavn upon us: which he strait expounds how he pleases. No evil can befall the Parlament or Citty, but he positively interprets it a judgement upon them for his sake; as if the very manuscript of Gods judgements had bin deliverd to his custody and exposition. But his reading de-
15 clares it well to be a fals copy which he uses; dispensing oft'n to his own bad deeds and successes the testimony of Divine favour, and to the good deeds and successes of other men, Divine wrath and vengeance. But to counterfet the hand of God is the boldest of all Forgery: And he, who without
20 warrant but his own fantastic surmise, takes upon him perpetually to unfold the secret and unsearchable Mysteries of high Providence, is likely for the most part to mistake and slander them; and approaches to the madness of those reprobate thoughts, that would wrest the Sword of Justice out of
25 Gods hand, and imploy it more justly in thir own conceit. It was a small thing to contend with the Parlament about sole power of the Militia, when we see him doing little less then laying hands on the weapons of God himself, which are his

judgements, to weild and manage them by the sway and bent of his own fraile cogitations. Therfore *they that by Tumults first occasion'd the raising of Armies,* in his doome *must* needs *be chastn'd by thir own Army for new Tumults.*

5   First note heer his confession, that those Tumults were the first occasion of raising Armies, and by consequence that he himself rais'd them first, against those supposed Tumults. But who occasion'd those Tumults, or who made them so, being at first nothing more then the unarmed and peaceable
10 concours of people, hath bin discust already. And that those pretended Tumults were chastiz'd by thir own Army for new Tumults, is not prov'd by a Game at Tictack with words; *Tumults and Armies, Armies and Tumults,* but seemes more like the method of a Justice irrational then Divine.

15 If the Citty were chast'nd by the Army for new Tumults, the reason is by himself set down evident and immediat, *thir new Tumults.* With what sense can it be referrd then to another far-fetchd and imaginary cause that happ'nd so many years before, and in his supposition only as a cause. *Manlius*
20 defended the Capitol and the Romans from thir enemies the *Gauls: Manlius* for sedition afterward was by the Romans thrown headlong from the Capitol, therfore *Manlius* was punisht by Divine Justice for defending the Capitol: because in that place punishd for sedition, and by those whom he de-
25 fended. This is his Logic upon Divine Justice; and was the same before upon the death of Sir *John Hotham.* And heer again, *Such as were content to see him driv'n away by unsuppressed Tumults, are now forc'd to fly to an Army.* Was this

a judgement? was it not a mercy rather, that they had a noble and victorious Army so neer at hand to fly to?

From Gods Justice he comes down to *Mans Justice*. Those few of both Houses *who at first with-drew with him* from the vain pretence of Tumults, *were counted Desertors;* therfore those many must be also Desertors who with-drew afterwards from real Tumults: as if it were the place that made a Parlament, and not the end and cause. Because it is deny'd that those were Tumults from which the King made shew of being driv'n, is it therefore of necessity impli'd, that there could be never any Tumults for the future? If some men fly in craft, may not other men have cause to fly in earnest? But mark the difference between their flight and his; they soon return'd in safety to thir places, he not till after many years, and then a Captive to receive his punishment. So that their flying, whether the cause be consider'd or the event, or both, neither justifi'd him, nor *condemn'd themselves.*

But he will needs have *vengeance to pursue and overtake them;* though to bring it in, it cost him an inconvenient and obnoxious comparison, *As the Mice and Ratts overtook a German Bishop.* I would our Mice and Ratts had bin as Orthodoxal heer, and had so pursu'd all his Bishops out of *England;* then vermin had ridd away vermin, which now hath lost the lives of too many thousand honest men to doe.

He cannot but observe this Divine Justice, yet with sorrow and pitty. But sorrow and pitty in a weak and over-maister'd enemy, is lookt upon no otherwise then as the ashes of his revenge burnt out upon it self; or as the damp of a coold fury

when we say, it gives. But in this manner to sit spelling and
observing divine justice upon every accident & slight disturbance that may happ'n humanly to the affaires of men, is but
another fragment of his brok'n revenge: & yet the shrewdest
5 & the cunningest obloquy that can be thrown upon thir actions. For if he can perswade men that the Parlament and
thir cause is pursu'd with Divine vengeance, he hath attain'd
his end, to make all men forsake them, and think the worst
that can be thought of them.

10   Nor is he onely content to suborn Divine Justice in his censure of what is past, but he assumes the person of Christ himself to prognosticate over us what he wishes would come.
So little is any thing or person sacred from him, no not in
Heav'n, which he will not use, and put on, if it may serve
15 him plausibly to wreck his spleen, or ease his mind upon the
Parlament. Although if ever *fatal blindness* did both *attend
and punish* wilfulness, if ever any *enjoy'd not comforts,* for
neglecting counsel belonging to thir peace, it was in none
more conspicuously brought to pass then in himself: and his
20 predictions against the Parlament and thir adherents have
for the most part bin verify'd upon his own head, and upon
his cheif Counselors.

He concludes with high praises of the Army. But praises
in an enemy are superfluous, or smell of craft; and the Army
25 shall not need his praises; nor the Parlament fare worse for
his accusing prayers that follow. Wherin as his Charity can be
no way comparable to that of Christ, so neither can his assurance that they whom he seems to pray for, in doing what

they did against him, *knew not what they did.* It was but arrogance therfore, and not charity, to lay such ignorance to others in the sight of God, till he himself had bin infallible, like him whose peculiar words he overweeningly assumes.

---

5   XXVII. *Intitil'd to the Prince of Wales.*

WHAT the King wrote to his Son, as a Father, concerns not us; what he wrote to him, as a King of *England,* concerns not him; God and the Parlament having now otherwise dispos'd of *England.*
10 But because I see it don with some artifice and labour, to possess the people that they might amend thir present condition, by his or by his Sons restorement, I shall shew point by point, that although the King had bin reinstall'd to his desire, or that his Son admitted, should observe exactly all his Fathers
15 precepts, yet that this would be so farr from conducing to our happiness, either as a *remedy to the present distempers, or a prevention of the like to come,* that it would inevitably throw us back again into all our past and fulfill'd miseries; would force us to fight over again all our tedious Warrs,
20 and put us to another fatal struggling for Libertie and life, more dubious then the former. In which as our success hath bin no other then our cause; so it will be evident to all posteritie, that his *misfortunes* were the meer consequence of his perverse *judgement.*
25   First he argues from *the experience of those troubles* which both he and his Son have had, to the improvement of thir

pietie and patience: and by the way beares witness in his own
words, that the corrupt education of his youth, which was but
glanc'd at onely in some former passages of this answer, was
a thing neither of mean consideration, nor untruly charg'd
5 upon him or his Son: himself confessing heer that *Court de-
lights are prone either to root up all true vertue and honour,
or to be contented only with some leaves and withering formalities of them, without any reall fruits tending to the public
good:* Which presents him still in his own words another
10 *Rehoboam, soft'nd* by a farr wors Court then *Salomons, and
so corrupted* by *flatteries,* which he affirmes to be *unsepara-
ble,* to the overturning of all *peace,* and the loss of his own
honour and Kingdoms. That he came therfore thus bredd up
and nurtur'd to the Throne, farr wors then *Rehoboam,* un-
15 less he be of those who equaliz'd his Father to King *Salomon,*
we have heer his own confession. And how voluptuously,
how idlely raigning in the hands of other men, he either tyranniz'd or trifl'd away those seventeen yeares of peace, without care, or thought, as if to be a King had bin nothing els in
20 his apprehension, but to eat and drink, and have his will, and
take his pleasure, though there be who can relate his domestic
life to the exactness of a diary, there shall be heer no mention
made. This yet we might have then foreseen, that he who
spent his leisure so remissly and so corruptly to his own
25 pleasing, would one day or other be wors busied and imployd to our sorrow. And that he acted in good earnest what
Rehoboam did but threat'n, to make his little finger heavier
then his Fathers loynes, and to whip us with his two twisted

Scorpions, both temporal and spiritual Tyranny, all his
Kingdoms have felt. What good use he made afterward of
his adversitie, both his impenitence and obstinacy to the end
(for he was no *Manasseh*) and the sequel of these his medi-
5 tated resolutions, abundantly express; retaining, commending, teaching to his Son all those putrid and pernicious doc-
uments both of State and of Religion, instill'd by wicked
Doctors, and receav'd by him as in a Vessel nothing better
seasond, which were the first occasion both of his own and
10 all our miseries. And if he in the best maturity of his yeares
and understanding made no better use to himself or others
of his so long and manifold afflictions, either looking up to
God, or looking down upon the reason of his own affaires,
there can be no probability that his son, bred up, not in the
15 soft effeminacies of Court onely, but in the rugged and more
boistrous licence of undisciplin'd Camps and Garrisons, for
yeares unable to reflect with judgement upon his own condition, and thus ill instructed by his Father, should give his
mind to walk by any other rules then these bequeath'd him
20 as on his Fathers death-bed, & as the choicest of all that experience, which his most serious observation and retirement
in good or evil dayes had taught him. *David* indeed by suffering without just cause, learnt that meekness and that wisdom by adversity, which made him much the fitter man to
25 raigne. But they who suffer as oppressors, Tyrants, violaters
of Law, and persecutors of Reformation, without appearance
of repenting, if they once get hold againe of that dignity and
power which they had lost, are but whetted and inrag'd by

what they suffer'd against those whom they look upon as them that caus'd thir sufferings.

How he hath bin *subject to the scepter of Gods word and spirit,* though acknowledg'd to be the *best Goverment,* and what his *dispensation of civil power* hath bin, with what *Justice,* and what *honour to the public peace,* it is but looking back upon the whole catalogue of his deeds, and that will be sufficient to remember us. *The Cup of Gods physic,* as he calls it, what alteration it wrought in him to a firm *healthfulness* from any surfet, or excess wherof the people generally thought him sick, if any man would goe about to prove, we have his own testimony following heer, that it wrought none at all.

First, he hath the same fix'd opinion and esteem of his old *Ephesian* Goddess, call'd the *Church of England,* as he had ever; and charges strictly his Son after him to persevere in that Anti-Papal Scism (for it is not much better) as that *which will be necessary both for his soules, and the Kingdoms Peace.* But if this can be any foundation of the kingdoms peace, which was the first cause of our distractions, let common sense be Judge. It is a rule and principle worthy to be known by Christians, that no Scripture, no nor so much as any ancient Creed, bindes our Faith, or our obedience to any Church whatsoever, denominated by a particular name; farr less, if it be distinguisht by a several Goverment from that which is indeed Catholic. No man was ever bidd be subject to the Church of *Corinth, Rome,* or *Asia,* but to the Church without addition, as it held faithfull to the rules of

Scripture, and the Goverment establisht in all places by the
Apostles, which at first was universally the same in all
Churches and Congregations; not differing or distinguisht
by the diversity of Countries, Territories, or civil bounds.
5 That Church that from the name of a distinct place takes autority to set up a distinct Faith or Goverment, is a Scism
and Faction, not a Church. It were an injurie to condemn
the Papist of absurdity and contradiction, for adhering to his
Catholic Romish Religion, if we, for the pleasure of a King
10 and his politic considerations, shall adhere to a Catholic
English.

But suppose the Church of *England* were as it ought to be,
how is it to us the safer by being so nam'd and establisht,
when as that very name and establishment, by his contriving,
15 or approbation, serv'd for nothing els but to delude us and
amuse us, while the Church of *England* insensibly was almost chang'd and translated into the Church of *Rome*.
Which as every Man knows in general to be true, so the particular Treaties and Transactions tending to that conclusion,
20 are at large discover'd in a Book intitld the *English Pope*.
But when the people, discerning these abuses, began to call
for Reformation, in order to which the Parlament demanded of the King to unestablish that Prelatical Goverment, which without Scripture had usurpt over us, strait, as
25 *Pharoah* accus'd of Idleness the *Israelites* that sought leave to
goe and sacrifice to God, he layes faction to thir charge. And
that we may not hope to have ever any thing reform'd in
the Church either by him or his Son, he forewarnes him,

*That the Devil of Rebellion doth most commonly turn him-
self into an Angel of Reformation*: and sayes anough to
make him hate it, as the worst of Evils, and the bane of his
Crown: nay he counsels him to *let nothing seem little or des-*
5 *picable to him, so as not speedily and effectually to suppress
errors and Scisms.* Wherby we may perceave plainly that our
consciences were destin'd to the same servitude and persecution, if not wors then before, whether under him, or if it
should so happ'n, under his Son; who count all Protestant
10 Churches erroneous and scismatical, which are not episcopal.
His next precept is concerning our civil Liberties; which by
his sole voice and predominant will must be circumscrib'd,
and not permitted to extend a hands bredth furder then his
interpretation of *the Laws already settl'd.* And although all
15 human laws are but the offspring of that frailty, that fallibil-
ity, and imperfection which was in thir Authors, wherby
many Laws, in the change of ignorant and obscure Ages,
may be found both scandalous, and full of greevance to their
Posterity that made them, and no Law is furder good, then
20 mutable upon just occasion, yet if the removing of an old
Law, or the making of a new would save the Kingdom, we
shall not have it unless his arbitrary voice will so far slack'n
the stiff curb of his prerogative, as to grant it us; who are as
free born to make our own laws, as our fathers were who
25 made these we have. Where are then the English Liberties
which we boast to have bin left us by our Progenitors? To
that he answers, that *Our Liberties consist in the enjoyment
of the fruits of our industry, and the benefit of those Laws*

to which we our selves have consented. First, for the in-
joyment of those fruits, which our industry and labours
have made our own upon our own, what Privilege is that,
above what the *Turks, Jewes,* and *Mores* enjoy under the
5 Turkish Monarchy? For without that kind of Justice, which
is also in *Argiers,* among Theevs and Pirates between
themselvs, no kind of Goverment, no Societie, just or unjust
could stand; no combination or conspiracy could stick together. Which he also acknowledges in these words: *That if*
10 *the Crown upon his head be so heavy as to oppress the whole*
body, the weakness of inferiour members cannot return any
thing of strength, honour, or safety to the head; but that a
necessary debilitation must follow. So that this Liberty of the
Subject concerns himself and the subsistence of his own regal
15 power in the first place, and before the consideration of any
right belonging to the Subject. We expect therfore somthing
more, that must distinguish free Goverment from slavish.
But in stead of that, this King, though ever talking and protesting as smooth as now, sufferd it in his own hearing to be
20 Preacht and pleaded without controule, or check, by them
whom he most favourd and upheld, that the Subject had
no property of his own Goods, but that all was the Kings
right.

Next for the *benefit of those Laws to which we our selves*
25 *have consented,* we never had it under him; for not to speak
of Laws ill executed, when the Parlament, and in them the
people have consented to divers Laws, and, according to our
ancient Rights, demanded them, he took upon him to have a

negative will, as the transcendent and ultimat Law above all
our Laws; and to rule us forcibly by Laws to which we our
selves did not consent, but complain'd of. Thus these two
heads wherein the utmost of his allowance heer will give our
5 Liberties leave to consist, the one of them shall be so farr
onely made good to us, as may support his own interest, and
Crown, from *ruin* or *debilitation;* and so farr Turkish Vassals enjoy as much liberty under *Mahomet* and the Grand
Signor: the other we neither yet have enjoyd under him, nor
10 were ever like to doe under the Tyranny of a negative voice,
which he claimes above the unanimous consent and power of
a whole Nation virtually in the Parlament.

In which negative voice to have bin cast by the doom of
Warr, and put to death by those who vanquisht him in thir
15 own defence, he reck'ns to himself more then a negative
Martyrdom. But Martyrs bear witness to the truth, not to
themselves. If I beare witness of my self, saith *Christ,* my
witness is not true. He who writes himself *Martyr* by his own
inscription, is like an ill Painter, who, by writing on the
20 shapeless Picture which he hath drawn, is fain to tell passen-
gers what shape it is; which els no man could imagin: no
more then how a Martyrdom can belong to him, who therfore dyes for his Religion because it is *establisht.* Certainly if
Agrippa had turn'd Christian, as he was once turning, and
25 had put to death Scribes and Pharisees for observing the Law
of *Moses,* and refusing Christianitie, they had di'd a truer
Martyrdom. For those Laws were establisht by God and
Moses, these by no warrantable authors of Religion, whose

Laws in all other best reformed Churches are rejected. And
if to die for an establishment of Religion be Martyrdom,
then Romish Priests executed for that, which had so many
hundred yeares bin establisht in this Land, are no wors Mar-
5 tyrs then he. Lastly, if to die for *the testimony of his own
conscience,* be anough to make him Martyr, what Heretic
dying for direct blasphemie, as som have don constantly, may
not boast a Martyrdom? As for the constitution or repeale of
civil Laws, that power lying onely in the Parlament, which
10 he by the verry law of his coronation was to grant them, not
to debarr them, nor to preserve a lesser Law with the contempt and violation of a greater, it will conclude him not so
much as in a civil and metaphoricall sense to have di'd a Martyr of our Laws, but a plaine transgressor of them. And
15 should the Parlament, endu'd with Legislative power, make
our Laws, and be after to dispute them peece meale with the
reson, conscience, humour, passion, fansie, folly, obstinacy,
or other ends of one man, whose sole word and will shall baf-
fle and unmake what all the wisdom of a Parlament hath bin
20 deliberatly framing, what a ridiculous and contemptible
thing a Parlament would soon be, and what a base unworthy
Nation we, who boast our freedom, and send them with the
manifest peril of thir lives to preserve it, they who are not
mark'd by destiny for Slaves, may apprehend. In this servil
25 condition to have kept us still under hatches, he both resolves
heer to the last, and so instructs his Son.

As to those offerd condescensions of *Charitable conniv-
ence, or toleration,* if we consider what went before, and what

follows, they moulder into nothing. For what with not suffering *ever so little* to *seem a despicable* scism, without effectual suppression, as he warn'd him before, and what with *no
opposition of Law, Goverment, or establisht Religion* to be
5 permitted, which is his following proviso, and wholly within
his own construction, what a miserable and suspected toleration, under Spies and haunting Promooters we should enjoy,
is apparent. Besides that it is so farr beneath the honour of a
Parlament and free Nation, to begg and supplicat the God-
10 ship of one fraile Man, for the bare and simple toleration of
what they all consent to be both just, pious, and best pleasing
to God, while that which is erroneous, unjust, and mischeivous in the church or State, shall by him alone against them
all, be kept up and establisht; and they censur'd the while for
15 a *covetous, ambitious, & sacrilegious faction*.

Another bait to allure the people, is the charge he laies
upon his Son, to be tender of them. Which if we should beleeve in part, because they are his Heard, his Cattell, the Stock
upon his ground, as he accounts them, whom to wast and de-
20 stroy would undoe himself, yet the inducement which he
brings to move him, renders the motion it self somthing suspicious. For if Princes *need no Palliations,* as he tells his Son,
wherfore is it that he himself hath so oft'n us'd them? Princes
of all other men, have not more change of Rayment in thir
25 Wardrobes, then variety of Shifts and *palliations* in thir solemn actings and pretences to the People.

To try next if he can insnare the prime Men of those who
have oppos'd him, whom, more truly then his meaning was,

he calls the *Patrons and Vindicators of the People,* he gives out *Indemnity,* and offers *Acts of Oblivion.* But they who with a good conscience and upright heart, did thir civil duties in the sight of God, and in thir several places, to resist Tyr-

5 anny, and the violence of Superstition banded both against them, he may be sure will never seek to be forgiv'n that, which may be justly attributed to thir immortal praise; nor will assent ever to the guilty blotting out of those actions before men, by which thir Faith assures them they chiefly stand

10 approv'd, and are had in remembrance before the throne of God.

He exhorts his son *not to study reveng.* But how far he, or at least they about him, intend to follow that exhortation, was seen lately at the *Hague,* & now lateliest at *Madrid:*

15 where to execute in the basest manner, though but the smallest part of that savage & barbarous revenge which they doe no thing els but *study* & contemplate, they car'd not to let the world know them for profess'd Traitors & assassinaters of all Law both Divine and human, eev'n of that last and most ex-

20 tensive Law kept inviolable to public persons among all fair enemies in the midst of uttermost defiance and hostility. How implacable therfore they would be, after any termes of closure or admittance for the future, or any like opportunity giv'n them heerafter, it will be wisdom & our safety to beleeve

25 rather and prevent, then to make triall. And it will concerne the multitude, though courted heer, to take heed how they seek to hide or colour thir own fickleness and instability with a bad repentance of thir well-doing, and thir fidelity to the

better cause; to which at first so cherfully and conscien-
tiously they joyn'd themselves.

He returnes againe to extoll *the Church of England,* and
againe requires his Son by the joynt autority of *a Father and*
5 *a King, not to let his heart receive the least check, or disaffec-*
tion against it. And not without cause, for by that meanes
having sole influence upon the Clergy, and they upon the
people, *after long search and many disputes,* he could not
possibly find a more compendious and politic way to uphold
10 and settle Tyranny, then by subduing first the Consciences of
Vulgar men, with the insensible poyson of thir slavish Doctrin: for then the bodie and besotted mind without much Re-
luctancy was likeliest to admitt the Yoke.

He commends also *Parlaments held with freedome and*
15 with *Honour.* But I would ask how that can bee, while he
onely must be the sole free Person in that number; and would
have the power with his unaccountable denyall, to dishonour
them by rejecting all thir Counsels, to confine thir Law-giv-
ing power, which is the Foundation of our freedom, and to
20 change at his pleasure the very name of a Parlament into the
name of a Faction.

The conclusion therfore must needs be quite contrary to
what he concludes; that nothing can be more *unhappy,* more
dishonourable, more unsafe *for all,* then when a wise, *grave,*
25 *& honourable Parlament* shal have labourd, debated, argu'd,
consulted, and, as he himself speakes, *contributed* for the
public good *all thir Counsels in common,* to be then frustrated, disappointed, deny'd and repuls'd by the single whiffe

of a negative, from the mouth of one wilfull man; nay to be
blasted, to be struck as mute and motionless as a Parlament
of Tapstrie in the Hangings; or els after all thir paines and
travell to be dissolv'd, and cast away like so many Naughts
5 in Arithmetick, unless it be to turne the O of thir insignifi-
cance into a lamentation with the people, who had so vainly
sent them. For this is not to *enact all things by public consent,* as he would have us be perswaded, this is to enact nothing but by the privat consent and leave of one not negative
10 tyrant; this is mischeif without remedy, a stifleing and obstructing evil that hath no vent, no outlet, no passage through:
Grant him this, and the Parlament hath no more freedom
then if it sate in his Noose, which when he pleases to draw
together with one twitch of his Negative, shall throttle a
15 whole Nation, to the wish of *Caligula* in one neck. This with
the power of the Militia in his own hands over our bodies and
estates, and the Prelats to enthrall our consciences either by
fraud or force, is the sum of that happiness and liberty we
were to look for, whether in his own restitution, or in these
20 precepts giv'n to his son. Which unavoidably would have set
us in the same state of miserie, wherein we were before; and
have either compell'd us to submitt like bond slaves, or put
us back to a second wandring over that horrid Wilderness of
distraction and civil slaughter, which, not without the strong
25 and miraculous hand of God assisting us, we have measur'd
out, and surviv'd. And who knows, if we make so slight of
this incomparable deliverance, which God hath bestowd upon
us, but that we shall like those foolish *Israelites,* who depos'd

God and *Samuel* to set up a King, *Cry out* one day *because of
our King,* which we have bin mad upon; and then God, as
he foretold them, will no more deliver us.

  There remaines now but little more of his discours, wher-
5 of yet to take a short view will not be amiss. His words make
semblance as if he were magnanimously exercising himself,
and so teaching his Son, *To want as well as to weare a Crown;*
and would seem to account it *not worth taking up or enjoying
upon sordid, dishonourable, and irreligious termes;* and yet
10 to his very last did nothing more industriously then strive to
take up and enjoy againe his sequesterd Crown, upon the
most sordid, disloyal, dishonourable, and irreligious termes,
not of making peace onely, but of joyning and incorporating
with the murdrous Irish, formerly by himself declar'd against,
15 for *wicked and detestable Rebells, odious to God and all good
Men.* And who but those Rebels now, are the chief strength
and confidence of his Son? while the Presbyter Scot that
wooes and solicits him, is neglected and put off, as if no
termes were to him sordid, irreligious and dishonourable, but
20 the Scotish and Presbyterian, never to be comply'd with, till
the feare of instant perishing starve him out at length to some
unsound and hypocriticall agreement.

  He bids his Son *Keep to the true principles of piety, vertue, and honour, and he shall never want a Kingdom.* And
25 I say, People of *England,* keep ye to those principles, and ye
shall never want a King. Nay after such a faire deliverance
as this, with so much fortitude and valour shown against a
Tyrant, that people that should seek a King, claiming what

this Man claimes, would shew themselves to be by nature slaves, and arrant beasts; not fitt for that liberty which they cri'd out and bellow'd for, but fitter to be led back again into thir old servitude, like a sort of clamouring & fighting brutes, 5 broke loos from thir copyholds, that know not how to use or possess the liberty which they fought for; but with the faire words & promises of an old exasperated foe, are ready to be stroak'd & tam'd again, into the wonted and well pleasing state of thir true Norman villenage, to them best agreeable.

10 The last sentence, wheron he seems to venture the whole waight of all his former reasons and argumentations, *That Religion to thir God, and loyalty to thir King cannot be parted, without the sin and infelicity of a People,* is contrary to the plaine teaching of Christ, that *No man can serve two* 15 *Masters,* but, if he hold to the one, he must reject and forsake the other. If God then and earthly Kings be for the most part not several onely, but opposite Maisters, it will as oft happ'n, that they who will serve thir King must forsake thir God; and they who will serve God must forsake thir King; which 20 then will neither be thir sin, nor thir infelicity; but thir wisdom, thir piety, and thir true happiness; as to be deluded by these unsound and suttle ostentations heer, would be thir misery; and in all likelyhood much greater then what they hitherto have undergon: if now againe intoxicated and 25 moap'd with these royal, and therfore so delicious because royal rudiments of bondage, the Cup of deception, spic'd and temperd to thir bane, they should deliver up themselves to these glozing words and illusions of him, whose rage

and utmost violence they have sustain'd, and overcomm so
nobly.

XXVIII. *Intitl'd Meditations upon Death.*

IT might be well thought by him who reads no furder
then the Title of this last Essay, that it requir'd no
answer. For all other human things are disputed, and
will be variously thought of to the Worlds end. But this business of death is a plaine case, and admitts no controversie:
In that center all Opinions meet. Nevertheless, since out of
those few mortifying howrs that should have bin intirest to
themselves, and most at peace from all passion and disquiet,
he can afford spare time to enveigh bitterly against that Justice which was don upon him, it will be needfull to say somthing in defence of those proceedings; though breifly, in
regard so much on this Subject hath been Writt'n lately.

It happn'd once, as we find in *Esdras* and *Josephus,* Authors not less beleiv'd then any under sacred, to be a great and
solemn debate in the Court of *Darius,* what thing was to be
counted strongest of all other. He that could resolve this, in
reward of his excelling wisdom, should be clad in Purple,
drink in Gold, sleep on a Bed of Gold, and sitt next *Darius.*
None but they doubtless who were reputed wise, had the
Question propounded to them. Who after som respit giv'n
them by the King to consider, in full Assembly of all his
Lords and gravest Counselors, returnd severally what they

thought. The first held that Wine was strongest; another that the King was strongest. But *Zorobabel* Prince of the Captive Jewes, and Heire to the Crown of Judah, being one of them, proov'd Women to be stronger then the King, for that he
5 himself had seen a Concubin take his Crown from off his head to set it upon her own: And others besides him have lately seen the like Feat don, and not in jest. Yet he proov'd on, and it was so yeilded by the King himself, & all his sages, that neither Wine nor Women, nor the King, but Truth, of
10 all other things was the strongest. For me, though neither ask'd, nor in a Nation that gives such rewards to wisdom, I shall pronounce my sentence somwhat different from *Zoro-babel;* and shall defend, that either Truth and Justice are all one, for Truth is but Justice in our knowledge, and Justice is
15 but Truth in our practice, and he indeed so explaines himself in saying that with Truth is no accepting of Persons, which is the property of Justice; or els, if there be any odds, that Justice, though not stronger then truth, yet by her office is to put forth and exhibit more strength in the affaires of man-
20 kind. For Truth is properly no more then Contemplation; and her utmost efficiency is but teaching: but Justice in her very essence is all strength and activity; and hath a Sword put into her hand, to use against all violence and oppression on the earth. Shee it is most truely, who accepts no Person, and
25 exempts none from the severity of her stroke. Shee never suffers injury to prevaile, but when falshood first prevailes over Truth; and that also is a kind of Justice don on them who are so deluded. Though wicked Kings and Tyrants

counterfet her Sword, as som did that Buckler, fabl'd to fall
from Heav'n into the Capitol, yet shee communicates her
power to none but such as like her self are just, or at least will
do Justice. For it were extreme partialitie and injustice, the
5 flat denyall and overthrow of her self, to put her own authentic Sword into the hand of an unjust and wicked Man, or so
farr to accept and exalt one mortal person above his equals,
that he alone shall have the punishing of all other men transgressing, and not receive like punishment from men, when
10 he himself shall be found the highest transgressor.

   We may conclude therfore that Justice, above all other
things, is and ought to be the strongest: Shee is the strength,
the Kingdom, the power and majestie of all Ages. Truth her
self would subscribe to this, though *Darius* and all the Mon-
15 archs of the World should deny. And if by sentence thus
writt'n it were my happiness to set free the minds of English
men from longing to returne poorly under that Captivity of
Kings, from which the strength and supreme Sword of Justice hath deliverd them, I shall have don a work not much
20 inferior to that of *Zorobabel:* who by well praising and extolling the force of Truth, in that contemplative strength conquer'd *Darius;* and freed his Countrey, and the people of God
from the Captivity of *Babylon.* Which I shall yet not despaire to doe, if they in this Land whose minds are yet Cap-
25 tive, be but as ingenuous to acknowledge the strength and
supremacie of Justice, as that heathen king was, to confess
the strength of truth: or let them but as he did, grant that,
and they will soon perceave that Truth resignes all her out-

ward strength to Justice: Justice therfore must needs be strongest, both in her own and in the strength of Truth. But if a King may doe among men whatsoever is his will and pleasure, and notwithstanding be unaccountable to men, then contrary to this magnifi'd wisdom of *Zorobabel,* neither Truth nor Justice, but the King is strongest of all other things: which that Persian Monarch himself in the midst of all his pride and glory durst not assume.

Let us see therfore what this King hath to affirm, why the sentence of Justice and the weight of that Sword which shee delivers into the hands of men, should be more partial to him offending, then to all others of human race. First he pleades that *No Law of God or man gives to subjects any power of judicature without or against him.* Which assertion shall be prov'd in every part to be most untrue. The first express Law of God giv'n to mankind, was that to *Noah,* as a Law in general to all the Sons of men. And by that most ancient and universal Law, *whosoever sheddeth mans blood, by man shall his blood be shed;* we find heer no exception. If a king therfore doe this, to a King, and that by men also, the same shall be don. This in the Law of *Moses,* which came next, several times is repeated, and in one place remarkably, *Numb.* 35. *Ye shall take no satisfaction for the life of a murderer, but he shall surely be put to death: the Land cannot be cleansed of the blood that is shedd therein,* but by the blood of him that shed it. This is so spok'n, as that which concern'd all *Israel,* not one man alone to see perform'd; and if no satisfaction were to be tak'n, then certainly no exception. Nay the King,

when they should set up any, was to observe the whole Law, and not onely to see it don, but to *do it; that his heart might not be lifted up above his Brethren,* to dreame of vain and reasonless prerogatives or exemptions, wherby the Law it
5 self must needs be founded in unrighteousness.

And were that true, which is most fals, that all Kings are the Lords Anointed, it were yet absurd to think that the Anointment of God, should be as it were a charme against Law; and give them privilege who punish others, to sin
10 themselves unpunishably. The high Preist was the Lords anointed as well as any King, and with the same consecrated oile: yet *Salomon* had put to death *Abiathar,* had it not bin for other respects then that anointment. If God himself say to Kings, *Touch not mine anointed,* meaning his chos'n
15 people, as is evident in that Psalme, yet no man will argue thence, that he protects them from Civil Laws if they offend, then certainly, though *David* as a privat man, and in his own cause, feard to lift his hand against the Lords Anointed, much less can this forbidd the Law, or disarm justice from having
20 legal power against any King. No other supreme Magistrate in what kind of Goverment soever laies claim to any such enormous Privilege; wherfore then should any King, who is but one kind of Magistrat, and set over the people for no other end then they?
25 Next in order of time to the Laws of *Moses,* are those of Christ, who declares professedly his judicature to be spiritual, abstract from Civil managements, and therfore leaves all Nations to thir own particular Lawes, and way of Goverment.

Yet because the Church hath a kind of Jurisdiction within her own bounds, and that also, though in process of time much corrupted and plainly turn'd into a corporal judicature, yet much approv'd by this King, it will be firm anough and valid against him, if subjects, by the Laws of Church also, be *invested with a power of judicature* both without and against thir King, though pretending, and by them acknowledg'd *next and immediatly under Christ supreme head and Governour.* *Theodosius* one of the best Christian Emperours having made a slaughter of the *Thessalonians* for sedition, but too cruelly, was excommunicated to his face by Saint *Ambrose,* who was his subject: and excommunion is the utmost of Ecclesiastical Judicature, a spiritual putting to death. But this, yee will say, was onely an example. Read then the Story; and it will appeare, both that *Ambrose* avouch'd it for the Law of God, and *Theodosius* confess'd it of his own accord to be so; *and that the Law of God was not to be made voyd in him, for any reverence to his Imperial power.* From hence, not to be tedious, I shall pass into our own Land of *Britain;* and shew that Subjects heer have exercis'd the utmost of spirituall Judicature and more then spirituall against thir Kings, his *Predecessors.* *Vortiger* for committing incest with his daughter was by *Saint German,* at that time his subject, cursd and condemnd in a Brittish Counsel about the yeare 448; and thereupon soon after was depos'd. *Mauricus* a King in *Wales,* for breach of Oath and the murder of *Cynetus* was excomunicated, and curst with all his offspring, by *Oudoceus* Bishop of *Landaff* in full Synod, about the yeare 560;

and not restor'd, till he had repented. *Morcant* another King in *Wales* having slain *Frioc* his Uncle, was faine to come in Person and receave judgement from the same Bishop and his Clergie; who upon his penitence acquitted him, for no other
5 cause then lest the Kingdom should be destitute of a Successour in the Royal Line. These examples are of the Primitive, Brittish, and Episcopal Church; long ere they had any commerce or communion with the Church of *Rome*. What power afterward of deposing Kings, and so consequently of putting
10 them to death, was assum'd and practis'd by the Canon Law, I omitt as a thing generally known. Certainly if whole Councels of the Romish Church have in the midst of their dimness discern'd so much of Truth, as to decree at *Constance,* and at *Basil,* and many of them to avouch at *Trent* also, that a
15 Councel is above the Pope, and may judge him, though by them not deni'd to be the Vicar of Christ, we in our clearer light may be asham'd not to discern furder, that a Parlament is, by all equity, and right, above a King, and may judge him, whose reasons and pretensions to hold of God onely, as his
20 immediat Vicegerent, we know how farr fetch'd they are, and insufficient.

As for the Laws of man, it would ask a Volume to repeat all that might be cited in this point against him from all Antiquity. In Greece, *Orestes* the Son of *Agamemnon,* and by
25 succession King of *Argos,* was in that Countrey judg'd and condemn'd to death for killing his Mother: whence escaping, he was judg'd againe, though a Stranger, before the great Counsel of *Areopagus* in *Athens.* And this memorable

act of Judicature, was the first that brought the Justice of that grave Senat into fame and high estimation over all *Greece* for many ages after. And in the same Citty Tyrants were to undergoe Legal sentence by the Laws of *Solon*. The Kings

5 of *Sparta,* though descended lineally from *Hercules* esteem'd a God among them, were oft'n judg'd, and somtimes put to death by the most just and renowned Laws of *Lycurgus;* who, though a King, thought it most unequal to bind his Subjects by any Law, to which he bound not himself. In

10 *Rome* the Laws made by *Valerius Publicola* soon after the expelling of *Tarquin* and his race, expell'd without a writt'n Law, the Law beeing afterward writt'n, and what the Senat decreed against *Nero,* that he should be judg'd and punish'd according to the Laws of thir Ancestors, and what in like

15 manner was decreed against other Emperours, is vulgarly known; as it was known to those heathen, and found just by nature ere any Law mentiond it. And that the Christian Civil Law warrants like power of Judicature to Subjects against Tyrants, is writt'n clearly by the best and famousest

20 Civilians. For if it was decreed by *Theodosius,* and stands yet firme in the Code of *Justinian,* that the Law is above the Emperour, then certainly the Emperour being under Law, the Law may judge him, and if judge him, may punish him proving tyrannous: how els is the Law above him, or to what

25 purpose. These are necessary deductions; and therafter hath bin don in all Ages and Kingdoms, oftner then to be heer recited.

But what need we any furder search after the Law of

other Lands, for that which is so fully and so plainly set
down lawfull in our own. Where ancient Books tell us, *Brac-
ton, Fleta,* and others, that the King is under Law, and inferiour to his Court of Parlament; that although his place *to*
5 *doe Justice* be highest, yet that he stands as liable *to receave
Justice,* as the meanest of his Kingdom. Nay *Alfred* the most
worthy King, and by som accounted first absolute Monarch
of the Saxons heer, so ordain'd: as is cited out of an ancient
Law Book call'd the *Mirror,* in *Rights of the Kingdom,* p. 31.
10 where it is complain'd on, *As the sovran abuse of all,* that *the
King should be deem'd above the Law, whereas he ought be
subject to it by his Oath:* Of which Oath anciently it was the
last clause, that the King *should be as liable, and obedient to
suffer right, as others of his people.* And indeed it were but
15 fond and sensless, that the King should be accountable to
every petty suit in lesser Courts, as we all know he was, and
not be subject to the Judicature of Parlament in the main
matters of our common safety or destruction; that he should
be answerable in the ordinary cours of Law for any wrong
20 don to a privat Person, and not answerable in Court of Parlament for destroying the whole Kingdom. By all this, and
much more that might be added as in an argument over-
copious rather then barren, we see it manifest that all Laws
both of God and Man are made without exemption of any
25 person whomsoever; and that if Kings presume to overtopp
the Law by which they raigne for the public good, they are
by Law to be reduc'd into order: and that can no way be more
justly, then by those who exalted them to that high place.

For who should better understand thir own Laws, and when
they are transgrest, then they who are govern'd by them, and
whose consent first made them: and who can have more right
to take knowledge of things don within a free Nation, then
5 they within themselves?

Those objected Oaths of Allegeance and Supremacy we
swore, not to his Person, but as it was invested with his Autority; and his autority was by the People first giv'n him conditionally, in Law and under Law, and under Oath also for
10 the Kingdoms good, and not otherwise: the Oathes then were
interchang'd, and mutual; stood and fell together; he swore
fidelity to his trust (not as a deluding ceremony, but as a real
condition of thir admitting him for King; and the Conqueror
himself swore it ofter then at his Crowning) they swore
15 Homage, and Fealty to his Person in that trust. There was
no reason why the Kingdom should be furder bound by
Oaths to him, then he by his Coronation Oath to us, which
he hath every way brok'n; and having brok'n, the ancient
Crown-Oath of *Alfred* above mention'd, conceales not his
20 penalty.

As for the Covnant, if that be meant, certainly no discreet
Person can imagin it should bind us to him in any stricter
sense then those Oaths formerly. The acts of Hostility which
we receav'd from him, were no such dear obligements that
25 we should ow him more fealty and defence for being our
Enemy, then we could before when we took him onely for a
King. They were accus'd by him and his Party to pretend
Liberty and Reformation, but to have no other end then to

make themselves great, and to destroy the Kings Person and autority. For which reason they added that third Article, testifying to the World, that as they were resolvd to endeavor first a Reformation in the Church, to extirpat Prelacy, to pre-
5 serve the Rights of Parlament, and the Liberties of the King-dom, so they intended, so farr as it might consist with the preservation and defence of these, to preserve the Kings Per-son and Autority; but not otherwise. As farr as this comes to, they Covnant and Swear in the sixth Article to preserve and
10 defend the persons and autority of one another, and all those that enter into that League; so that this Covnant gives no un-limitable exemption to the Kings Person, but gives to all as much defence and preservation as to him, and to him as much as to thir own Persons, and no more; that is to say, in order
15 and subordination to those maine ends for which we live and are a Nation of men joynd in society either Christian or at least human. But if the Covnant were made absolute, to pre-serve and defend any one whomsoever, without respect had, either to the true Religion, or those other Superiour things
20 to be defended and preserv'd however, it cannot then be doubted, but that the Covnant was rather a most foolish, hasty, and unlawfull Vow, then a deliberate and well-waighd Covnant; swearing us into labyrinths, and repugnances, no way to be solv'd or reconcil'd, and therfore no way to be kept:
25 as first offending against the Law of God, to Vow the abso-lute preservation, defence, and maintaining of one Man though in his sins and offences never so great and hainous against God or his Neighbour; and to except a Person from

Justice, wheras his Law excepts none. Secondly, it offends
against the Law of this Nation, wherein, as hath bin prov'd,
Kings in receiving Justice, & undergoing due tryal, are not
differenc'd from the meanest Subject. Lastly, it contradicts
5 and offends against the Covnant it self, which Vows in the
fourth Article to bring to op'n trial and condign punishment
all those that shall be found guilty of such crimes and Delin-
quencies, wherof the King by his own Letters and other undeniable testimonies not brought to light till afterward, was
10 found and convicted to be cheif actor, in what they thought
him at the time of taking that Covnant, to be overrul'd onely
by evil Counselers. And those, or whomsoever they should
discover to be principal, they vow'd to try, *either by thir own
supreme Judicatories,* for so eev'n then they call'd them, *or
15 by others having power from them to that effect.* So that to
have brought the King to condign punishment hath not
broke the Covnant, but it would have broke the Covnant to
have sav'd him from those Judicatories, which both Nations
declar'd in that Covnant to be *Supreme* against any person
20 whatsoever. And besides all this, to sweare in covnant the
bringing of his evil counselers and accomplices to condign
punishment, and not onely to leave unpunisht and untoucht
the grand offender, but to receive him back againe from the
accomplishment of so many violences and mischeifs, dipt
25 from head to foot and staind over with the blood of thousands that were his faithfull subjects, forc'd to thir own defence against a civil Warr by him first rais'd upon them, and
to receive him thus, in this goarie pickle, to all his dignities

and honours, covering the ignominious and horrid purple-
robe of innocent blood that sate so close about him, with the
glorious purple of Royaltie and Supreme Rule, the reward of
highest excellence and vertue here on earth, were not only
5 to sweare and covnant the performance of an unjust Vow, the
strangest and most impious to the face of God, but were the
most unwise and unprudential act as to civil goverment. For
so long as a King shall find by experience that doe the worst
he can, his Subjects, overaw'd by the Religion of thir own
10 Covnant, will only prosecute his evil instruments, not dare
to touch his Person, and that whatever hath bin on his part
offended or transgress'd, he shall come off at last with the
same reverence to his Person, and the same honour as for
well doing, he will not faile to finde them worke; seeking
15 farr and neere, and inviting to his Court all the concours of
evil counselers or agents that may be found: who tempted
with preferments and his promise to uphold them, will hazard easily thir own heads, and the chance of ten to one but
they shall prevaile at last, over men so quell'd and fitted to be
20 slaves by the fals conceit of a Religious Covnant? And they
in that Superstition neither wholly yeilding, nor to the utmost resisting, at the upshot of all thir foolish Warr and expence, will finde to have don no more but fetchd a compass
only of thir miseries, ending at the same point of slavery, and
25 in the same distractions wherin they first begun. But when
Kings themselves are made as liable to punishment as thir
evil counselers, it will be both as dangerous from the King
himself as from his Parlament, to those that evil-counsel him,

and they who else would be his readiest Agents in evil, will then not feare to disswade or to disobey him, not onely in respect of themselves and thir own lives, which for his sake they would not seem to value but in respect of that danger 5 which the King himself may incurr, whom they would seem to love and serve with greatest fidelitie. On all these grounds therfor of the covnant it self, whether religious or political, it appeares likeliest, that both the English Parlament, and the Scotch Commissioners thus interpreting the Covnant (as in- 10 deed at that time they were the best and most authentical interpreters joyn'd together) answerd the King unanimously, in thir Letters dated *Jan.* 13th 1645. that till securitie and satisfaction first giv'n to both Kingdoms for the blood spilt, for the Irish Rebels brought over, and for the Warr in *Ireland* 15 by him fomented, they could in no wise yeild thir consent to his returne. Here was satisfaction, full two yeares and up- ward after the Covnant tak'n, demanded of the King by both Nations in Parlament, for crimes at least Capital, wherwith they charg'd him. And what satisfaction could be giv'n for 20 so much blood, but Justice upon him that spilt it? Till which don, they neither took themselves bound to grant him the exercise of his regal Office by any meaning of the Covnant which they then declar'd (though other meanings have bin since contriv'd) not so much regarded the safety of his per- 25 son, as to admitt of his return among them from the midst of those whom they declar'd to be his greatest enemies; nay from himself as from an actual enemy, not as from a king, they demanded security. But if the covnant all this notwith-

standing swore otherwise to preserv him then in the preservation of true religion & our liberties, against which he
fought, if not in armes, yet in resolution to his dying day, and
now after death still fights against in this his book, the cov-
5 nant was better brok'n, then he sav'd. And god hath testi-
fi'd by all propitious, & the most evident signes, whereby in
these latter times he is wont to testifie what pleases him; that
such a solemn, and for many Ages unexampl'd act of due
punishment, was no *mockery of Justice,* but a most gratefull
10 and well-pleasing Sacrifice. Neither was it *to cover their
perjury* as he accuses, but to uncover his perjury to the Oath
of his Coronation.

The rest of his discours quite forgets the Title; and turns
his Meditations upon death into obloquie and bitter vehe-
15 mence against his *Judges and accusers;* imitating therin, not
our Saviour, but his Grand-mother *Mary* Queen of Scots, as
also in the most of his other scruples, exceptions and evasions:
and from whom he seems to have learnt, as it were by heart,
or els by kind, that which is thought by his admirers to be the
20 most vertuous, most manly, most Christian, and most Mar-
tyr-like both of his words and speeches heer, and of his answers and behaviour at his Tryall.

It is a sad fate, he saith, *to have his Enemies both accusers,
Parties, and Judges.* Sad indeed, but no sufficient Plea to ac-
25 quitt him from being so judg'd. For what Malefactor might
not somtimes plead the like? If his own crimes have made
all men his Enemies, who els can judge him? They of the
Powder-plot against his Father might as well have pleaded

the same. Nay at the Resurrection it may as well be pleaded, that the Saints who then shall judge the World, are *both Enemies, Judges, Parties, and Accusers.*

So much he thinks to abound in his own defence, that he
5 undertakes an unmeasurable task; to bespeak *the singular care and protection of God over all Kings,* as *being the greatest Patrons of Law, Justice, Order, and Religion on Earth.* But what Patrons they be, God in the Scripture oft anough hath exprest; and the earth it self hath too long groan'd
10 under the burd'n of thir injustice, disorder, and irreligion. Therfore *To bind thir Kings in Chaines, and thir Nobles with links of Iron,* is an honour belonging to his Saints; not to build *Babel* (which was *Nimrods* work the first King, *and the beginning of his Kingdom was Babel*) but to destroy it,
15 especially that spiritual *Babel:* and first to overcome those European Kings, which receive thir power, not from God, but from the beast; and are counted no better then his ten hornes. *These shall hate the great Whore,* and yet *shall give thir Kingdoms to the Beast that carries her; they shall com-*
20 *mitt Fornication with her,* and yet *shall burn her with fire,* and yet *shall lament the fall of Babylon,* where they fornicated with her. *Rev.* 17. & 18. chapt.

Thus shall they be too and fro, doubtfull and ambiguous in all thir doings, untill at last, *joyning thir Armies with the*
25 *Beast,* whose power first rais'd them, they shall perish with him by the *King of Kings* against whom they have rebell'd; and *the Foules shall eat thir flesh.* This is thir doom writt'n, *Rev.* 19. and the utmost that we find concerning them in

these latter days; which we have much more cause to beleeve, then his unwarranted Revelation here, prophecying what shall follow after his death, with the spirit of Enmity, not of Saint *John*.

5   He would fain bring us out of conceit with the good *success* which God hath voutsaf'd us. Wee measure not our Cause by our success, but our success by our cause. Yet certainly in a good Cause success is a good confirmation; for God hath promis'd it to good men almost in every leafe of 10 Scripture. If it argue not for us, we are sure it argues not against us; but as much or more for us, then ill success argues for them; for to the wicked, God hath denounc'd ill success in all that they take in hand.

He hopes much of those *softer tempers,* as he calls them, 15 and *less advantag'd by his ruin, that thir consciences doe already* gripe them. Tis true, there be a sort of moodie, hotbrain'd, and alwayes unedify'd consciences; apt to engage thir Leaders into great and dangerous affaires past retirement, and then, upon a sudden qualm and swimming of thir conscience, 20 to betray them basely in the midst of what was cheifly undertak'n for their sakes. Let such men never meet with any faithfull Parlament to hazzard for them; never with any noble spirit to conduct and lead them out, but let them live and die in servil condition and thir scrupulous queasiness, if no in-25 struction will confirme them. Others there be in whose consciences the loss of gaine, and those advantages they hop'd for, hath sprung a sudden leake. These are they that cry out the Covnant brok'n, and to keep it better slide back into neu-

trality, or joyn actually with Incendiaries and Malignants. But God hath eminently begun to punish those, first in *Scotland,* then in *Ulster,* who have provok'd him with the most hatefull kind of mockery, to break his Covnant under pre-
5 tence of strictest keeping it; and hath subjected them to those Malignants, with whom they scrupl'd not to be associats. In God therfore we shall not feare what their fals fraternity can doe against us.

He seeks againe with cunning words to turn our success
10 into our sin. But might call to mind, that the Scripture speakes of those also, who *when God slew them, then sought him;* yet did but *flatter him with thir mouth, and ly'd to him with thir tongues; for thir heart was not right with him.* And there was one, who in the time of his affliction trespass'd
15 more against God; *This was that King Ahaz.*

He glories much in the forgivness of his Enemies; so did his Grandmother at her death. Wise men would sooner have beleev'd him had he not so oft'n told us so. But he hopes to erect *the Trophies of his charity over us.* And Trophies of
20 Charity no doubt will be as *glorious* as Trumpets before the almes of Hypocrites; and more especially the Trophies of such an aspiring charitie as offers in his Prayer to share Victory with Gods *compassion,* which is over all his works. Such Prayers as these may happly catch the People, as was in-
25 tended: but how they please God, is to be much doubted, though pray'd in secret, much less writt'n to be divulg'd. Which perhaps may gaine him after death a short, contempt-ible, and soon fading reward; not what he aims at, to stirr

the constancie and solid firmness of any wise Man, or to un-
settle the conscience of any knowing Christian, if he could
ever aime at a thing so hopeless, and above the genius of his
Cleric elocution, but to catch the worthles approbation of an
5 inconstant, irrational, and Image-doting rabble; that like a
credulous and hapless herd, begott'n to servility, and inchanted with these popular institutes of Tyranny, subscrib'd
with a new device of the Kings Picture at his praiers, hold out
both thir eares with such delight and ravishment to be stig-
10 matiz'd and board through in witness of thir own voluntary
and beloved baseness. The rest, whom perhaps ignorance
without malice, or some error, less then fatal, hath for the
time misledd, on this side Sorcery or obduration, may find
the grace and good guidance to bethink themselves, and
15 recover.

The End.

NOTES

THE TENURE OF KINGS AND MAGISTRATES

THE *Tenure of Kings and Magistrates* was first published in London in 1649, printed by Matthew Simmons "at the Gilded Lyon in Aldersgate Street." Internal evidence indicates that it was composed during the trial of Charles I, which began on January 20 and concluded in the execution of the king on January 30. On the title-page of the copy in the Thomason Collection appears in Thomason's autograph the date, February 13. The only acknowledgment of authorship which appears in the book itself is found on the title-page in the words, "The Author, J. M." The initial "M." was expanded by Thomason in his copy to "Milton." Milton himself states in the *Second Defence* that, after the execution of Charles, he published a book to show "what might lawfully be done against tyrants." The first edition of this work was followed in about a year by a second, which is extant in two slightly different states. On the title-page of the first, represented by a copy in the New York Public Library, the book is said to have been printed "at the Gilded Lyon in Aldersgate Street," and the date is given as 1649. On the title-page of the second, represented by a copy in the Yale University Library, the book is said to have been printed "next doore to the Gil-Lyon in Aldersgate Street," and the date is 1650. In each state the title-page is otherwise identical with that of the first edition except for the addition of the words, "Published now the second time with some additions, and many Testimonies also added out of the best & learnedest

Protestant Divines asserting the position of this book." A copy of the second edition in its second state is found in the Thomason Collection with the date, "February 15," entered on the title-page in Thomason's hand. The text of the second edition varies from the first in what appear to be casual differences in spelling and punctuation, in occasional changes of phraseology, in a few slight additions throughout the work, and in the addition at the end of several pages of testimonies of Protestant divines referred to in the title-page. Except for the title-page, the second state of the second edition varies from the first only at two points and then only in spelling.

The text of the present edition has been set up from a photostat of the Yale copy of the second or 1650 state of the second edition. A few turned letters and other slight typographical errors have been silently rectified. A few obvious mistakes in spelling and punctuation have been corrected and recorded in the notes. The text as given has been collated with the New York Public Library copy of the first or 1649 state of the second edition and with the Yale copy of the first edition of 1649. A copy of the first edition in the New York Public Library appears to be identical with the Yale copy. In the notes to the present edition the Yale copy of the first edition is referred to as 1, the New York Public Library copy of the first state of the second edition as 2, and the Yale copy of the second state of the second edition as 3. With the exceptions mentioned above, the notes record all variants. When no contrary indication appears, the variant recorded is to be found only in 1.

Page 1

—1 men] Men   —2, 14, 15, 18, 19 thir] their   —3 Custom] custome   —4 better,] better   —6 doors] doores   —14 Maisters] Masters   —16 Tyrants] Tirants   alwayes] alwaies —17 *Loyalty,*] *Loyalty*   —18 somtimes] sometimes

Page 2

—1, 8, 10, 15, 16, 18, 25 thir] their   —1 vertue] vertue, —2 writt'n] written   —3 *Jer.* 48.19.] Jer. 48.10.   —4, 6, 12 only] onely   —4 thraldoms] thraldomes   People] people —7 mischiefs] mischiefes   —8 world] World   born] borne —9 disannointed] disanointed   Pulpits] Pulpits,   —10 real] reall —14 necessary] necessarie   —15, 17, 25 own] owne   —18 accessory;] accessory,   —19 Lawes] Laws   —21 Traytors death,] traytors death   don] done   —23 flash] flash,   —26 half] halfe   —27 wickednes] wickednesse   —28 joyn'd] join'd   causes,] causes

Page 3

—1 whereof] which they   capable] capable of   —2 If] NO PARAGRAPH   —3 wherof] whereof   draws] drawes   —4 Goverment] Government   downfal] downfall   —5, 9, 11, 14, 15, 22 thir] their   —5 families] Families   —6 enterprize] Enterprize   —6, 27 be] bee   —7 Vulgar] vulgar   —8 irrational] irrationall   privileges] Privileges   customs] customes   forms] formes   —9 entanglement] intanglement   Iniquity] iniquitie —10 thir] 1, 2 their   —11 beene] been   —12 mean] meane Warr] Warre   —13 disposal] disposall   —14, 21 suddain] suddaine   —17 talk] talke   —18 tryal] tryall   superior] superiour   —19 mortal] mortall   —20 will] wil   certainly] certainely   —21 grown] growne   —22 pitty] pity   true,] true   —23 shallowness] shallownesse   —24 carnal] carnall pomp] pompe   —26 begett] beget   discord] commotions —27 Name] name

Page 4

—2 farr] farre   —4 read] read,   —6 *Agag;*] *Agag,* vilifying] villifying   —7 *Jonathans,*] *Jonathans*   —8 niceness] nicenesse   —9, 22 thir] their   —9 Covnant wrested,] Covnant: —14 cours] course   —15 actions,] actions   form] forme —16 Custom] Custome   —17 swerve,] swerve   Majesty] majesty   —19 forms] formes   and] &   —22 equal] equall —26 thir ... assistance] their assistance   &] and   —27 wherin] wherein   Victory] Victorie   —28 only] onely

PAGE 5

—1 immediat] immediate   excercise supream power,] exercise supreame power;   —2 equal] equall   —5 Scarcrowes] Scar crowes —5, 8 counsel] counsell   —6 empty] emptie   —9 madness] madnesse   —10, 11, 14, 23 thir] their   —13 thir] their owne —14 duty] dutie   —15 perseverance,] perseverance   unmasku-line] unmasculine   —17 fashion sake] fashion-sake   privat] private   publist] publish't   —18 himself] himselfe   —20 be] bee   —22 self-repugnance] selfe-repugnance   —23 boldness] boldnesse   —25 verity] veritie   —26 Faces] faces

PAGE 6

—1 Provincial] Provinciall   —2 deep] deepe   —3 scandal] scandall   —4 exclaim] exclaime   —5 less] lesse Party] party —6 Houses,] Houses   —7 Superior] 1, 2 Superiour   —8 good,] good   —9 evil] evill   —10 universal] universall   —13 &] and   —14 upon] on   —15 Tribunal] Tribunall National] Nationall   —16 less] lesse   —18 lad'n] laden   —19 King-doms] Kingdomes   —19, 22 be] bee   —20 now,] now —21 Sovran] Sovrane   —22 anointed] Annointed   —24 use-less] uselesse   —25 deny] denie   —26 dignity] dignitie —27 own] owne   —28 determin'd] determind

PAGE 7

—1 general discours] generall discourse   —2 proof] proofe determin] determine   —4 less] lesse   —6 find] finde   —8 massachers] massacres   —9 pawn] pawne   —11 Citties] Cities he] hee   —15 human] humane   —16 evil] evill   —21 downe] downe,   original] originall   —22 wherfore] wherefore thir] their   —23 Tyranny] tyranny   —24 depos'd] deposed punish'd] punishd   —26 Scisms] Schismes   —27 calumniat] calumniate

PAGE 8

—6 himself] himselfe   —7 born] borne   —8 liv'd] livd so. Till] so, till   —16 som] some   —17 restrain] restraine —18 right.] right: —21 own] owne   Judge] judge   —25 call'd] calld   —28 been] bin

PAGE 9

—4 himself] himselfe   —5 Persons] persons   civil] civill —7 govern'd] governd   —8 equity] equitie   own] owne —11 tryal] tryall   —13 Laws] Lawes   fram'd,] fram'd —15 man,] man   —17–19 While . . . Magistrate.] NOT IN 1 —21 constrain'd] constraind   —23 thir] their   —27 made,]

made to] tq oft-times] oft times
—4 threatn'd] threatn.d, —6 *Parliament*] *Parlament* —7–8
not . . . but] NOT IN I —8 French] NOT IN I —9 farr] farre
—12 ev'n] eev'n —14 Peoples] peoples thir] their —16–
17 known . . . besides the] German —20 unsworn] unsworne
—21 compell'd the] compelld a —24 only] onely transferr'd]
transferrd —25 People,] 2, 3 People, 1 people
—2 People] people —3 own] owne causes,] causes —4
Titles] titles Sov'ran] Sovran natural] naturall —5 Em-
perours] Emperors —7 Christians,] Christians —9 Asia,]
Asia —10 King] King, —11 Authors] authors —13
Crown] crown —14 Subject] subject —15 sould.] sould,
—17 either but] but either —19 certain] certaine —20 himself,] himselfe —22 proportional] proportionall —25 dignitie]
dignity —27 follows] followes —28 ouerturning] overturning government] goverment
—1 cov'nants] covnants —7 mortal] mortall —8 Parasites]
parasites —8–13 *Aristotle . . . men.*] NOT IN I —13 And
surely no] And no Prince,] Prince —14 *Cæsars*] *Cæsars,*
—17 Brethren] brethren only] onely —18 glory;] glory,
—19 pleasure,] pleasure vermin] vermine —20 Feet] feet
trod on] injurd —21 Men] men —22 wisdom] wisdome
mind,] mind —24 us,] us —26 imagin'd] imagind —27
sinn] sinne —28 Neighbour] neighbor Law] law
—2 therfore] therefore —7 pathetical] patheticall —9
poynt] point certain] certaine —11 Interpreters] interpreters
—12 *Tyranny*] *tyranny* —14 *unjustly,*] *unjustly* —15, 18
Trajan] *Traian* —16 drawn] drawne —19 yonger,] younger
—20 acknowledg'd] acknowledgd —23 and] & submitt]
submit —24 remains yet] remaines yet unrepeald —26 main-
tain] maintaine himself] himselfe —27 own imperial] owne
imperiall
—3 Beast] beast —5 originaly] originally —6, 16 own]
owne —9 liberty] libertie Men,] men —11 plain] plaine
—12 Scripture.] Scripture, —14 *mee.*] *mee* —16 Gover-
ment] goverment —17 People] people therfore] therefore

—18 form] forme   —19 displeas'd] displeasd   —24 King,]
King   he] hee   —25 especial] especiall   —26 Therfore]
Therefore   —27 2 *Sam.* 5. 3.] NOT IN 1
PAGE 15
    —1 People] people   —2 Therfore] Therefore   Crown]
Crowne   —4 *What*] *what*   —5 *Inheritance*] *inheritance*
Jesse?] *Jesse.*   —6 House] house   —7 depos'd] deposd
—7, 13 *Samuel*] *Samuell*   —8 misgoverment] misgovement
—10 expressly] expressely   —11 joyn'd] joynd   —12 som]
some   —14 govern'd] governd   —15 thir] their   —16
Numa,] *Numa*   —20 Prophet] Profet   —22 Brethren] breth-
ren   —24 himself] himselfe   —26 fit] fitt   —27 Coun-
selors] Counsellors
PAGE 16
    —2 scorn] scorne   God, not] God, and not   —6 subordinat,]
subordinat   is . . . call'd] is calld   —8 alike] NOT IN 1   —9
evil] evill   —10–13 But . . . men?] NOT IN 1   —13 *There*]
And *there*   —19, 26 Kingdoms] Kingdomes   —20 Devil]
Devill   *All*] *all*   —21 deliver'd] deliverd   *&*] *and*   —22,
23, 28 he] hee   —23 affirm'd;] affirm'd: —25 *seate*] *seat*
PAGE 17
    —1 evil;] evill,   —4 requir'd] requird   —5 ordain'd]
ordaind   —7 bee] be   —9 *concrete*] *concret*   —11 it;] it,
—12 least] lest   deceav'd] deceavd   —15 Devil] Devill
—19 saith] saith,   —20 *thee?*] *thee.*   —21 Kings] Kings,
in these days,] NOT IN 1   —22 Scripture,] Scripture   —25
them,] them;   —28 God,] God
PAGE 18
    —5 bee] be   —7 raigning] reigning   —8 deposing,] de-
posing   —11 was] was,   —12 conferr'd] conferrd   —13
imployed] imployd   —14 liberty] libertie   —15 Magistrates]
Magistrats   —21 Crown] Crowne   —26 murders,] 1 murders,
2, 3 murders   —27 massachers] massacres   —28 Provinces,]
provinces;
PAGE 19
    —2 father] Father   —7 own] owne   —9 show] shew
—10 in] is   —11 *Romans,*] *Romans*   witness,] witness   —14
tryal:] tryal;   —15 be] bee   —26 custom] custome
PAGE 20
    —4 years] yeares   present,] present   —5, 22 own] owne
—9 himself overturns] himselfe overturnes   —12 King,] King

look] looke   —15 League] league   —22 prerogative] prærog-
ative   —24 Subjects] subjects   —26 destroy'd,] destroy'd
lie] lye   —27 their] thir
PAGE 21
     —8 op'n] open   —10 defence,] defence   —11 civil] civill
warr] Warr   —13 therfore] therefore   —14 me,] me   remote,] remote   —16 neighbour] nighbor   —17 religious,]
religious   liberty] libertie   —22 whatever] whatsoever   —26
Sovran;] Sovran,   serv'd] servd   —27 we] wee
PAGE 22
     —2 Allegeance,] Allegeance   Subjects] subjects   —3 testify'd]
testifyd   —7 allowable] allowsble   —9 *Samuel*] *Samuell*
own] owne   —11 reason.] reason,   —12, 22 self] selfe
—17 seems] seemes   —18 natural] naturall   —23 Tyrant,]
Tyrant   —25, 26 privat] private   —27 peoples. But] peoples;
but
PAGE 23
     —3 Wee] We   —4 Tyrants,] tryants   —6 mind] minde
—7 autority] autoritie   Gentilism] Gentilisme   —8 flourish'd]
flourishd   —13 excercise] exercise   —16 Servant] servant
—18 Tyrant] tyrant   —19 *Fox, Luc.*] 1 *Fox, Luc.* 2, 3 *Fox Luc*
—19–22 So . . . protection.] NOT IN 1   —22 Mother] mother
—27 stil] still   —28 mischief] mischiefe
PAGE 24
     —5 Prelats] Prelates   —11 Tyranny,] tyranny   —12 requisite]
requisit   —14 Son] sonne   —16, 17 Subjects] subjects
—22 Emperor,] Emperor   —25 som] some   own] owne
—28 officer] Officer   call'd] calld   Palace,] palace
PAGE 25
     —1 solemnities] solemnitie   —5 will doubt] will needs doubt
—7 legal] legall
PAGE 26
     —4 Statesman,] Statesman   Commonwelth] Commonwealth
—5 *England,*] *England*   lawfull] lawful   —7 lerned] learned
—8 these days,] those days   —21 Britans] Britanes   —28 wors]
worse   heer] here   domestic] Domestic
PAGE 27
     —1 depos'd] deposd   —4 Protestant,] Protestant   —11,
18 precedent] president   —15 lately,] lately   —16 backsliders,]
backsliders   —22 op'n] open   —24 towards] toward   —25
Councel whither] Counsell whether   —28 The Scotch] the Scotch

PAGE 28

—5 soon] soone   betook] betooke   —6 certainly] certainely
—11 general] generall   maintained] maintaind   —12 &] and
—17 preferr'd] prefer'd   —18 Princes;] Princes,   —21 suffer,]
suffer   —22 he] hee   again] againe   —27 Common-welths.]
Common-welths,   —28 lerned] learned

PAGE 29

—1 judgement] judgements   question,] question   —2 him-
self] himselfe   —4 lerned] learned   —6 own] owne   —9
Book] book   —12 doe,] doe   —17 prison,] prison   —18
depos'd] deposd   —20 Ambassadors] Embassadors   —21
alleg'd] alleag'd   —22 toward] towards   deserv'd] deservd;
—23 punish'd] punishd   —25 freedom] freedome   unkingd]
unKingd   —27 customs] customes

PAGE 30

—2 mutual] mutuall   —3 *Hist.*] 1 *Hist.* 2, 3 *Hist,*   —7 law]
Law   equal] equall   —8 strain] straine   —11-23 Which
... Son.] NOT IN 1   —28 many times] oft'n   &] and

PAGE 31

—1 depos'd] deposd   —3 this,] this   world] World
—5 Neighbours] neighbours   —7 mean] meane   —9 when as]
whenas   —14 maintain'd] maintaind   lawful] lawfull   —18,
20 own] owne   —20 turn'd] turnd   —22 rightful] righful
—25 observ'd] observed

PAGE 32

—1 submitt] submit   —3 Subject] subject   Therfore] Therefore   —5, 6 establish'd] establishd   —7 unlawful] unlawfull
—14 years] yeares   —22 faithful,] faithful   —25 thir Oath]
their Oath]   —27 petition'd?] petitiond

PAGE 33

—1 &] and   —2 undenyably] undeniably   —3, 11 depos'd]
deposd   —5 dignity] dignitie   —6 sincerity] sinceritie
—7 success] 1 success, 2, 3 sucess   —8 subordinat] subordinate
—9 concerne] concern   —16 take] takes   —20 autority]
autoritie   —21, 28 years] yeares   —21 remov'd] removd
extinguishd] extinguish   —22 speak] speake   —25 Oaths]
Oathes   —27 termes] tearmes   —28 Warr;] 1, 2, 3 Warr

PAGE 34

—1 outlaw'd] outlawd   —2 clear] cleare   —3 avers] averse
—10, 18 be] bee   —11 we] wee   —21-23 Have ... Delinquent,] Have they not converted his revenue to other uses, and detain'd
from him

PAGE 35

—2 be] bee   —3 him, &] him and   forbidd] forbid
—9 remorse,] remorse   —16 man,] man   —17, 21 he] hee
—19 favour] favor   & ... & ... &] and ... and ... and   —20
mischief,] mischief   —24 me] mee   justice] Justice   —27
better] better,

PAGE 36

—7 again] againe   —8 vertue,] vertue   declar'd] declard
—10 Supreme;] Supreme,   —13 goe] go   —14 mouths]
mouthes   —19 Covnant,] Covnant   —20 sort,] sort   —21
feare,] feare   —23 when as] whenas   —24 things,] things
—27 kills] kils

PAGE 37

—2 be] bee   —4 sett] set   —6 prison,] prison   —13
prov'd] provd   —20 sentenc'd] sentencd   —21 Reprobats]
Reprobates   own] owne   —24 himself] himselfe   —24–25
but ... counselers] but against his evill Councel   —25, 27 &] and
—25 wherfore] wherefore   —26 office] Office   —28 therfore]
therefore

PAGE 38

—2 certain destruction;] certaine destruction,   —5 reviv'd]
revivd   —8 over,] over   thing,] thing   —10 person,]
person   Law,] Law   —11 Subject,] Subject   —14 doom]
doome   —15, 25 own] owne   —17 arraign'd] arraignd   &]
and   —18 Ahab] *Ahab*   Antiochus] *Antiochus*   —23 dissention;] dissention,   —25 disciplin] discipline   —28 laid] layd

PAGE 39

—3 for,] for   —7 Gospel] Gospell   —11 sav'd] savd
aime,] aime   —12 God,] God   —13 will] wil   —14–
15 giving ... noisemakers] looking after these firebrands   —18
Supreme] supreme   —23 leader] leader,   —27 wherein]
wherin

PAGE 40

—7 subordinat,] subordinate   —21 tyrants;] tyrants?   —26
milde &] mild and   it,] it   —27 tryal] tryall   Kings,] Kings
who] that

PAGE 41

—2 &] and   —3 out-cries and] out-crys &   —4–10 Though
... death.] NOT IN 1   —11 doe] do   —11, 13 precedent]
president   —15 honour,] honour   —17 heretofore,] heretofore
—18 dominion,] dominion   —19 fortitude,] fortitude   —24

mankinde,] mankind   —25 men,] men   —28 believe] beleive
and faithfull] & faithful

PAGE 42

—1 misledd] misled   —4 things,] things   —9 argument,]
argument   —12 own doings,] owne doings   —13 men,] men
—14 passion,] passion   —15 associats,] 1, 2 associats   —21, 22
them,] them   —22 therfore] therefore,   —23 be] bee
—25 provok'd] provokd   —27 informe] inform

PAGE 43

—1 receav'd] receavd   —3 chief] cheif   —11 ruin] ruine
final] finall   —12 which,] which   —13 State,] State
—14, 19 Armes] armes   —17 *David,*] *David*   —17–19 whose
... instruct us,] NOT IN 1   —19 when] after   he] hee   —23
own] owne   —26 on,] on   accomodation,] accomodation

PAGE 44

—1 somthing] something   —4 harder,] harder   —7 odd]
od   —13 learn] learne   —19 rav'nous] ravnous   —25 renounc'd] renouncd

PAGE 45

—3 Church-discipline] Church discipline   —4 belly-cheare]
belly cheare   —7 observe,] observe   —14 &] and   —16
sinns] sins   wherof] whereof   —17 wicked ones] NOT IN 1
immediatley] immediately   —20 op'n] open   —23 blasphem'd]
mock'd   traduc'd] NOT IN 1   —24 people.] people. *The End.*
—24–p. 57, l. 12 And ... *The End*   NOT IN 1

EIKONOKLASTES

EIKONOKLASTES was published in London in 1649, "the Author *I. M.* . . . . Printed by Matthew Simmons, next dore to the gilded Lyon in Aldersgate street." It was composed as a reply to *Eikon Basilike,* which was attributed at the time to Charles I and published immediately after his execution on January 30, 1649. On the title-page of the copy of the *Eikon Basilike* in the Thomason Collection there appears in Thomason's hand the date, February 9, and on the title-page of a copy of *Eikonoklastes* the date, October 6. Milton indicates in his preface that he wrote the book upon the instance of the Council of State. He says in the *Second Defence,* "I was ordered to answer it [*Eikon Basilike*]; and opposed the Iconoclast to his Icon." In composing the work he appears to have made use of *Eikon Alethine,* an anonymous reply to *Eikon Basilike,* which was published earlier in the same year and a copy of which is found in the Thomason Collection, dated by Thomason, August 26 (Loewenhaupt, Studies in Philology, XX, 28–51). A second edition of *Eikonoklastes* appeared in 1650, "The Author J. M. . . . Publish'd now the second time, and much enlarg'd . . . Printed by T. N. [probably Thomas Newcome] and are to be sold by Tho. Brewster and G. Moule at the three Bibles in Pauls Church-Yard near the West-end." This edition differs from the first in occasional changes of spelling, punctuation and phraseology, and in a number of additions made to the text.

The text of the present edition has been set up from a photostat of an original copy of the second edition in the Yale University Library. This has been compared with a copy in the New York Public Library, with which it seems to be identical. The text as here given has been collated with that of an original copy of the first edition in the Columbia University Library, which has been compared and found to be identical with a copy in the New York Public Library. A few typographical errors have been silently rectified. The notes which follow record such slight emendations as have been made and the variants found in the first edition. The first edition of 1649 is referred to as 1, the second edition of 1650 as 2.

PAGE 63

—1 person] Person   —2 final] finall   —3 self] selfe
—4 discours] discourse   —9 thir Favourers] their Favorers
—10 privat] private   —20 custom] custome   —23 mortal]
mortall   —24 seems] seemes   —26 behalf] behalfe Common-
wealth] Common-wealth

PAGE 64

—1 appears] appeares   —3 Regal] regall   —5 own] owne
designes,] designes;   —8 mindes] minds   —16 misaffirm'd]
misaffirmd   —19 self] selfe   —19–25 save . . . to] stuft with
naught els but the common grounds of Tyranny and Popery, sugard a
little over; or   —28 in] 1 in   2 in in

PAGE 65

—1–16 And though . . . contented with.] NOT IN 1   —17 And]
NO PARAGRAPH IN 1   —19 evil Goverment] evill Government
—20 behalf] behalfe   been] bin   —22 unfortunat] unfortunate
—25 adversaries] Adversaries   —27 himself] himselfe

PAGE 66

—1 advocat] advocate   —1, 12, 15, 24, 27 own] owne   —8
form] forme   —18 Book] Booke   —18, 20 speak] speake
—18, 25 evil] evill   —20 plain] plaine   —21, 26 himself]
himselfe   —25 Counsellors,] Counsellors   —26 he] hee
—27 laid] layd

PAGE 67

—1 unhappines] unhappiness   —2 onely] only   —3 own]
owne   —6–11 Yet . . . book.] NOT IN 1   —13 intended,]
intended   —15 been] bin   —16 we finde] wee find   will]
Will   —17, 24 hee] he   —24 himself] himselfe   —25
appears] appeares

PAGE 68

—1 *negarunt*;] *negarunt,*   That] that   —2 he] hee   —3
sense] sence   —4 minde] mind   —5 wee] we   —8 Book]
Booke   —9 befool] befoole   —11 were] were,   —14 old]
olde   Twelf-nights] Twelfe-nights   —17 thir] their   —19
title] Title   —21 certainly] certainly,   —22 answer] Answer
—25 took courage,] tooke courage   —26 People] people   —28
kinde] kind   idolizing] Idolizing

PAGE 69

—2 faithful] faithfull   —5 *Momfort*] *Momfort,*   —5, 6
Earl] Earle   —7 now,] now   —8 retain] retaine   —9
Freedom] freedome   —10 rest,] rest   —12 Memory] memory

—14 Liberties,] Liberties   British] Brittish   —17 natural] naturall   —17 English-man] Englishman   —18 First,] First —19 Pulpit stuff] Pulpit-stuffe   —20 perpetual] perpetuall —21 whose] and thir   —23 self-denial] selfe-denyall   —25 several] severall   —26 own] owne   —28 break] breake

PAGE 70

—3 him;] him,   —4 tyrannical] Tyrannicall   universal] universall   —6, 26 evil] evill   —11 begott] begot   —13 fears] feares   —14 Whenas] When as   —15 Sword-men] swordmen   Suburb-roysters] Suburb roysters   —18 attempt,] attempt   —20 Peace] peace   —22 field] feild   —25 wisdom] wisdome   wilfulness] willfullness   —26 piety] pietie   —28 chief] cheife

PAGE 71

—1 honour'd] honourd   —2 designes;] designes,   —3, 6, 13 thir] their   —4 whom] whome   —8 *Hom. Iliad.*] Hom. Iliad.   —10 fear] feare   —13 Loyaltie] loyaltie   —16 Arms] Armes   —19 think] thinke   —20 vain she bears] vaine shee beares   —22 political] politicall   —24 grief] griefe —26 hair;] haire: —26–p. 72, l. 3 an...them.] Which observation, though made by a Common Enemie, may for the truth of it heerafter become a Proverb.

PAGE 72

—4 undoubtedly] NOT IN 1   —5 vulgarly] Vulgarly   —8 main contents] maine Contents   —10 men] Men   —11 testimony] Testimony   —13 fair] faire   —14 fairly] fairely   —19 be-witch'd] bewitchd   —20 blinde] blind   beleef] beleefe   —21 charm] charme   —23–p. 74, l. 17 This...themselves.] NOT IN 1

PAGE 75

—1 Ἐικονοκλάϛης] *ΕΙΚΟΝΟΚΛΑΣΤΗΣ*   —4 layes] laies —20 preach] Preach   discours] discourse

PAGE 76

—2 hopes] hopes,   —8 Father;] Father.   —8–9 concerning ...us.] NOT IN 1   —11 former:] former.   —12 year] yeare Raign] Raigne   —13 seems] seemes   —14 he] hee   —17 Parlaments,] Parlaments;   —20 complain] complaine   —21 despaire] dispaire   —25 Ship-money] Ship-mony

PAGE 77

—4 interest] interest,   —5 plainly] plainely   —6 be] bee —10 Money] Mony   —11 *chois*] *choise*   —13 State,] State own] owne   —17 maintain] maintaine   —19 afterward] afterwards —23 breaks] breakes —27 Army,] Army accord,] accord

Page 78

—1 general] genarall people] people, —2 regality] regalitie —3 extremity] extremitie summon'd] summond —6 them,] them —9 or] 1 or 2 ot —11 hee] he —23 affairs] affaires —25 mediocrity] mediocritie remembrance] remembrance, —27 affirms] affirmes —28 *always*] *alwayes*

Page 79

—1, 2 hee] he —3 he] hee —5 hear] heare —7 *Parlaments,*] *Parlaments* —11 several] severall —14 been qualify'd] bin qualifi'd —16 fear] feare poverty] povertie —19 wherfore] wherefore —23 *fear'd*] *feard* —26 obstinacy, Reason] obstinacy reason —28 him] him, Crown] Crowne

Page 80

—1 Passion, Prejudice] passion, prejudice Faction] Faction, —3 *hear*] *heare* —4 carry'd] carri'd Letters] Letters, —5 divert] divert, —7 Religion] Religion, —9 were,] were —11 judgment] judgement —12 vain] vaine —22 Posterity] Posteritie —24 privat] private

Page 81

—2 he] hee —7 *sence*] *sense* —8 himself] himselfe —14 *regulations.*] *regulations,* —17 taken] tak'n —18 Clergy] Clergie —19 over burd'n'd] over-burd'n'd —23 Jiggs] Jigs May-poles] Maypoles publish'd] publisht —28 general] generall

Page 82

—2 disclaim] disclaime —4 heer hee] 1 heer hee 2 heerh ee —4 envie] envy under-Officers] under Officers —15 hee] he —16 *be*] *bee* —19 Earl] Earle —20 stil] still —23 reason] reason, been] bin —24 intal'd] intailed

Page 83

—4–10 He . . . Law.] NOT IN 1 —19 section] Section —21 admire,] admire —27 ord'nary] ordnary

Page 84

—11 &] and —23 third,] third. —27 *Freinds*] *Freinds,* *enemies*] *Enemies* —28 1,] 1.

Page 85

—9 praying therfore] Praying therefore —17 prayer] Prayer —18 offer'd] offerd —24 howr] hower —26 for] as saintly] Saintly

PAGE 86

—1 of a] 1 of a   2 a of   —2 fiction] Woman   heathen] Heathen   &] and   —3 but] but in   vain] vaine   Sr] Sir —4 kind] kinde   —7–p. 87, l. 4 They . . . God.] NOT IN 1   —13 of] 1 if   —18 *Aegyptian*] 1 *Aegyhtian*   —22 digression] 1 digrsesion

PAGE 87

—4 Yet hardly it] It hardly   —5 (though . . . thing)] NOT IN 1 —6 kind of] NOT IN 1   laughter] laughter,   —6–7 at . . . cousenage:] NOT IN 1   —7 trampl'd] acted   —8 tragically] Tragically,   —8–9 world . . . exit] World at last with such a ridiculous exit   —9 Deifying] deifying   —10 him] him,   pretious] NOT IN 1   —12 with shame,] with shame and confusion.   —12– 18 if . . . Zeal.] NOT IN 1   —19 to let] that lett   fal] fall —19 trapp] Trapp   —20 expos'd] expos'd   derision;] derision, —21 men] Men   —24 God] God,   buzzard] Buzzard —25–p. 89, l. 14 fitt . . . poverty.] that would be serv'd and worshipt with the polluted trash of Romances and *Arcadias*, without discerning the affront so irreligiously and so boldly offerd him to his face.

PAGE 89

—15 generall] general   prayers,] Prayers;   speciall] special —16 *Arcadian* prayer] Arcadian Prayer   Captivity,] Captivity; —17 undeceave] undeceive   esteeme wee] esteem we   —17–p. 90, l. 14 For . . . People] NOT IN 1

PAGE 90

—15 we] wee   —19 Parlament:] Parlament;   prayer] Prayer   —25 Christ'ndom] Christ'ndome

PAGE 91

—10 stil] still   mans] Mans   —11 bin always] always bin —14 Authority] Autority   —15 privat] private   —21 one of his Prayers] his Prayer

PAGE 92

—2 endeavor'd] endeavour'd   between] betweene   —3 counceld] counseld   —7 alledg'd and] alleg'd &   —10 discours] discourse   —13 Courtiers] 1 Courtiers   2 Coutiers   —17 sign] signe   —24 information] 1 information   2 imformation   —25 else] els   —28 pick'd] pickd

PAGE 93

—5 half] halfe   —7 he] hee   —8 *Earl*] *Earle*   —10 himself] himselfe   —17 &] and   —20 receav'd &] receav'd, and   —22 himself] himselfe   —23 real] reall   —25 con-

science?] conscience,   —26 ensuing] insuing
PAGE 94
    —1 Conspirators] Conspiratours   —10, 12 himself] himselfe
—14 oppression] opression   —15 Scolastic] Scholastic   —25
deceive] deceave   —27 &] and
PAGE 95
    —4 himself] himselfe   —6 malefactor] Malefactor   doubt-
less] doutless   —8 he had] hee had   —10 Kingdoms] Kingdomes   —11 Tyranny:] Tyranny,   —14 els,] els   —18
finde] find
PAGE 96
    —6 Pharises] Pharisees   —8 Gnatt] Gnat   —11 ruin] ruine
Kingdoms] Kingdomes   —12 certainly] certainely   —14
wholsom] wholesom   —15 Kingdoms] Kingdomes   —16 con-
cele] conceale   —20 imply'd] impli'd
PAGE 97
    —2, 15 himself] himselfe   —4 his] his his   —10 plainly]
plainely   —11 judgment] judgement   —15 treasonous]
Treasonous   —18 any] any other   —22 last,] last   —24
Kingdoms] Kingdomes   —28 *evidence*] 1 *evidence* 2 e-evidence
PAGE 98
    —7 Rebels] Rebells   —9 wherof] whereof   —13 thought]
thinks   —14 beleif] beleife   —21 *enemies*] *Enemies*   —24
himself] himselfe
PAGE 99
    —4 ev'n] eev'n   —11 himself] himselfe   —18 hunderd]
hundred   —22 *us'd,*] *us'd*   —25 tampering] tampring
PAGE 100
    —4 *repulse*] *repuls*   —6 wherfore] wherefore   —9 des-
perate] desperat   would] 1 would 2 wculd   —14 Law.] Law:
he] hee   —21 *men:*] *Men:*   —24 People,] People.   —24–
27 but . . . Tower.] NOT IN 1
PAGE 101
    —3 guilty] guiltie   —5 *he*] *hee*   —11 jealousie.] jealousie?
—15 *justifiable*] *justifyable*   —23 onely,] onely   Pursivant]
Pursivant,
PAGE 102
    —3 himself] himselfe   —19 suspicions] suspitions   —20
Councel] Counsel   —21 own] owne   —23 business] buisness
prov'd,] prov'd   —24 soldiers] Soldiers   Papists] Papists,
—25 King,] King   —27 manner.] 1 manner. 2 manner,

PAGE 103

—6 own] owne —19 himself] himselfe

PAGE 104

—8 inveigh] enveigh —13 fear] feare —18 himself] himselfe —25 &] and —26 spoil] spoile —27 up,] up

PAGE 105

—2 foul] foule K.] King —2–9 tempts . . . he] NOT IN 1 9, 19 &] and —9–10 by . . . Hinderson,] NOT IN 1 —11 only] onely —21 self] selfe

PAGE 106

—5 Guard] Guard, —20 sat] sate —21 King,] King —22 wherof] whereof —23 Earl] Earle —27 *White Hall*] *Whitehall*

PAGE 107

—1 entertaind] entertain'd —9 slight] sleight —18 Tumult] Tumult, —21 Tumults,] Tumults —25 extreme] extreme,

PAGE 108

—3 self] selfe —9 milde] mild —10 releef] releefe —16, 26 *&*] *and* —16 *Authority*] *Autority* —23 That] *That* —28 People] people thir] their

PAGE 109

—1 unarm'd] unarmed —8 City] Citty Kingdome] Kingdom —13 shook] shooke —14 *earthquake,*] *earthquake*; —17 arm'd] armd —19 him] him, —20 Party] party —24 suspicion] suspition —25 mischeifs] mischeifes —26 Tumults] tumults —28 *Houses*] *houses*

PAGE 110

—4 Law] law —5 Religion] religion —8 *schismatical*] *schismaticall* —9 *government ecclesiastical*] *goverment ecclesiasticall civil*] *civill* —11 goodness] goodnes —12 People,] People —14 innovations] 1 innovations 2 innovasions —15 down] downe High Commission] High-Commission —17 enveighs] inveighs —23 Tumults] tumults —28 wholsome] wholesome Politic] politic

PAGE 111

—1 *WhiteHall*] *Whitehall* —2 we] wee —6 own] owne —14 Country] Countrie Tyranniz'd] tyranniz'd —17 men into slavery] Men to be Slaves —23 for] 1 for 2 fcr —24 warr?] Warr. —28 *chiefe*] *cheife*

PAGE 112

—3 Money] Mony —6 people] People —7 emboldn'd]
embold'nd who,] who —10 less] lesse thir] their —22
assaults,] assaults —23 Rufflers,] Rufflers;

PAGE 113

—2 justice] Justice —2–3 *In . . . of*] NO ITALICS IN 1 —3
Naboth] *Naboth* —3–4 *shall . . . thine.*] NO ITALICS IN 1 —9
self-undoing] selfe-undoing —10 immediatly] immediately
—12 pulld] pull'd —14 *streets*] *Streets* —21 hee] he
—22 commit] committ himself] himselfe —27 *he*] *hee*

PAGE 114

—6 colour pretence —9 *scuffling*] *Scuffling* —19, 26 he]
hee himself] himselfe —22 fear] feare —23 meditations.]
1 meditations. 2 meditations,

PAGE 115

—9 *gardens*] Gardens —12 Garden,] Garden —14 *he*]
hee —19 sat] sate —25 us?] us. —26 members] Members

PAGE 116

—3 instead] in stead —4 prayes] prays —7 people]
People —9 *And*] *and* this] this, —10–14 THe . . .
necessary;] THE Bill for Triennial Parlaments was doubtless a good
Bill, and the other for setling this was at that time very expedient;
—14 Words] words —17 affirms] affirmes —20 himself]
himselfe —23 wee] we

PAGE 117

—3 year] yeare —4–26 From . . . liberalitie.] NOT IN 1
—26 other act] second that] 1 that 2 that, —27 &] and

PAGE 118

—3 War] Warr —5 own] owne —8 this] that —11
a] this —12 setling] settling —13 malady,] malady
—18 himself] himselfe —22 *Act*] *act* —23 six] three
—25 boon] boon,

PAGE 119

—8 people] People —10 denyal] denyall —13 he] hee
—28 grievances] greevances &] and

PAGE 120

—3, 4 he] hee —7 bill] Bill —10 people] People
—16 And] and —18 Parlament,] Parlament —24 Lawes]
Laws

PAGE 121

—16 Crown] Crowne —17 wherupon,] wherupon —18

Parlament,] Parlament   —23 reason] to reason   Autoritys] to Autorities   —28 people,] people

PAGE 122

—5 *continual*] *continuall*   —6 Common wealth,] Commonwealth   —9 *Act*] *act*   —14 dutie] duty   —22 Parlament;] Parlament,   —25 extirpat] extirpate   —27 fatuity] fatuitie

PAGE 123

—2 peace,] peace;   —6 *tumults*] *Tumults*   —14 lik'n'd] lik'n'd,   —16 he] hee   —18 *not:*] *not.*   —22 in] to doe —23 unwonted] unwonted,   nice,] nice

PAGE 124

—4 *down*] *downe*   —5 we] wee   himself] himselfe   —10 Palace,] Palace   —13 *by the wayes*] *by wayes*   sin] sinn —14 himself] himselfe   —16 scannd] scand   —20 he] hee —25 shut] shutt

PAGE 125

—1 *his*] *His*   —3 he begins] Hee beginns   —4 Poetical] Poeticall   —6 hearing him] him hearing   —12 *stai'd*] *stay'd* *driven*] *driv'n*   —16 he] hee   *wherin*] *wherein*   —17 *own*] *owne*   —21 *principal*] *principall*

PAGE 126

—2 sat] sate   Parlament] Parlament,   —5 Favorite;] Favorite, —13 King,] King   —14 tumults] Tumults   —15 leav] leave —17 unskilful] unskilfull   —20 not] NOT IN 1   —21 plaid] plai'd   —22 King ?] 1 King?   2 King   —27 Church Discipline] Church-Discipline

PAGE 127

—10 peoples] Peoples   —12 denial] deniall   —13 people] People   —15 bondage;] bondage,   *Were*] *were*   —19 outballance] out-ballance   —24 case] cases   —25–p. 128, l. 4 And . . . ruin.] NOT IN 1

PAGE 128

—6 our] public   —9 reason] reason,   and mature wisdom] NOT IN 1   —20 were it] it were   —21 Major] major   —22 one single] any one   —23 that,] that   —26 he] hee   —27 Kingdom] Kingdome

PAGE 129

—2 he] hee   —5 equivalent] equal   —7 it:] it.   —7– 13 much . . . remediless.] NOT IN 1   —14 maintains] maintaines —23 safety?] safety.   —24 Kingdom] Kingdome   whence] Whence

PAGE 130

—15 denials] denialls   —25–28 He . . . vassals.] NOT IN 1

PAGE 131

—2 *that*] *That*   —8 *injoying*] *enjoying*   —14 beasts] Beasts   —28 himself] himselfe

PAGE 132

—1 Man,] Man   —2 himself] himselfe   —8 we] wee —9 and of his] and his   —19 office;] Office,   —21 Parlament,] Parlament;   —22 he] hee   —26 unphilosophical] un-philosophicall

PAGE 133

—1 their] thir   —7 Politics,] Politics: —19 only] onely to] 1 to 2 to to   people] People   —23 negative] Negative

PAGE 134

—6 wholsom] wholesome   —9 command,] command.   —10– 17 not . . . him.] NOT IN 1   —17 *He*] *Hee*   —24–27 he . . . foresee;] a whole Nation be ruin'd,

PAGE 135

—1 Man;] Man,   —3, 7 he] hee   —5 fit] fitt   —14 renounce] 1 renounce 2 ronounce   thir] their   —25 be] bee

PAGE 136

—9 &] and   —12 *concurr'd*] *concur'd*   —13 selfconceited] self-conceited   —15 *himself*] *himselfe*   —21 *Church*] *Church,* —26 Right] right

PAGE 137

—13 *Crown*] *Crowne*   —17 *Factions,*] 1 *Factions,* 2 *Factions.* —19 chois] choise

PAGE 138

—2 rightfully] righfully   —3 we] wee   —8 *not:*] 1 *not:* 2 *not,*   —13 concerns] concernes   divulge] 1 divulge 2 divulc —14 vertues] 1 vertues 2 vergtues   —23 shal] shall   —26 warr] Warr   subjects] Subjects

PAGE 139

—3 least] lest   —5 yeare] year   —10 means] meanes —21 Parlament,] Parlament:

PAGE 140

—4 *Allegiance*] *Allegeance*   —10 prayes] praies   —15 the Popes *Nuntio*,] and the Popes *Nuntio* here,   —16 and . . . Mother] NOT IN 1   —19 duely] duly

PAGE 141

—2 Puritants] Puritans   —2–3 the . . . Court,] NOT IN 1

—12 Magazin] magazin —14 *England*] England causless]
causeless —15 Subjects] subjects —18 sale] saile —22
Hull] Hull —25 Houses] houses

PAGE 142

—2 own] owne —3 sir] Sir House] house —4, 14,
28 *Hull*] Hull —5 Train'd] train'd —5–11 For . . . party]
Neither had the King before that time omitted to attempt the same, first
by Colonel *Legg*, one of those who were imploy'd to bring the Army up
against the Parlament, then by the Earle of *Newcastle* under a disguise.
—10 latter] PROBABLY SHOULD READ former that place (l. 11) RE-
FERS TO HULL, IN OPERATIONS AGAINST WHICH NEWCASTLE WAS ENGAGED
IN 1643. —12 wherin] wherein K.] King —15–17 And
. . . parts.] NOT IN 1 —20 *Ireland*;] Ireland, —21 Rebels]
rebels wors] worse —24 2000.] 2000 200.] 200 —25
Magazin] magazin —28 remoove] remoov

PAGE 143

—1 *London*] London denial] deniall —2 *Hull*] Hull
400.] 400 —9 Traitor] traitor —10 iniquitie] iniquity
—22 *self*] selfe

PAGE 145

—1 Jewels] Jewells —2 Town] Towne —6 own,] own;
suspicious] suspitious —24 evill] evil

PAGE 146

—23 general] generall —24 judgement] judgment —26
divided] *devided* —27 *divided*] *devided*

PAGE 147

—1 *his*] *the* —2 *Father*] *father* —7 some] som —8
a Disciple] the Disciple —13 wherof] wheref —14 fansy]
fancy —22 wherof] whereof Whole] whole —27 his]
this

PAGE 148

—3 workes] works —11 and] & —15 *we*] *wee* —19
praises] prayses —28 worse] wors

PAGE 149

—6 *dispute*] 1 *dispute* 2 *dspute* —9 end] end, —11,
13 own] owne —12 reserve not] doe not reserve —15 we]
wee —16 *Vaine Repititions*] *Vain Repitions*

PAGE 150

—5–6 How . . . take] But heer a mortal man takes —10 *listing*]
Listing raising] Raising —18 *Tumults*,] *Tumults*; —19
peace] Peace —24 he] hee

Page 151

—1 *be*] *bee*   —8 man] Man   —9, 23 he] hee   —10 whenas] when as   —19 Courtiers] Courtiers,   —20 Bishops,] Bishops   —24 people] People   —25 God,] God   —28 people] People

Page 152

—2 Prelats] Prelats,   —4, 14 he] hee   —5 himself] himselfe   —6 conscience,] conscience;   —16 duty] duty,   —20 *Subjects*] *Subjects*,   —23 person] Person   —25 Hee] He —27 *and Plenty*] *Plenty*   —28 Counsel-Table] Counsel Table

Page 153

—26 *Irish*] NOT IN 1   —28 Houses?] Houses.

Page 154

—2 Clergy] clergy   —3 covetousnes] covetousness   —7 Tyranny] Tyrany   —13 *miscariages* onely] *miscarriages* only —15 counsels] councels   —16 men,] *Men*   & practise] and practice   al] all   —17 frequently avowing he] he frequently avow'd and   —18 himself;] himself,   —18–21 and . . . sins.] NOT IN 1   —21 The persons also] and whose Persons   —23 never,] never   —24 punishment] Punishment   —26 he] hee —27 *What widdows*] *what Widows*

Page 155

—1 protected] protected,   —3–6 (with . . . persecution,] NOT IN 1   —9 affirmes] affirmes,   —16 persecution] Persecution —17 yeares] Yeares   —26 *He*] *Hee*   —28 prosecute] Prosecute

Page 156

—1, 5 own] owne   —8 *not*] *not*,   —16 *he*] *hee*   —17 he] hee   —22–24 though . . . continu'd.] NOT IN 1.   —24 Not] not

Page 157

—7 justice] Justice   —12 Reformation] reformation   —15 wherin, he] wherein, hee   —17, 18 *ruin*] *ruine*   —25 12.] 12 —26 thir] their

Page 158

—2 will] wil   —3 Injustice to appeach] Injustice in   —9 Bil] Bill   —12 sense] sence   Malignancy] 1 Malignancy 2 Malignacy   —13 Parlament,] Parlament: —20 wholsom] wholsom   —21 reformed;] reformed,   —22 *own*] *owne*

Page 159

—1 *judgement*] *judgment*   —4 admitt] admit   —10 popery]

Popery rememberd] remembred   —12 *Lawes*] *lawes*   —16
absurrd] abur'd   —19 literal] litteral   —20 all;] all.
—20–23 both . . . *formality*.] NOT IN I
PAGE 160

1–7 And . . . establishment.] NOT IN I   —14 impris'nments]
Impris'nments   —15 wherwithall] wherewithall   —17 upon]
on the   —19 till] til   —24 *firm*] firme   —25 *thir*] *their*
PAGE 161

—2 we] wee   small] NOT IN I   integrity] the integrity
—4 he] hee   —12 Parlament;] Parlament,   —13 means]
meanes   —16 &] *and*   —21 *Delinquents*] *delinquents*
—22 Delinquency] delinquency   Tumults] tumults   —27
offer'd] offerd   —28 Episcopal] episcopal
PAGE 162

—3 Covnant] Cov'-nant   —4 *liberties*] *liberties*,   —8 *Refor-*
mation] *reformation*   —12 brotherly] Brotherly   —15 *Jewes*]
Jews   —24 *betweene*] *between*
PAGE 163

—1 *som men*] *some Men*   —4 not] Not   —6 *half*] *halfe*
—12 God,] God   —18 *people*] *People*   —26 heare] hear
PAGE 164

—12 thir] their   Rights,] Rights   —12 diminishing] de-
minishing
PAGE 165

—1–4 while . . . sitting.] and Soldiers billeted in all parts,   —4
The] the   —5 property] propertie   —6 Subject] subject
—7 overspread] overspredd   —10 Nation] Nation,   —10–11
not . . . self,] NOT IN I   —11 Arms] Armes   —18 untill] until
—20 Pacification:] Pacification.   —20–24 The . . . himself.] NOT
IN I   —27 Earl] Earle
PAGE 166

—2 warr] Warr   —3 *Denmark,*] *Denmark*   —4 parlament;]
Parlament,   —4–6 and . . . then] NOT IN I   —13 Counsels]
Councels   —14 dismiss'd,] dismiss'd   —22 divers] diverse
sent] sent;   —22–24 with . . . City.] NOT IN I   —24 The]
the   —26 hunderds] hundreds   —28 more,] more;   —28–
p. 167, l. 11 of . . . but] NOT IN I
PAGE 167

—11 inhabitants] Inhabitants   —13 peace,] peace.   —13–
14 and . . . listed.] NOT IN I   —16 or . . . first,] NOT IN I
—21 House] house   —22 practices] Practices   Town] Towne

—23 Counsels] Councels   considerd] considered

Page 168

—3 wherof] whereof   —5 selves] selvs   —15 their] thir
—22 then] then,

Page 169

—3 Jewels] Jewells   —5 Morter-peeces] 1 Morter-peeces   2
Morters-peeces   —8 Teares;] Teares,   —13 help] helpe
—16 *Peoples,*] *Peoples*   —23 *hand*] *hands*   —27 presump-
tion] Presumption

Page 170

—1 who] that   —18 selves] selvs   he] hee   —21 which]
Which   —27 authority] autority   —28 Sword] sword   Law]
law

Page 171

—4 dispose;] dispose,   —5–6 in a lump] NOT IN 1   —9–
10 would . . . law,] were that power of the Sword higher then the power
of Law,   —10 &] and   —11–13 in . . . absolutely] NOT IN 1
—13–19 And . . . Yet] NOT IN 1   —19 such] Such   all] NOT
IN 1   —22 understanding,] understanding;   —24 knows]
knowes   —26 is,] is   —28 warr] Warr

Page 172

—4 *mouthes*] *mouths*   Mouthes] Mouths   —6 hees] Hees
shees] Shees   there] ther   —10 Counsel] Councell   —12
&] and   —14 debate] theme   —24 King,] King   —27
perjurie] *Perjurie*

Page 173

—6 not] and not   —11 himself] himselfe   —12 &] and
—13 fear] feare   —16 hands? It] hands, it   —19 terms]
termes   —22 wherewithall] wherwithall   —23 warr] Warr
—24 *him,*] *him*   —25 *Heaven*] *Heav'n*

Page 174

—1 publick] public   —9 &] and   —11 *rate,*] *rate*   —15
we] wee   —20 he] hee   —23 years] yeares

Page 175

—2, 9 he] hee   —3 cals] calls   *soul*] *soule*   —5
offerd] *offer'd*   *requital*] *requitall*   —6 satiate] satiat   man]
Man   —7 king] King   millions yearly] Millions yearely,
—8 what . . . crook,] NOT IN 1   —12 Revennue] Revenue
—16 Parlament,] Parlament   —18 conditional] conditionall
—19 contest] contest,   good;] good,   —22 abrogate,] abrogate
—24 grows] growes   —27 being] beeing

PAGE 176

—2 self] selfe   —8 them,] them;   —17, 19 he] hee
—19 Kingdom] kingdom

PAGE 177

—1, 3, 5, 6, 16, 21, 22 he] hee   —23 him,] him

PAGE 178

—1 parlament] Parlament   —2 chief] cheif   —3 will] NOT
IN 1   —4 real,] real;   —6 remorseless] remorceless   —8
he] hee   —11 *policy*,] *policy*   —14 denyal] denyall
—18 sake,] sake;   indifferent,] indifferent   —19 sake:] sake,
—24 find] finde

PAGE 179

—6 councel] counsel   —12 *him*.] *him*;   —15 suspicion,]
suspition   —17 means] meanes

PAGE 180

—8 enjoynes] enjoyns   —9 satisfi'd,] satisfi'd   —10 Superior]
superior   —14 Slaves,] Slaves: —18 petition'd] Petition'd
King,] King   —19 *absurd*] absur'd   —20 absurd] absur'd
he] hee   —22 man,] man   —23 will,] will;   —24 sovran]
Sovran   —26 Laws] Lawes   —27 therfore] therefore

PAGE 181

—1 Kings,] Kings   —4 King,] King   law] law,   —10,
13 he] hee   —13 teachers] Teachers   —21 resembl'd]
resembled   —26 him] him,

PAGE 182

—2 Reason,] Reason   —5 satt] sate   propound;] propound,
—6, 14, 22 he] hee   —12 *done*] *don*   —15 *advantages*]
advantage   —22 lookd] look'd   —24 greevance] greevance,

PAGE 183

—1 worke] work   —2 alleges] alleges,   —8 practise]
practice   —12 imitation,] imitation   —14 despair'd] dispair'd
—18 scism] Scism   —22 mention] mention,   —24 *Government*] *Goverment*   —27 But] but

PAGE 184

—6 admitt] admit   Reformation] Refcrmation   —13 *by
Lawes*] *by the Lawes*   —20 an] a   —28 *thir*] *their*

PAGE 185

—1 concernd] concer'd   —10 them] him   Faction] faction,
—19 and] of   —27 reason,] reason   —28 the . . . wind-eggs.]
can produce no Law:

Page 186
—9 which,] which —10 being,] being —21 Tyrannical]
tyrannical *joynt*] joint —22 *part;*] part, —27 &] and
Page 187
—4 Cities] Citties —17 he] hee
Page 188
—5 principl's] principl's, —7 *ask*] *aske* —11 sollicitous]
solicitous —15 *Ireland*] *Ireland,* 154000.] 154000 —15–
16 in . . . onely,] NOT IN I —17–18 which . . . great,] NOT IN I
—21 sprung,] sprung; was] was, —24 Irish,] Irish
Page 189
—1 own] owne —2 irreconcileable] irreconcilable —4
aid] aide —9 neither] nether —10–17 And . . . declares]
NOT IN I —19–22 And . . . House.] NOT IN I —23 Autority]
autority
Page 190
—1 Rebels] Rebells —13 Rebelion] Rebellion —14 evidence.] evidence: —16 findes] finds —20 indulgences]
indulgencies —25 up,] up —25–26 either . . . hand,] NOT
IN I —26 onely army] only Army
Page 191
—4 he] hee —17 K.] King, —21 Papists] Papists,
—21–22 which . . . disband,] NOT IN I —23 With] And with
them,] them come,] come —24–25 which . . . complotting,]
NOT IN I —25 do] doe —26 som] NOT IN I —26–27 &
. . . natures] NOT IN I —27 Parlmt.] Parlament, —27–28 &
. . . Masters.] NOT IN I —28 agrees &] NOT IN I
Page 192
—1 were] should be —2 Arms] Armes —5 offerd] offer'd
—18 Massacher;] Massacher, —24 recourse] recours —25–
p. 193, l. 5 Besides . . . *England.*] NOT IN I
Page 193
—6 onely] only —11 *Instigator*] *instigator* —13–14 with
. . . speedily] NOT IN I —15 all] NOT IN I —17 his bare deniall]
the bare denyall of one man, —18 can . . . countervaile;] cannot in
any reason countervaile. and . . . cause.] NOT IN I —19 thinkes]
thinks —21 *authority*] *autority* —24 tenderd] tender'd
—26 receavd] receav'd
Page 194
—1, 27 Rebels] Rebells —6 threatn'd] threat'nd —9 He]
Hee —11 Offender;] Offender, —17 own] owne —20

weake] weak —22 do] doe —23 tyrant] Tyrant well]
wel —26 said] sayd
PAGE 195
—5 Rebells] Rebels fee'd] feed —8 perhaps,] perhapps
—9–10 nay . . . that] NOT IN 1 —18 *rigor*] *rigour* —24
common-Prayer-Book] Common-Prayer-Book
PAGE 196
—2 to be their] to their BUT 1 HAS to be AS CATCHWORD. —6
shivering] trembling —7 that] as that —16–20 which . . .
many.] whom hee seems heer to compassionat. The particulars are too
well known to be recited, and too many. —22, 26 he] hee
PAGE 197
—4 findes] finds —5 threatn'd] threat'nd —9 *unevangeli-cal*] *unevangelicall* —15 his zeale] his own zeale —17, 20
City] Citty —25 Tribe?] Tribe, —26 *Jabesh Gilead*]
Jabesh-Gilead
PAGE 198
—4, 5, 11, 22 he] hee —4 raised] intended —5 all,] all;
—8, 12, 27 *he*] *hee* —8 perhaps] perhapps —14 *stream*]
streame —25 He] Hee
PAGE 199
—6 we] wee —11 mannaging] managing —16 plaine]
plain —19 own] owne —20 discoverd] discover'd
PAGE 200
—5–16 But . . . irreligious?] NOT IN 1 —18 Protestations]
Remonstrances —27 preacher] Preacher —28 bee] be
PAGE 201
—1 *beleives*] *beleeves* —2 *embroyle*] *embroile* *kingdoms*]
Kingdoms —3 beleive] beleeve —4 publishd] publish'd
—11 he] hee —13 ye] yee —16 *or*] or
PAGE 202
—2 thir] their —3 strange,] strange where Men] to Men
who —4 contemplat] contemplate —8 thir] their —15
revennue] revenue —18–p. 203, l. 10 Indeed . . . Yet] NOT IN 1
PAGE 203
—10 this ignorant] This ignorance —14, 18 he] hee —15
bounty,] bounty; *favours*] *favours,* —22 hands,] hands;
—23 *interest*] *Interest* —25 fals] false —27 wherwith]
wherewith
PAGE 204
—5 he] hee —9 *setling*] *settling* —20 &] and score]

engrave   —22 stopd] stop'd   —27 he] hee   —28 obstinate]
obstinat
PAGE 205
    —4 we] wee   —8 sat] sate   —17 Parlaments;] Parlaments,
—18 come] com   —23 turne] turn   —25 furious] 1 furious
2 rſiousfu   of] 1 of 2 o   —26 Pupil] Pupill
PAGE 206
    —2 &] and   —5 Episcopacie] Episcopacy   —8 we] wee
times,] times   —11 likeliest] likliest   —17 *England*] *England,*
—20 Scripture,] Scripture   —26 *zeal*] *zeale   concernd*] *concern'd*
PAGE 207
    —1, 25 he] hee   —2 zeal] zeale   —5 Head] head   —7
be] bee   —11 deliverd] deliver'd   —13 Spirit] spirit
—14 doubtful] doubtfull   —16 tyrannical] Tyrannical   —25
we] wee
PAGE 208
    —3 call'd] call'd in   —4 help] helpe   —5 *thir*] *their
we*] *wee*   —6 Presbytery,] Presbytery   —16 implor'd,]
implor'd   —21 *Piety*] *Pietie   Loyalty*,] *Loyalty*   —27
friendship] freindship
PAGE 209
    —2 Theme] theme   · Discours] discourse   Matter] matter
—5 *souls*] *soules*   —7 antiquity] antiquitie   —15 years]
yeares   —17 *unsatisfied*] *unsatisfi'd*   —22 he] hee
PAGE 210
    —2 *legal*] *legall*   —7 Jews] Jewes —17 and our encourage-
ment NOT IN 1   —18 Church Goverment] Church-Goverment
—26 returns] returnes
PAGE 211
    —1 fear] feare   —3 the] 1 the 2 the the   —6 truly]
truely   —8 preservd] preserv'd   —14 general] generall
—16 kinde] kind   —23 *himself*] *himselfe*
PAGE 212
    —3, 27 he] hee   —6 *Word*] *word*   —7 fansi'd] fanci'd
learned] lerned   —12 Rebel] Rebell   —13 returns again]
returnes againe   —14 vows] vowes   —17 &] and   —20
main] *maine*   —24 we] wee
PAGE 213
    —4 revennue] revenue   —9 means] meanes   —10 *Bread*]
bread   —13 way,] way   —24 him] him,   —26 *down*]

downe   loyalty] *loyaltie*
PAGE 214

—1 Water-works] Waterworks   Engines] Engins   —10 we]
wee   —14 *tranquilitie*] *tranquillitie*   —17 he be cast] 1 he be
cast 2 he cast   *increase*] *encrease*   —18 *storm,*] *storm;*   con-
troversy] controversy,   —20 yeres] yeares   —22 &] and
—24 wel] well   —27 judgement] judgment
PAGE 215

—5 guilded] gilded   —16 men,] men;   —21 nobler]
Nobler
PAGE 216

—3, 4, 12, 20, 27 &] and   —6 appear] appeare   —7
Parlament] Parlament,   —8 lernt] learnt   —9 *ther*] *there*
—9 *samenes*] *sameness*   —10 *allegeance & subjection*] *Allegeance
and Subjection*   —11 puritans] Puritans   —12 realm]
Realm *Scotl.*] *Scotland,*   —13 liturgie] Liturgie   king] King
—14 episcopacie] Episcopacie   monarchie] Monarchie   —15
religion] Religion   duty & allegeance] Duty and Allegeance   —16
do court maxims] doe Court Maxims   court] Court   —17 king]
King   —18 courtier] Courtier   —19 wel] well   —20
religions] Religions   —21 Religious] religious   —25 letter]
Letter   —26 protestants] Protestants   religion] Religion
—27 papists] Papists   —28 protestancy] Protestancy
PAGE 217

—7, 13 &] and   —14 some] som   —16 bad] badd
—16, 20 he] hee   —27 miscall'd,] miscall'd   —28 Goverment,] Goverment;
PAGE 218

—4 summ] sum   —4–8 limit . . . to] regulate and limit his
negative voice, and   —21 is,] is   —23–25 And . . . superior.]
NOT IN 1   —26 Finally,] Finally   —27 mis-goverment] misgoverment
PAGE 219

—2 *self*] *selfe*   *Splendour*] *splendour*   —3 *fatal*] *fatall*
—8 *speak*] *speake*   —13 *from*] *frow*   til] till   —14 *wel*]
well   seems] seemes   —20 *Common-Prayer*] *Common-prayer*
—22 Apostolicall] aposolicall
PAGE 220

—3 fear] feare   —10 *these*] *those*   *their*] *thir*   —11
vein] *veine*   —22 fear] feare   model'd] modell'd   —24
people] People

PAGE 221

—4 autority] authority   —6 Priest] Preist   —7 evident,]
evident   —12 sett] set   —13 Prayers and that] 1 Prayers and
that 2 Prayers that   —18 we] wee   —20 God.] 1 God. 2 God
We] Wee   —22 wee] we   —26 own] owne

PAGE 222

—3 rather] rather   —5 variety] varietie   —6 ask] aske
giv'n] given   —9 praier] Prayer   —11 Priests] Preists
—15 sett] set   —24 onely] only

PAGE 223

—4 Gift,] Gift.   —5–6 to . . . publicly.] NOT IN 1   —7
onely] only   —8 formal] formall   superficial] superficiall
—9 sett] set   &] and   —11 these,] these   —14 easilie]
easily   —15 sympathy] simpathy   —18 again] againe

PAGE 224

—2 sett] set   —3 alwaies] allwaies   —4 Mass-Book] Mass
Book   —8 daily] dailie   —15 God,] God   —16 Ecclesias-
tical] Ecclesiasticall   —18 ask] aske   —22 them,] them
—23 Christ,] Christ   —24 them,] them;

PAGE 225

—6 Common-Prayer] Commonprayer   —9 doubtful] doubtfull
—10 Wee] we   —11 Prayer] Praier   sett Forms] set Formes
—13 lays] layes   he] hee   —14 lawful] lawfull   —17 wors]
worse   —17–18 unless . . . them.] NOT IN 1   —20 Church-
Goverment] Church Goverment   —24 Pietie] Piety

PAGE 226

—8 We] Wee   History] Story   —12 dreadful] dreadfull
—13 Kingdom,] Kingdom   —14 break] breake   —15 Dominion.] 1 Dominion. 2 Dominion,   —18 ruin] ruine   —23 he]
hee   —25 shun] prevent   &] and

PAGE 227

—7 preacht] Preacht   —8 apprehensions] thoughts   —9
himself] himselfe   —21 He] Hee

PAGE 228

—2 fansie] fancy   —4 Prelats] Prelates   —6 Trentine
storie] History of Trent   —10 principal] principall   —12
extirpating] removal   —14 bee] be   —19 he] hee   —22
thanksgiving] thanks-giving   —23 victorie] victory   —28
Episcopacie] Episcopacy   wee] we

PAGE 229

—1 mental] mentall   —5 urg'd.] urg'd: —6 reports]

pretends   distinctly] NOT IN I   none;] none,   —8 years]
yeares   —16 Protestant] protestant   —17 Histories] histories
—19 Historie] history   informs] informes   —22 preciselie]
precisely   —23 extraordinarie] extraordinary   —25 &] and
the] and   —28 charity] charitie   Prelatie] Prelaty
PAGE 230
—4 Ecclesiastical storie] Ecclesiasticall story   —5 fals] false
—6 over-confident] overconfident   —7 Twelve hundred] twelve
hunderd   seventh] Seaventh   —8 Arabia,] Arabia   —13 add]
ad   —15 years] yeares   —17 Episcopacie] Episcopacy   —20
years] yeares   Historie] History   —22 mischeivous] mischevous
—26 he] hee   —28 testimonie] testimony
PAGE 231
—1 onely roaves at heer] cites here   —3 thing,] thing;
—12 posteritie] posterity   —13 Apostolical] Apostolicall   —17
obstinacie] obstinacy   —17, 19, 25 Episcopacie] Episcopacy
—22 denial] deniall   —23 thir] their   —25 endeavours]
indeavours
PAGE 232
—1 imparitie] imparity   —5 sobrietie] sobriety   —6 insti-
tution] Institution   —7, 10 far] farr   —8 Reformed] reformed
—11 Episcopacie] Episcopacy   —13 Reformed] reformed
—16 handful] handfull   —19 he] hee   —26 &] and
—28 Reformed] reformed
PAGE 233
—1 conformitie] conformity   —4 return] returne   —7
Clergie] Clergy   arm] arme   —8 he] hee   —9 terms]
termes   —10 dignitie] dignity   —12 we] wee   perhaps]
perhapps   —13 bee] be   minde] mind   —18 Episcopacie]
Episcopacy   —21 thir] their   —25 joint] joynt   —28
Episcopacie] Episcopacy
PAGE 234
—5 Slaves;] Slaves,   —10, 27, 28 he] hee   —15 years]
yeares   —24 manners, who] manners who,
PAGE 235
—3 him,] him   heer] heer,   times,] times   —4 Praiers]
Prayers   —14 it] it,   —17 War] Warr   —19 wors mis-
chiefs] worse mischeifs   —22 he] hee   —24–p. 236, l. 3 had
. . . obscure;] taking the advantage of a Mist, the fittest weather for
deceit and treachery,

Page 236

—6 quartering] Quartering —9 Military] Martial —11 treating] treating, with his subjects,] NOT IN 1 —17 blood,] blood. —18 and ... treat.] NOT IN 1 —23 successful] successfull unsuccessful] unsuccessfull —25 he] hee far] farr

Page 237

—4 *opportunities:*] *opportunities.* —5–18 and ... dissention.] NOT IN 1 —23 and] & —25 judge] judge, —26 rightful] rightfull —28 &] and

Page 238

—1 far] farr —4 King;] King, —7 borrowd Rights] borrow'd rights —10 power] autority —10, 13 he] hee —16 *places*] *Places* gave] gave, —20 Rebels] Rebells —25 stood;] stood:

Page 239

—4, 12 Rebels] Rebells —13 happines] happiness —14 Hatchet] Hatches —16 *allay'd*] *allayd* —17 open'd] op'nd —18 lay'd] layd —24 *unsuccessfullness*] *unsuccessfulness*

Page 240

—3 Principal] principal —7–13 And ... *Fight*,] But that his *lowest Ebb* could not be *lower then a Fight*, —16 *treat:*] *treat*; —20 prayer] Prayer —21 treaties] Treaties —23 Prayer] Praier —25 he] hee —26 Houndslow] Hounds-low

Page 241

—5 claim] claime —9 Scripture] 1 Scripture 2 Scrip- —13 we] wee —14, 20 he] hee —18 fear] feare —20 bear] beare

Page 242

—9 wee] we —9, 19, 20 bee] be —17 he] hee —18 world] World —27 beleef] beleif —28 men] Men

Page 243

—4 bee] be —17 *Life*] *life* —19 but] but, said] sayd —20 *Cause:*] *Cause*; —21 *fierceness*] *feirceness* —24 Sail Saile —27 he] hee

Page 244

—1 he] hee —27 pray'd] prayd —28 For] for

Page 245

—7 Parlament;] Parlament, —8 self] selfe —13 pious,] pious —20 he] hee —21 War] Warr —28 *he yeelded*] *hee yeilded* fear] feare

PAGE 246

—1 he] hee   perhaps] perhapps   —2 deliverd] deliver'd
—9 *he*] *hee*   —18 leven] levens,   —24 prayer] Prayer
—27, 28 he] hee

PAGE 247

—13 may] may,   —15 zeal] zeale   —19 fears] feares
—24 *work*] *worke*   —26 Pope] Pope,

PAGE 248

—16 been] bin   —18 rather;] rather,   —20 bee produc'd]
be produc'd,   —23 zeal] zeale   —25 *deceitful*] *deceitfull*

PAGE 249

—8 Hypocrits] Hypocrites   —9 bee] be   seen] seene
—12 som] some   —15 kinde] kind   —17 years] yeares
—18 still] NOT IN 1   —21 knowing,] knowing   —23 years]
yeares   concernd,] concernd   —24 it,] it

PAGE 250

—5, 17, 20, 23 he] hee   —7 *sett*] *set*   —12 *own*] *owne*
—14 *Spain*] *Spaine*   —16 we] wee   —20 hazard] hazzard

PAGE 251

—3 *Naesby*] *Naseby*   —5 all] al   —6 Protestations] protestations   —8 straight] streit   —9 pernitious] pernicious
—9 &] and   —9 dishonorable peace] dishonourable Peace
—10 solicited] sollicited   soliciting] solliciting   —11 he] hee

PAGE 252

—2 do] doe   —6 state] State   —12 already] alreadie
—19 Estates,] Estates;   —21 managing] mannaging   —24
Duke] Dukes   —28 wherwith] wherewith

PAGE 253

—23 *Bees*] *Bee's*   —24 here] heer

PAGE 254

—13 licentious] 1 licentious   2 tious   BUT 2 HAS licenti- AS
CATCHWORD   —21, 22, 24, 28 he] hee

PAGE 255

—1 and] *and*   —2 cloth] cloath   —3 Prayer] Prayer,
Discours?] Discours.   —8 do] doe   —10 the . . . will,] his
Servants and Vassals,   —11 him,] him   —11–13 as . . . Crown.]
for the Liberty of thir Country.   —16 for *necessitie*] For *necessity*
—21, 23 he] hee   —23 shewes] shews

PAGE 256

—4 an] a   —10 hazardous] hazzardous   —12 yeelding;]
yeelding: —13 Loyalty] loyalty   —20 fatal] fatall   —26
he] hee

Page 257

—8 man] Man   —11 we] wee   —13 &] and   —23 *England*] England

Page 258

—2 Counsel] Councel   —6 Ave's;] Ave's,   —7 *Counselors*] *Councellors*   —9 worlds] Worlds   —23 answering] Answering

Page 259

—16 know, and] know &   —20 Yeoman-Ushers] Yeomen Ushers —21 prayers] Prayers   —25 kings] Kings   king] King —26 &] and   child] Child

Page 260

—1, 8 &] and   —1 closetwork] Closet- work   principles] Principles   —2 tyranny & superstition] Tyrannie and Superstition —5 zealous persons] Zealous Persons   —6 instruct] Instruct religion] Religion   —7 soule] Soule   —8 cure] Cure —9 evil] evill   —17 *me good*,] *mee good*   —19 Mosaical] Mosaicall   —23 Office] office   —26, 28 he] hee

Page 261

—1 some] som   —4 it,] it   —7 he] hee   —18 *me*;] *me*,   —20 Parallel] Parallell   —26 go] goe   —27 divising] devising

Page 262

—6 we] wee   —10 People] people   —11 kings] Kings —18 Closet Chaplain] Closet-Chaplain   *prayers*] *Prayers*   —22 own] owne   —27 *spiritual*] *spirituall*

Page 263

—2 Lamp] lamp   —10 he] hee   —14 place] place, —24 Ministers,] Ministers   —24-25 ye . . . bellies,] NOT IN 1 —26 your wares,] NOT IN 1   —27 Cordials] Cordials,   in print,] NOT IN 1   &] and   —28 widows] Widdows

Page 264

—6 Holmby] Holmby.   —17 borrowd,] borrowd   own] own,   —19 said] sayd

Page 265

—1 *sind*] *sin'd*   —6 me] mee   —12 *Sackcloth*] *sackcloth* —18 said] sayd   *sind*] *sin'd*   —25 he] hee   —27 prayer:] prayer,

Page 266

—3 &] and   —5 person;] person,   —7 to] eev'n to —8 very] NOT IN 1   God,] God;   the next] the very next —9 she] shee   —18 Vowes;] Vowes,   —20 Vow'd] vow'd —21 Vow] vow

PAGE 267

—5 *he*] *hee*   —8 in State] in the State   —28 Law,] Law

PAGE 268

—3 compelld] compell'd   —4 Shewbread] Shew-bread
—6 necessity] necessitie   —7 oft times] ofttimes   —9 *he*] *hee*
—17 deliverd] deliver'd

PAGE 269

—11 God] God,   —13 *People*] *people*   —15 Vows] Vowes
—21 brethren] Brethren   &] and   —22 falling out,] falling,
out   —23 judge] Judge,   wel] well   —26 know,] know

PAGE 270

—2 Army,] Army   —8 them] them,   —12 expens]
expence   —14 matchles] matchless   —16 Countrymen,]
Country men   —18 hight] height   —20 some] som

PAGE 271

—5 surprisal] surprisal,   —14 He] Hee   —15 overul'd]
overrul'd   —18 undoubtedly] undoutedly   —22 hope] hope,
—15 overul'd] overrul'd   —18 undoubtedly] undoutedly
—22 hope] hope,

PAGE 272

—8 he] NOT IN 1   —10 Heavn] Heav'n   —14 deliverd]
deliver'd   —23 approaches] approches   reprobate] reprobat
—25 Gods hand] Gods own hand   thir] his

PAGE 273

—1 judgements] judgments   —6 he] hee   —12 Tictack]
Tic-tack   —21 Romans thrown] 1 Romans thrown   2 Roman
throwns   —23 Capitol:] Capitol,

PAGE 274

—6 with-drew] withdrew   —10 therefore] therfore   —14
years] yeares   —26 weak] weake   over-maister'd] overmaister'd

PAGE 275

—2 divine justice] Divine Justice   —2, 4, 5 &] and   —5
obloquy] obloquie   —6 he] hee   —10 suborn] suborne
—15 plausibly] plausibly,   —19 conspicuously] evidently

PAGE 276

—2 therfore,] therfore   charity,] charity   —5 *Intitl'd*]
Intitl'd   —18, 19 again] againe

PAGE 277

—7 *only*] *onely*   —8 *public*] *pubilc*

PAGE 278

—8 receav'd] receiv'd   —14 son] Son   —20 his ... death-

bed] the death-bed of his Father &] and —22 dayes] days
—26 persecutors] persecuters
PAGE 279
—1 suffer'd] suffer'd, —2 sufferings] suffrings —12 we]
wee —17 Scism] Scisme —19 kingdoms] Kingdoms
PAGE 280
—2 Apostles,] Apostles; —7 injurie] injury —16 in-
sensibly] NOT IN 1 —17 and translated] NOT IN 1 —20
intitld] intitl'd —28 he] hee
PAGE 281
—2 *himself*] *himselfe* —6 and] & —10 episcopal]
Episcopal —15 laws] Laws —16 wherby] whereby —22
far] farr —23 prerogative] Prerogative —24 laws] Laws
fathers] Fathers —25 we] wee
PAGE 282
—1 *we*] *wee* —3 Privilege] privilege —5 Monarchy?]
1 Monarchy? 2 Monarchy, —6 Theevs] Theeves Pirates]
Pirats —7 themselvs] themselves —21 favourd] favour'd
—27 people] People —28 he] hee
PAGE 283
—15, 24 he] hee —18 He] Hee —20 tell] tel —28
Religion] religion
PAGE 284
—1 all] al —8 Martyrdom] martyrdom —10 verry law]
very Law coronation] Coronation —16 peece meale] peice-
meale —24 servil] servile
PAGE 285
—4 *Goverment*] *Government* —9 supplicat] supplicate
—13 church] Church —15 &] *and* faction] *Faction* —16
bait] baite —22 *Palliations*] *palliations* —23 Princes] Princes,
PAGE 286
—1 Vindicators] vindicators he] hee —12 He] Hee
son] Son *reveng*] *revenge* far] farr —14 *Hague,*] *Hague;*
—14–21 & ... hostility.] and by what attempts were likewise made in
other places. —22 therfore] NOT IN 1 —22–24 after ...
heerafter,] NOT IN 1 —23 *opportunity*] 2 *opprotunity* —24
&] and —25 rather] rather, triall] tryall —28 repentance]
1 repentance 2 repentatnce
PAGE 287
—11 thir] their —25 &] *and* shal] *shall* —26 himself

speakes] himselfe speaks   —27 *thir*] *their*   —28 disappointed]
disapointed
PAGE 288
　　—1 wilfull] willfull   —7 to] *to*   —10 stifleing] stifling
—16 of the Militia] of Militia   —18 sum] summ   —20 son]
Son   —21 miserie] misery   wherein] wherin   —22 bond
slaves] bond-slaves   —26 out,] out;   —27 bestowd] bestow'd
—28 we] wee
PAGE 289
　　—6 he] hee   —16 Rebels] Rebells   —17 Son?] Son;
—18 solicits] sollicits   —20 Scotish] Scottish   Presbyterian,]
Presbyterian.   —20—22 never . . . agreement.] NOT IN 1
PAGE 290
　　—4 servitude] bondage   &] and   —5 loos] loos,   from
thir copyholds,] NOT IN 1   —6 for;] for.   —6—9 but . . .
agreeable.] NOT IN 1   —10 seems] seemes   —15 *Masters*]
Maisters   —16 then] then,   —17 onely,] onely   —19
God] God,   —21 happiness;] happiness: —23 misery;]
misery.   —23—p. 291, l. 2 and . . . nobly.] NOT IN 1
PAGE 291
　　—5 reads] Reads   —7 answer] Answer   —9 death] Death
—11 howrs] howers   —12 passion] passion,   —13 enveigh]
inveigh   —14 somthing] something   —17 *Esdras*] *Esdras,*
—22 next *Darius*] next to *Darius*   —25 full] ful   —26
Counselors] Counsellors
PAGE 292
　　—3 being] beeing   —8 &] and   —18 truth] Truth
—24 truely] truly   —26 falshood] 1 falshood   2 fashood
PAGE 293
　　—4 do] doe   —7 person] Person   —14 self] selfe
—17 returne] return   —19 deliverd] deliver'd   —20 *Zorobabel* :] 1 *Zorobabel:*   2 *Zorobabel.*   —26 heathen king] Heathen
King   —27 truth] Truth
PAGE 294
　　—12 pleades] pleads   —16 general] generall   —17 Sons]
sons   *whosoever*] *Whosoever*   —19 find] finde   king] King
therfore] therefore   —26 shed] shedd
PAGE 295
　　—2 *do*] *doe*   —16 Laws] Lawes   —17 *David*] David
—20 legal] legall   —22 King,] King   —23 people] People
—27 Civil] civil

Page 296

—4 approv'd] approov'd   —9 one . . . Emperours] the Emperour
—14 Read] Reade   —16 confess'd] confest   —19 *Britain*]
Brittain   —20 shew] show   —21 spirituall] spiritual   —22
Predecessors] *Predecessours*   —23 daughter] Daughter,   *Saint*]
Saint   subject] Subject   —24 cursd] curs'd   condemned]
condemn'd   Counsel] Councel   —25 thereupon] therupon
—26 Oath] Oath,
Page 297

—2 Uncle] Unkle   —13 discern'd] discernd   decree] Decree
Page 298

—4 Legal] Legall   —6 judg'd,] judg'd   —10 *Publicola*]
Publicola,   —10–12 soon . . . writt'n,] NOT IN 1   —12 Senat]
Senate   —13 he] hee   —16 known;] known.   —16–17
as . . . it.] NOT IN 1   —17 Christian] NOT IN 1   —28 Law]
Laws
Page 299

—2 own] owne   —7 absolute] 1 absolute   2 abolute   —9
Mirror,] Mirror;   —18 he] hee
Page 300

—4 Nation,] Nation   —9 Law,] Law   —12 trust (]
trust;   —13 thir] their   —14 Crowning)] Crowning:
—17 he] hee   —18 broken;] broken: —24 receav'd]
receiv'd
Page 301

—2 autority] Autority   —3 resolvd] resolv'd   —4 extirpat]
extirpate
Page 302

—3 &] and   tryal] tryall   —5 Vows] vows   —6 trial]
triall   condign] condigne   —8 undeniable] undenyable
—10 actor,] actor   —11 onely] only   —12 Counselers. And]
Counselers; and   —13 principal] principall   —20–p. 303,
l. 28 And . . . security.] NOT IN 1
Page 304

—28 But . . . notwithstanding] And if the Covnant
Page 305

—1 preserv] preserve   —2 religion &] Religion and   liberties]
Liberties   —3 armes] Armes   resolution] Resolution   —4
against] against,   book] Book   covnant] Covnant   —5 god]
God   —6 propitious, &] propitious and   the most] NOT IN 1
—10 *their*] *thir*   —15, 23 accusers] Accusers

Page 306

—11 *Chaines*] *chaines*   —13 *Babel*(] *Babel,*   work] work, —14 *Babel*)] *Babel,*   —16 power,] power;   —22 *Rev. . . . chapt.*] NOT IN 1   —28 *Rev.* 19.] NOT IN 1   we] wee

Page 307

—2 here] heer   —7 cause] Cause   —23 spirit] Spirit —24 servil] servile

Page 308

—4 mockery] mockerie   —7 therfore] therefore   —9, 16 He] Hee   —23 works] Works   —24 happly] perhaps People] people   —28 he aims] hee aimes

Page 309

—5 rabble;] rabble.   —5–11 that . . . baseness.] NOT IN 1 —12 some] som

COLUMBIA UNIVERSITY PRESS
Columbia University
New York

———

FOREIGN AGENT
OXFORD UNIVERSITY PRESS
Humphrey Milford
Amen House, London, E.C.